NO PLACE LEFT
TO BURY THE DEAD

NO PLACE LEFT
TO BURY
THE DEAD

DENIAL, DESPAIR, AND HOPE IN THE AFRICAN AIDS PANDEMIC

NICOLE ITANO

ATRIA BOOKS

New York • London • Toronto • Sydney

ATRIA BOOKS

A Division of Simon & Schuster, Inc.
1230 Avenue of the Americas
New York, NY 10020

First Atria Books hardcover edition November 2007

ATRIA BOOKS and colophon are registered trademarks of Simon & Schuster, Inc.

For information about special discounts for bulk purchases,
please contact Simon & Schuster Special Sales at •
1-800-456-6798 or business@simonandschuster.com.

Designed by Dana Sloan

Manufactured in the United States of America

1   3   5   7   9   10   8   6   4   2

Library of Congress Cataloging-in-Publication Data
Itano, Nicole.
No place left to bury the dead : denial, despair, and hope in the African AIDS
pandemic / by Nicole Itano.
p.   cm.

1. AIDS (Disease)— Southern Africa.   I. Title.

RA643.86.S6I83 2007
362.196'979200968—dc22

2007034598

ISBN-13: 978-0-7432-7095-3
ISBN-10:   0-7432-7095-9

For Barnaby

CONTENTS

NO PLACE LEFT
TO BURY THE DEAD

INTRODUCTION

B Y THE TIME I first stepped off the plane in Johannesburg in early 2001, at the beginning of what was to be a five-year stay there, a new sense of urgency had arisen over the issues of AIDS. In part, the country had finally awoken to the sheer magnitude of the crisis. By then, South Africa was home to an estimated five million HIV-positive people, more than any other nation in the world. But I suspected the real reason for the new energy was that, finally, it seemed something tangible could be done to halt the epidemic: treatment.

Efforts to prevent the spread of the disease had always seemed depressingly ineffectual and immeasurable; for two decades infection rates had largely continued their upward momentum. Most Africans did not even know their HIV status, and for those who did know they were infected there were few treatment options available; most were simply sent home to die. Communities were staggering under the weight of the sick, dying, and orphaned. The epidemic seemed unstoppable.

The five years that I spent living in South Africa and working there and in neighboring countries, however, was a period of enormous change and new optimism. Treatment that had seemed impossible in Africa just a few years before was becoming possible.

A new grassroots activism arose around AIDS, new international money poured in, and treatment centers opened across the continent. In the jumble of new initatives, some projects were ill conceived, and there was much overlap and duplication. But for the first time in nearly two decades, progress was being made.

This book tells the stories of three families and their communities during this period of enormous change, although I try to put their experiences into a broader context and to show how the epidemic unfolded in Africa. I spent more than a year—between 2004 and 2006—visiting the three communities I've written about in this book, talking to ordinary people, community leaders, and activists. Much of the time I spent simply observing, and to a degree participating in, the daily life of the families who generously allowed me to chronicle their lives. I ate meals with them, helped wash their laundry and harvest their fields, and even occasionally slept at their houses. My goal was to try to paint a picture of how real people and real communities were dealing with the epidemic, not based on a single snapshot in time but over a period as they adjusted and dealt with the virus.

The three families whose stories comprise the bulk of this book do not represent the most extreme or tragic cases. In many ways, the stories I have chosen to tell are quite ordinary. Some of the people on whom I've focused are even relatively prosperous or fortunate within the context of their communities. As you will see, however, all the families have been stricken not once, but many times by the epidemic. Often I discovered the other cases of HIV/AIDS only much later, after I had spent many months with the family. But increasingly, in the nations of Southern Africa particularly, few families remain unscathed. In these cultures where familial ties and responsibility include not just sisters and brothers, but cousins many generations removed, there are few people who have not lost some relative and many who have lost more than one.

The main characters in this book are predominately women. In part this was out of necessity—it is largely women who are willing to talk about the epidemic—but it also reflects the fact that in Africa it is women who are bearing the brunt of the epidemic. They are caring for the sick and orphaned, and they are dying in larger numbers and at earlier ages. For the women I met, the AIDS epidemic was intricately entwined with abuse, alcoholism, poverty, and hunger. It was rarely, if ever, simply a matter of choice.

From the beginning, I also did not feel that, ethically or emotionally, I could watch someone die and do nothing to help. Therefore I chose to work in places and with families that would likely be able to avail themselves of new treatments as they became available. As a result, this book is less about dying from AIDS than living with it. For many of those I met, however, the line between life and death was often perilously thin.

Often this process was difficult to witness: I saw families crumble and disperse and watched young women I had come to care about return again and again to abusive situations where they put themselves at risk of being infected. I sometimes despaired and frequently felt helpless. The challenges, for the families and their communities, at times seemed insurmountable. In the three places themselves—located in the Southern African countries of Lesotho, South Africa, and Botswana—I often encountered a similar bewilderment. Few understood, much less knew, how to stop the slow disintegration of their communities.

I was painfully aware throughout the process of researching and writing this book of the limitations of my own perspective. I was an outsider, a wealthy Westerner. In a region with a deep and divisive racial past, I was also a "white" person writing about black subjects, with all the cultural baggage that entailed. Although I do not classify myself as white—my mother is of Japanese heritage and my father of mixed Mexican and European—in the context of Africa I am very aware that I am usually identified as such. In writing this book I chose to use a limited first-person narrative, so that I could explain as much as possible the relationship I had with my subjects. I knew that, given the long-term nature of my involvement with them, I would be unable to stay true to the traditional ethic of journalistic noninvolvement, an ethic I have come to suspect, in any case. Inevitably, though, given the difficult nature of this subject and the many cultural and economic divides that lay between us, finding the appropriate relationship was often difficult, and I didn't always succeed. I have tried to be honest about these failures in part because I think the readers of this book deserve to know, and in part because I think they are themselves instructive.

Given the enormous cultural divides between myself and those I was writing about, there is much that I struggled to understand and probably more that I misinterpreted. Yet I think there is an even greater danger in not trying to understand each other. How can we begin to break down such barriers if we are too afraid of giving offense to confront our differences? I hope one day an African writer will tackle this subject and write the story of AIDS on the continent from an inside perspective. For now, though, I have tried to keep an open mind so as not to let my preconceptions color my views. In some cases, people I spoke to made sweeping statements about their own people and culture that may seem offensive in our Western, politically correct culture. In some cases I disagreed with these statements, and in others thought they contained elements of truth. But in general, I have chosen not to edit these and to let people speak with their own voice about their own lives and struggles.

In the course of researching and writing this book I found more questions than answers, but I also discovered that much of what we had thought was unshakable truth about AIDS in Africa might not be so uncomplicatedly true after all.

PART I
DENIAL
MASERU, LESOTHO

1

MALESHOANE

O N   A   W A R M October day in 2003, a young
woman named Adeline Majoro made her way across Maseru, the
capital city of a small mountain kingdom at the tip of Africa called
Lesotho. A hint of spring was in the air, but the land lay parched
after several years of drought. Most of the city was brown: dusty dirt
roads, mud-colored mountains, gray-brown concrete buildings. As
she usually did, Adeline walked a few blocks down a rutted lane
from the single room where she lived alone, to a main road. There
she waited for one of the run-down, sagging Toyota vans, called
taxis, that serve as the main form of transportation in the city.

On most days Adeline caught a taxi to the city center, where she
taught business and accounting to high school students not much
younger than herself. That October day, however, Adeline had
steeled herself to make a journey she had been avoiding for weeks.
She climbed into a taxi and headed to a small mission clinic on the
other side of the city for the results of an AIDS test.

Then just twenty-two years old, Adeline had a broad face, wide
hips, and a big, ever-present smile. She dressed conservatively,
avoiding the tight, revealing clothes popular among many of her
contemporaries. Her mode of dress reflected a certain seriousness in
her character. Adeline knew what she wanted from life and worked

hard to get it; she had no time to spend at bars or looking for men. During the day she taught, and at night she took classes on a government scholarship to become a chartered accountant. At home, in the village where she was born, she had a young son who lived with her mother.

Like most Basotho [1]—the collective name used for the people of her country—Adeline was born in a rural area but had been lured to the city in hope of a better life. In 1966, when Lesotho was granted its independence by Great Britain, its capital of Maseru was a sleepy colonial town of about 15,000 whose grandest buildings were a handful of administrative structures built from yellow sandstone hewn from the local mountains. There was a single hotel and a handful of paved roads. In the four decades since, Maseru has sprawled outward from a small center. Today it is home to around 170,000 people and is the only city of any size in a country that remains largely agrarian. [2] But beyond the loud and bustling city center, which now awkwardly pairs those original buildings with a handful of modern office blocks and run-down shopping centers, Maseru still has a rural feel. In the neighborhoods that ring the center, such as the one where Adeline lived and the one to which she headed for her test results, the houses were scattered over the landscape rather than squeezed in close together in the manner of a classic slum.

When Adeline arrived later that warm morning at Maluti clinic, a simple, crowded health center run by the Seventh-day Adventist Church, a nurse recognized her. To the annoyance of those already in the waiting room, many of whom had been there for hours, she was ushered immediately into a private consulting room. "Maybe they were afraid I would run away," she laughed ruefully when she recalled the incident to me many months later.

Adeline had started several years earlier on the journey that had brought her to that small clinic. Over the previous few years there had been small signs that all was not well, each on its own easy to dismiss. First she suffered from strange sores under her arms, then a series of painful abdominal cramps. She sought the services of a traditional healer for a burning outbreak of herpes and, finally, was plagued by itchy and puffy eyes that she initially attributed to an allergy.

In the beginning, Adeline tried to convince herself that it was nothing but stress, that her body was simply worn down from the heavy burden of work and school and motherhood. She rose at dawn most days and often went to bed after midnight, studying by the light of a bare bulb in her single room. She had never been sickly, though, and repeated bouts of bad health worried her. She began to fear that something more serious lay beneath her health problems.

The allergy-like symptoms finally drove Adeline to confront her fear. In the weeks before she went for an HIV test, she was sent repeatedly back to the clinic, where she was prescribed various syrups and pills. But nothing seemed to help. "I would wake up and my eyes were sore and puffy," she recalled later. "I was going to the doctor every week, but nothing he gave me helped."

During the two years that her health had spiraled downward, no doctor ever suggested to Adeline that she get an AIDS test, although some of her symptoms, particularly the "herps," as she called it, are common opportunistic infections associated with HIV infection. Once she even asked a physician if she should get tested. She was breast-feeding when sores appeared under her arms and so asked the doctor she went to see, a private practitioner in the platinum-mining city of Rustenburg in the neighboring Republic of South Africa (where she had been then living), if she should have an HIV test done. He said no. She asked if she should stop breast-feeding and again he said no. She stopped anyway, on the advice of her mother.

That was in 2001 and AIDS was running rampant across Southern Africa. Less than a year earlier, Nelson Mandela had called the epidemic "one of the greatest threats humankind has faced" at a huge international AIDS conference held in Durban, South Africa.[3] Yet Adeline's doctor discouraged her from taking steps to learn her status. Perhaps he felt helpless in the face of this incurable, deadly disease. Believing that there was no treatment he could offer his patients if they did test positive, he may have thought it better that they not know. In this he would not have been alone. Many doctors, aid workers, and government officials across the continent felt the same way; throughout the epidemic, Africans in even the hardest-hit communities were often discouraged from learning their status.

That would later prove to be one of the biggest mistakes made in combating AIDS in Africa.

It was in Adeline's nature, however, to confront the truth. Listening to the radio in South Africa one day she had heard that abdominal cramps could be associated with HIV. The increasing number of posters and signs around Maseru urging people to use condoms and not discriminate against HIV-positive people were also hard to ignore. By 2001, the seed of doubt was planted. Two years later, it had grown into a gnawing fear.

It was the end of September 2003 when Adeline finally made her way to the Seventh-day Adventist clinic which was then one of the few places in the country where HIV tests were performed. On that first visit, a nurse had explained the difference between HIV and AIDS, and told her that even if she were infected with the virus, she might not have AIDS yet. She described how the test worked and asked Adeline if she was sure she wanted to take it. The nurse drew some blood and told her to return in a few days. Tests that gave results in minutes were already being used in wealthier parts of the world, but such new technology had yet to reach that small mission clinic. To determine if she was infected, Adeline's blood had to be sent to a laboratory in another part of the city, and she would have to return. Many patients who found the courage to come for the test never came back for their results; Adeline nearly became one of them. For weeks she delayed her return. "I was scared to go back. Every day I told myself I should go for the results, but I was so afraid." Three weeks later, when she finally found the courage to come for the results, she found herself sitting in a plastic chair in the clinic's bare consulting room, bracing herself to hear news that deep down she thought she already knew.

"You have the *maleshoane*," the nurse told her gently. The two women were alone in a consulting room of a mission clinic, but even there the nurse spoke in metaphors, referring to her patient's sickness by the name of an insect pest. Perhaps the nurse thought it would help soften the blow if the evil remained unspoken. Or perhaps, even at that small mission clinic in a tiny nation at the heart of the epidemic, the sickness in the young woman's blood remained too taboo to be named.

For Adeline, though, the meaning was clear enough. In her blood flowed the deadly human immunodeficiency virus, or HIV, the virus that causes AIDS. Despite the nurse's gentleness, the words were a sentence of death. For even in those days, in the third year of the new millennium, there was little hope in Lesotho, one of the world's smallest and poorest nations, for those who tested HIV-positive. She would, she thought, fail her parents, who had sacrificed so much to give her a better life. Her son, just two years old, would grow up an orphan. And she would die.

Adeline thinks she cried, although she cannot recall precisely. The nurse tried to give her hope. She told Adeline she knew people who had been tested years earlier and were still healthy. If she ate well, got plenty of rest, and avoided stress, she too could still have years of life ahead of her. Then she referred Adeline to an associated hospital, more than an hour's drive away, that was also run by the Seventh-day Adventist Church and had the country's only AIDS program. If she had enough money, perhaps they could give her some treatment. Her own small clinic had nothing more to offer.

As she emerged from the consulting room, almost an hour after she had entered, Adeline heard the grumbles of a group of women outside. "Look at her," she heard one complain. "We came here early and she came late but took the whole day." Adeline walked out without a word and made her way into the hot, dusty streets of Maseru.

I MET ADELINE in June 2004, about eight months after her test, through a small organization of people living with AIDS called Positive Action. We were introduced by an articulate, wiry young man named Koali Job, who had left behind a life of boozing and womanizing after he tested positive and become one of a handful of openly HIV-positive people in Lesotho, which was belatedly trying to come to terms with the epidemic.

Not long before I met her she had left her teaching job and found a new position as the bookkeeper for a small catering company, called In 'n' Out Catering, that operated out of the back of a bar. At night she still took her accounting classes. Koali took me to meet Adeline at her new workplace, where we bought meat from a nearby butcher and watched it being grilled on an outside barbecue.

Adeline struck me, in that first meeting, as confident and well-spoken, with a naturally optimistic disposition. During the time I spent with her, she never once shed tears for herself, though she had plenty of reasons for self-pity. Adeline did not fit any of the stereotypes about women with AIDS. She was not a prostitute, barmaid, or loose woman, just a good girl who had had the bad luck to fall in love with the wrong man.

She told me some of her story that first day, as smoke curled off the cooking meat, letting off a mouth-watering smell. Other parts came out over the successive weeks and months, often as we sat eating in her small home with South African soaps blaring from the television. On the afternoon she learned she was HIV-positive, Adeline told me, she returned to her school and taught the remainder of the day's classes. She stumbled blindly through the rest of the week and then made a slow, agonizing journey home to Ha'Senekane to inform her family of the news.

Adeline told me she felt she had failed them as well as herself. She was an only child and much adored by her parents. But her mother, a seamstress who sewed traditional dresses, and her father, a gold miner in South Africa who was home for the weekend, told her they were proud of her for being open with them. Later, after he had returned to South Africa, Adeline's father wrote her a letter telling her how much it meant to him that she had trusted them with this information. That, she said, was itself an extraordinary act: "My father is not a letter writer."

The support from her family improved her spirits. She was soon also befriended by an openly HIV-positive young woman in her accounting class. The woman introduced her to Positive Action, but died a few months later. Her death frightened Adeline, but she tried to rationalize it. Although the woman was open about her status, she continued to drink alcohol and eat poorly. Adeline told herself that she would survive because she would live positively.

Positive Action, and particularly Koali, became important sources of support in those early days. He introduced her to his church, a small evangelical outfit called Fill the Gap, and helped her through those rough first few months. "Having other positive people to talk to—that made a big difference," Adeline said. "It made me realize that I could keep living."

When I met her in the year after she learned she was HIV-positive, Adeline appeared to be in good health, especially compared to how she described her health before her diagnosis. The mysterious, allergy-like symptoms had disappeared and she felt less tired. No one would have been able to tell by looking at her that she was infected; Adeline certainly didn't look like the victim of a disease that had been nicknamed "slim" in parts of Africa. She was plump, with large breasts and a healthy appetite. Once, when I went to a clinic with her, the nurse pinched her fondly and exclaimed: "Ah, this one is healthy. See how big she is!" She quickly sobered after skimming through Adeline's medical card, which bore a small, seemingly innocuous notation from her visit to the Maluti clinic, marking her HIV status.

Adeline's outward appearance of well-being, I would soon learn, masked her fragile health. After her positive test, she went to a mission hospital where she had a CD4 count, a common test that measures how far the disease has progressed. It examines how many disease-fighting white blood cells, known as T-helper cells, remain in the blood. Healthy people have CD4 counts of above 500, meaning that for every cubic millimeter of blood an individual has at least 500 T-helper cells. Anyone with a CD4 count below 200 is considered not just to be HIV-positive, but to have full-blown AIDS. Someone with less than half the body's normal allotment of T-cells is extremely susceptible to infection, and without antiretroviral treatment (ART), would likely live less than two years.[4] Although I knew she had been symptomatic, I was still shocked when I learned that Adeline's test, taken a few months before I met her, showed a CD4 count of 111. I shouldn't have been, but I was. She seemed so healthy.

She had felt better since her diagnosis, though, and attributed her low CD4 count and prior illnesses to the stress of worrying whether she was infected. In a way, once her worst suspicions were confirmed, she was able to come to terms with her infection. "I sort of already believed I had the virus," she said. "So I was ready to accept the outcome."

There was probably an element of truth to this. After her test, Adeline took better care of herself. She tried to eat better and began taking vitamin supplements. But with her body's natural defenses so weakened, Adeline remained worryingly susceptible to infection. Many patients, it's true, waste away slowly over months or even years. Death, however, can also come swiftly with AIDS, on the wings of a single deadly, and often invisible, infection.

ADELINE WAS BORN on a wide, fertile plateau in Lesotho (pronounced Le-SOO-too), one of Africa's smallest nations. Landlocked and completely surrounded by South Africa, it sits at the tip of Africa in a mountain range known as the Maluti. It is a ruggedly beautiful country of jagged peaks and high, soaring plains whose people are known for their distinctive conical grass hats and the heavy woolen blankets they wear like cloaks in winter and summer.

With a population of just 2.2 million[5] and no real natural resources, except for a few diamonds located inconveniently high in the mountains and an excess of water, it is also, in terms of geopolitics, a thoroughly unimportant place. Until recently, when its astronomically high AIDS rate brought the country new attention, Lesotho's main claims to international fame were geographic. The country is one of only three enclave nations in the world (the other two nations that are completely surrounded by another country are the Vatican and San Marino, both located inside Italy). It also has the highest low point of any country in the world, 4,600 feet above sea level. Nearly 80 percent of the country lies above 5,900 feet, and much of it is covered in ancient, rocky mountains.[6]

Lesotho is also one of the world's poorest and least developed nations, and like much of sub-Saharan Africa, it has become poorer in the postcolonial period. In 1974, one in ten of the world's poor were African; today half are.[7] Disease, overpopulation, corruption, war, and political instability have all hampered the continent's growth, and many of those factors played a role in Lesotho. Before AIDS, though, the quality of life in Lesotho was on a slow, upward trajectory. Life expectancy had risen steadily, from 41.6 years in 1960 to 45.7 in 1990. More people had access to safe water and education, and despite opposition from the Catholic Church, contraception had become more widely used and the birth rate had begun to fall.[8] Today, by almost every indicator, the standard of life is declining.

The pressures on Lesotho are numerous and complex. Its population has doubled since 1970, putting enormous strain on the land and other resources. Across the country, once-fertile soil has been overgrazed and overworked, and the percentage of arable land has been steadily decreasing. Today only 11 percent of the country's land is suitable for cultivation.[9] In addition, the region as a whole has suffered from severe droughts, the most recent of which forced the country to turn to international food aid in 2002.

Perhaps most important to Lesotho's declining fortunes, however, has been the slow shrinkage of South Africa's gold industry. Once South Africa was the largest producer of gold in the world, most of which was dug up by foreign mine workers from surrounding countries, like Lesotho, that sat on the fringes of the continent's biggest economy. Many of the men in Adeline's family spent years in the mines. But over the past decade, South Africa's gold industry has struggled to compete globally and has shed tens of thousands of workers as it has shrunk. In 1995, 125,000 Basotho men toiled deep underground in South African mines; their earnings financed 50 percent of Lesotho's imports. By 2005, that figure had fallen to just over 54,000, and their contribution to imports had halved.[10]

Then there is AIDS, which reversed much of the progress made in Lesotho's early decades. Life expectancy has fallen to thirty-six years, and a child born today in Lesotho has a staggering 67 percent chance of dying before his or her fortieth birthday.[11] Like many of the countries in Southern Africa, during the 1990s Lesotho experienced a dramatic increase in the number of infected people. Today, around 23 percent of adults in the country are HIV-positive and almost a hundred thousand children have been orphaned by AIDS.[12]

In this new world, the members of Adeline's generation, in general, have bleaker prospects than their parents. By local standards, Adeline was not badly off. She had a comparatively well-paying job, a stable and loving family, and an education. But she had bigger ambitions. She was, she often joked, "on her way to the top."

Adeline's parents were solid, working-class folk. They were not highly educated themselves but, like many African parents, saw education as a ticket to a better life and worked hard to ensure that Adeline could get the best. She went away to a boarding school—there was no high school in her village—where she studied according to the internationally accepted Cambridge method, developed in Great Britain. Inspired by one of her teachers, when she finished there she went to Maseru to take a year-long accounting class and then won a scholarship to study to become a chartered accountant.

At the time we were introduced, in mid-2004, Adeline lived in a tiny single room in an outlying neighborhood of Maseru called Ts'enola, about three miles from the city center. Her room was one in a long concrete row, each with a door facing a dirt street that became impassable during summer rains. A double bed, always neatly made, filled half the room. In addition to the bed, she owned a large, worn wooden cabinet, overflowing with clothes, a plastic table and two chairs, a stereo, a two-burner hot plate, and an electric kettle. The only decoration was a slightly tattered poster of a little boy in his underwear, showing his privates to a similarly clad little girl: "Facts of Life," it read in bold lettering. Water came from a tap outside, and the toilets were outhouses on the other side of the yard. In its favor, though, the room had electricity, run off a small meter recharged with vouchers bought at local stores.

A few months after we met, Adeline moved to a larger place, on the same road, with two large rooms. The rent was more than twice that of her old home—almost $40 a month, compared to the $15 she had paid before—but the new place was far larger. Not long afterward she bought a television and refrigerator, and her home was always stocked with food. By many measures, Adeline was lucky.

She never went hungry and had, compared to many of her neighbors, an enviable number of material possessions. Yet she still paid less for rent in a month than I regularly spent for dinner on a single evening. And sometimes, near the end of the month, she would struggle to find the 50 cents she needed to pay the taxi fare to work. Wealth and poverty, in a global sense, are highly relative.

When we met in mid-2004, though, Adeline felt as if she had hit a brick wall in terms of her career. The job at In 'n' Out Catering was supposed to only be temporary while she looked for something better. She earned 1,500 maloti per month, about $235, a livable salary in Maseru, but that was still far less than the salaries of most of her classmates at the Lesotho Centre for Accounting Studies. Often the owner paid Adeline and the other employees late, causing much hardship. What she really wanted was a government job, which came with pension benefits and health care. Lesotho's government was desperately short of qualified accountants and bookkeepers, and officials had told members of the accounting technician course she had completed that they would soon be offered government jobs.

She and her classmates submitted their qualifications, but two years later Adeline was still being told their applications had yet to be processed. Nor did she have any success finding something better on her own. "I think sometimes that maybe my luck has run out," she said. She even wondered aloud whether she had been bewitched, then quickly dismissed the idea.

Adeline hoped that when she finished her studies and became a chartered accountant things would change. Unlike many of the women who lived nearby, many of whom worked in struggling textile factories, she had, at least until AIDS cast a shadow over her dreams, reasonable aspirations of moving up in the world. Adeline's night course, preparation for the same exam that students in England take, cost about $2,700 a year, nearly her annual yearly salary. When, and if, she passed her course, she would have a ticket into the middle class. In South Africa, black chartered accountants, especially black women chartered accountants, were worth their weight in gold.

I often worried that she pushed herself too hard, that the stress and lack of rest would send her over the edge and into an unstoppable downward spiral. Yet I could hardly fault her for working hard and for continuing to dream. Even as I worried, I admired her strength and unwillingness to give in to the virus in her blood. "I'm fighting to show that I can still succeed," she told me once. "An HIV-positive person is not a disabled person. I still have my dreams."

2

FROM THE PLACE WHERE THE FISHES SWIM

———————————————————————————————

B Y THE TIME Adeline walked out of that busy Maseru clinic in October 2003, burdened with the knowledge that she carried in her blood a terminal disease, AIDS had already cut a deadly swath through Africa. In 2003, it was well-entrenched in Lesotho. For more than two decades, AIDS had been spreading out across the continent from its birthplace somewhere in Central Africa.[1] The first signs of the new epidemic, however, had come in the early 1980s.

American doctors first connected the dots and noticed a pattern in the strange medical cases that were trickling into doctor's offices in California and New York. In the early eighties, the gay sexual revolution was in full swing. An affluent, extravagant decade that celebrated excess had begun.

In this tumultuous time, American doctors noticed a rash of *Pneumocystis carinii* pneumonia cases, in which a normally harmless fungus suddenly began filling the lungs of young men, choking their breathing. Such cases had previously been seen only in severely immune-compromised individuals, usually cancer patients undergoing intense chemotherapy. Around the same time, dermatologists began seeing unusual cases of a rare cancer, known as Kaposi's sarcoma, which was usually seen only in Central Africans and middle-aged men of Italian and Jewish descent. Both diseases were suddenly appearing in young, otherwise healthy white men. The only apparent connection between these patients was that they were all gay.

American doctors surmised that there must be some connection between the lifestyles of these gay men, many of whom had taken sexual liberation to new extremes, and their strange illnesses. Some doctors thought the symptoms might be related to nitrite inhalants, known as poppers, which many gay men used as a sexual stimulant. Others postulated that the men were suffering from short-circuited immune systems, the result of having bombarded their bodies with infectious diseases during the course of numerous, often anonymous, sexual encounters. The most frightening possible cause, however, was that a new infectious disease was running rampant in the United States.[2]

Across the Atlantic in Europe, similar cases had also been trickling into doctor's offices, although most would not be recognized as part of a larger epidemic until later. Some of them corresponded with the American pattern, appearing largely among gay men. There were other cases, though, some of which predated the earliest cases in the United States, that pointed to another source of the disease.

There was a Danish surgeon, Grethe Rask, who returned home in 1977 after spending the previous five years working in the Central African country of Zaire, now called the Democratic Republic of Congo. After several years of general fatigue, she was struck with a shortness of breath during a holiday in South Africa and flown home to Copenhagen, where in the course of the next few months her body succumbed to a wave of diseases that should not affect a woman of forty-seven: her mouth filled with yeast and staph infections that laid waste to her body. Finally, *Pneumocystis carinii,* that usually innocuous tiny fungus, suffocated her.[3]

The same year, a thirty-four-year-old Zairian woman came to Belgium, her country's former colonial power, to seek medical care for her three-month-old daughter. Like Rask, the infant was suffering from an oral yeast infection called candidiasis. The Zairian woman, a secretary at an airline company, had recently lost two children, one from a respiratory infection and the second from what doctors later recorded as septicemia, or blood poisoning. Both had also suffered from oral yeast infections. While in Belgium, the mother herself fell ill with fevers, fatigue, and headaches. She too deteriorated rapidly, victim to a series of inexplicable diseases. In addition to oral yeast infections, she had an outbreak of herpes, one of the illnesses Adeline would suffer from many years later, and became infected with *Cryptococcus neoformans,* a fungus usually seen in animals that attacks the respiratory and nervous systems. She also tested positive for E. coli, a strain of salmonella bacterium, a staph infection, and several other bacterial and viral agents. In February 1978, she returned to Zaire and subsequently died.[4]

Two other strange cases, both with African connections, appeared at a Paris hospital in the late 1970s with symptoms that baffled doctors. One was a thirty-two-year-old French woman who had lived in Zaire from 1971 to 1976 with her Congolese husband, the other a thirty-five-year-old Portuguese man who had driven a truck back and forth across Africa from Angola to Mozambique during the late 1960s and early 1970s.[5]

These two cases would later be retrospectively noted in medical journals by European scientists after the first reports of a new disease had crossed the Atlantic. It was the last case, of the Portuguese truck driver, that French doctor Jacques Leibowitch recalled when he first read in the *New England Journal of Medicine* about the strange outbreak of diseases among homosexual men in the United States in December 1981.[6] The man, "Monsieur F.," had begun seeking medical help in 1977 for recurrent, unexplainable infections. He too had *Pneumocystis carinii,* as well as *Candida albicans,* also a fungal infection, and papovavirus, which causes regular warts in most people but in his case had led to supersized growths on his hands, forearms, and legs. Finally, in 1979, Monsieur F. died of brain abscesses that were probably caused by the parasitic disease toxoplasmosis, a common infection in cats that usually causes few symptoms in humans. As he read about the new epidemic in America, Leibowitch realized his mysterious patient must have died from the same condition as the gay men in America.

As new cases appeared in America among intravenous drug users, hemophiliacs, and the female partners of drug users, doctors there began slowly expanding the list of suspected risk factors for the new disease. Realizing that it was affecting a broader spectrum of people, researchers dropped the initial term used to describe the new disease, Gay-related Immune Deficiency, or GRID. In its place the "4H" definition of AIDS was slowly developing: homosexuals, hemophiliacs, heroin users, and Haitians, the latter a designation that greatly angered officials in the poor Caribbean nation, who felt they were being blamed for an American problem. American homosexuals who frequently vacationed in Haiti, officials on the island claimed, had probably brought the new sickness to them.[7]

Across the Atlantic, European researchers, like Leibowitch, saw another connection: Central Africa. By 1982, scientists in Belgium and France were already talking about a potential African source of the disease. And unlike their American colleagues, they had no doubt that an infectious disease was at work.

The French launched an investigation into the epidemic in March 1982. Looking through recent medical records, they found suspected cases among twenty-two Africans and a Greek man who had lived in Zaire for twenty years, all of whom had been hospitalized between May 1979 and April 1983.[8] In the same period, Belgian doctors had noted at least a dozen Zairian patients with symptoms suggesting what was already being called AIDS.

If, as European doctors increasingly suspected, Africa was the source of the infectious agent, then the cases seen in Europe represented only a small fraction of what was likely a much larger epidemic in Africa. "Since only the better-off families of Zaire can afford medical care in Europe these patients may be just the tip of an epidemiological iceberg," wrote J. Vandepitte, then a doctor at St. Raphael University Hospital in Leuven, Belgium.[9] His words would prove to be prophetic, becoming in time a mantra for those who hoped to awaken the world's eyes to a looming threat.

In Africa itself, there were also signs, although only a handful of these ever made it into medical journals. For example, in the early

1980s researchers at Mama Yemo Hospital, in Zaire's capital city, Kinshasa, recorded an unusual surge of cases of cryptococcal meningitis, an opportunistic infection caused by a fungus that causes swelling in the brain and spinal cord and later became closely associated with AIDS.[10] Leibowitch writes in his book on the early history of AIDS, *A Strange Virus of Unknown Origin*, that in the late 1970s there were reports in French medical publications of the rise of a new, more virulent strain of Kaposi's sarcoma, the skin cancer that had initially tipped off American doctors.[11] In retrospect too, some doctors working in Central Africa in the late 1970s also recalled cases that were probably AIDS-related.

Yet it was not until the disease reached the shores of America that the pieces were put together and a pattern was seen to emerge, and even then it was several years after the first cases appeared that the picture became clear. Why in America and not Kinshasa or Paris or Antwerp? Perhaps a confluence of factors was at play. The early American cases were first recognized in closed communities, in gay-friendly cities among doctors who were themselves homosexual or known to be friendly and sympathetic to gay patients. This no doubt encouraged a connecting of the dots among doctors, who quickly began to suspect a connection between the cases. The heady environment of free love and the bathhouse culture of hard, anonymous sex, in which some men had hundreds of sexual partners in a single year, also likely amplified the epidemic, allowing the virus to spread more quickly than it did in other places. Where Europe saw a trickle of cases, America quickly experienced a flood. When the Morbidity and Mortality Weekly Report of the Centers for Disease Control (CDC) published the first academic account of the new gay disease on June 5, 1981, it mentioned five cases. A year later, the agency had reported 355 cases of the suspected new disease.[12]

American medical culture may have also contributed to the identification of the epidemic. In the competitive environment of medical academia, doctors were on the lookout for unusual cases, unsolved questions on which to launch a career. They had time to follow up on such patients, ask questions, and network with colleagues. The United States also had the world's best infectious disease tracking agency, the CDC. Though it initially struggled, for political reasons, to find enough funding to address the burgeoning AIDS crisis, the CDC was able to piece together bits of information coming in from around the country and put together a coherent picture.[13] When it took the lead on AIDS, in mid-1981, it approached the emerging epidemic with all the wisdom garnered from years of experience investigating strange outbreaks around the world.

The medical infrastructure in postcolonial Africa, in contrast, especially in the Central African countries where AIDS first emerged, was slowly crumbling. In the late 1970s, Zaire was being bankrupted by the American-supported dictator Mobutu Sese Seko, and neighboring Uganda was in the grip of civil war. In many rural areas, modern medical care was hard to find. When it was available it was generally administered at mission hospitals struggling to meet basic health needs and with little time, or training, for research. Patients were seldom tracked and few physicians—when there even were doctors—had much contact with their colleagues, in their own countries or abroad. Some research hospitals and medical schools still existed in major cities, but even these were suffering from the economic downturn of the postcolonial era. Such hospitals were of low priority to African leaders and since the study of infectious diseases, especially those that primarily plagued the developing world, had fallen out of fashion in the West, they received little support from richer countries.

Over the second half of the nineteenth and first half of the twentieth centuries, through a combination of improved sanitation and the development of antibiotics and vaccinations, life expectancy in the developed world rose dramatically and deaths from infectious disease nearly disappeared. By the 1950s, according to Laurie Garrett, author of *The Coming Plague,* science had declared a premature victory against microbes.[14] That many of these new advances had failed to trickle down to the world's poorest—in places such as Africa, where every year millions continued to die of treatable diseases like malaria, cholera, and measles—was largely ignored.

During the second half of the twentieth century, occasional outbreaks of bizarre and terrifying new diseases, such as the epidemic of the hemorrhagic fever caused by the Ebola virus that erupted in the Zairian region of Yambuku in 1976, captured international attention and gave rise to fears that perhaps nature had not yet been entirely conquered. Foreign doctors from the CDC and the World Health Organization (WHO) swooped in to control the disease's spread and then left again once the contagion had been contained. But such outbreaks were rare and failed to spread outside relatively confined areas; for the most part, infectious diseases that primarily affected the developing world were ignored.

AIDS was not even immediately recognized as a distinct new disease. It didn't burn through a community quickly, leaving a comprehensible chain of death that could clearly be attributed to an infectious disease. Nor did it cause dramatic, gory symptoms like the hemorrhagic bleeds of Ebola Fever; instead it manifested itself in a wide variety of symptoms connected only by an underlying immune suppression and detectable only with sophisticated modern tests that had been developed in the West just a few years previously. AIDS simmered rather than flared, the long latency between infection and illness enabling it to multiply before it could be detected. It was, in short, perfectly adapted to flourish in the Africa of the 1970s and '80s.

As the virus spread slowly out across Central Africa, local doctors failed to realize that a terrible new infectious disease had emerged, or if they did, their shouts for help never reached the outside world and have since been lost to history. By the time doctors in Europe realized that an epidemic was under way in Africa, the virus was already well entrenched. The stage for the tragedy to come was set.

DOWN AT THE southern end of the continent, Lesotho remained unaware of the brewing crisis farther north. If news of AIDS reached Lesotho at all in those years—and no one I met there could recall hearing of the disease until much later—it was dismissed as a disease of strange people in faraway places.

As the 1980s progressed and AIDS began its silent spread across the continent, the small country was consumed by its own troubles. The promise of independence had quickly soured, and Lesotho had descended into dictatorship. Four years after independence, the ruling party suppressed the results of an election, which they had probably lost. Over the following years, the civil service was purged of opposition supporters, which included a large percentage of the country's educated elite.[15]

In addition to its own political problems, Lesotho was caught in the middle of growing turmoil in neighboring South Africa, which was under increasing internal and international pressure over its policy of apartheid. Although it was an independent country, unlike the puppet black states established by the South African government as "homelands" for the country's African people, Lesotho was deeply dependent on South Africa for trade and employment. It was a tiny black speck in the midst of a mighty, white-ruled nation with a powerful and sophisticated military.

Although the Lesotho government had initially espoused a conciliatory policy toward apartheid South Africa, in the 1980s the country's authoritarian Prime Minister Leabua Jonathan grew increasingly belligerent toward the powerful neighbor. In 1982, he allowed communist countries to establish embassies in Lesotho and began sheltering members of the African National Congress (ANC)—the antiapartheid resistance movement—prompting several raids by South African commandos. One in 1982 killed forty-two people in Maseru, while another in late 1985 killed nine people, including six ANC members.[16] Although most Basotho supported the black liberation struggle in South Africa, they nevertheless worried that Jonathan's courting of South Africa's anger would backfire.

In early January 1986, South Africa decided that Lesotho had gone too far. In retaliation for Lesotho's protecting ANC "terrorists," South Africa imposed a blockade on Lesotho, cutting it off from the world as completely as an island nation might be when encircled by a mighty navy. As the blockade wore on, Lesotho began to run low on gasoline, medicine, and other supplies. Jonathan held a press conference saying that if Lesotho's traditional allies in the West would not help, he would turn for assistance to Soviet bloc nations. For the Lesotho military, which had always had a fragile relationship with the ruling party, it was the final straw.

About 150 soldiers, led by Major General Justin Lekhanya, surrounded the prime minister's office, and violent clashes erupted between members of the armed forces and the Youth League, a North Korean–trained militia loyal to Jonathan, resulting in the deaths of several people. Finally, on January 21, Radio Lesotho announced that Jonathan had been deposed and that the country's government was now in the hands of a military council led by Lekhanya and operating under the authority of the king, Moshoeshoe II.

It was a relatively bloodless coup, although there would later be several retaliatory killings against members of the former government. That day, however, there was more celebration than bloodshed. Citizens cheered in the streets as South Africans allowed a train full of fuel and other supplies to enter Maseru. The ANC fugitives were expelled from the country, flown out on a special chartered plane, though not handed over to South Africa.[17]

Seven days after the coup, Moshoeshoe II swore in a new, fourteen-member cabinet. To the post of minister of health, he appointed his personal physician, Thabo Makenete, a man who would soon become a lone voice warning of a coming plague. Little did anyone know then that AIDS had already made the long journey southward to Lesotho from the heart of Africa, or that it would soon become a health crisis on a magnitude never before seen in the small country.

Today Dr. Makenete is a soft-spoken older man who runs a small private practice in Maseru. His hair is peppered with gray and he walks slightly stiffly. He would like to retire, but the need for doctors in Lesotho is great, especially now, so he continues to run his own part-time practice on the ground floor of a sandstone building otherwise occupied by the offices of a diamond trader. We met there on a chilly morning, when the line in his waiting room had thinned.

Not long after he assumed his new post, Makenete traveled to a WHO-sponsored meeting where doctors and scientists warned that AIDS was the next plague. Although Makenete did not believe that AIDS would ever become a major problem for Lesotho, on his return he commissioned a small survey. The survey found three HIV cases, all African expatriates who were working in Lesotho. As he later recalled, and we have only his memory to rely on since I was unable to find any records of such a survey, two were teachers and the third a pilot. At least one, he believes, was from Tanzania, another was from Uganda, and the third was possibly from somewhere in West Africa. All three were eventually deported.

"We thought it was manageable," he said more than eighteen years later from the modest office of his private practice. "We thought it hadn't really come to Lesotho yet."

In response to these three cases, Makenete said, the ministry tried to do some minimal contact-tracing, but they didn't find any infected Basotho. Later, though, he said the three towns where the cases were discovered all had higher than average AIDS rates. Makenete quickly established a screening program for donated blood and formed a National AIDS Committee, which produced a plan for the prevention and control of AIDS. In a 1990 paper for the Development Bank of Southern Africa, well-respected University of Natal academic Alan Whiteside complimented Lesotho on its rapid response to the epidemic given the small number of reported cases, then only eleven.[18] But he warned that given its high rates of other sexually transmitted diseases, the impact of migrant labor, rapid urbanization, and high unemployment, the country was ripe for an epidemic of massive proportions. His warning was prescient. Nor would Lesotho continue its early progressive path.

In retrospect, Makenete now believes that the message he promoted in those early years was the wrong one. After those first identified cases, he went on the radio—which in Lesotho, as in many African countries where illiteracy is high and television penetration low, remains the most powerful form of disseminating information—and told Basotho to be wary of outsiders who might carry the disease. "We told people to receive foreigners with open arms, but closed thighs," Makenete said.

Those early warnings had at least one lasting impact. The first name for AIDS in Lesotho, and one that is still used to this day, was *mokakallane oa setla-bocha,* the "imported disease." In another version I heard it was called *kaotsi-eabosolla thlapi,* a disease from the place where the fishes swim. In landlocked Lesotho, many people could imagine no place farther away than the sea.

Makenete was also stymied in his early efforts to combat AIDS by the basic conservatism of the country and its rulers. Frank discussions of sex did not come easily in conservative Lesotho. Lekhanya and many of the other members of the military council were devout Catholics and staunchly anticommunist. Although the immediate cause of the 1986 coup was to end the blockade, Lekhanya and others in the military had long feared Jonathan's turn leftward. In toppling him, they called for a return to tradition and the elevation of the king to his rightful place as the country's true leader. But power struggles quickly paralyzed the new government.

Although the cabinet appointed by King Moshoeshoe II was technically in charge of the country, true power was held by Lekhanya's six-man military committee. Theoretically, the military council held only veto power, but in reality it formed an extra layer of bureaucracy in an already sluggish government. In addition, the last years of the 1980s were a period of tightened finances for the health department and other government institutions. Under the guidance of financial organizations like the International Monetary Fund and as part of a broader "structural adjustment program" intended to stabilize the country's economy and reduce poverty, Lesotho was encouraged to reduce spending by recouping more of the costs of basic services, such as health care and education, through fees.

The philosophy behind structural adjustment was that the economies of poor countries were at high risk of collapse and that in order to ensure long-term stability they needed to open their markets, reduce expenditures, and eliminate price controls and subsidies. Countries were required to make these changes in order to acquire loans from international lending agencies. Critics of the programs say they hurt the poor by raising barriers to basic services like health care and education and by wrenching open underdeveloped economies to competition from outside before they were properly prepared to compete.[19] In Lesotho, the immediate impact of these policies on the health system was stark. In 1988, the cost of a trip to a government health clinic or hospital doubled, and though the fees seem inconsequential to an outsider—the cost of a visit to a hospital for an adult increased from one maloti to two, still less than a dollar—the effect was to drive many people away from the formal health system. A study by the World Bank found that in some areas, use of public health facilities fell 50 percent after the price increases.[20]

The conservatism of the new regime also made it difficult to talk openly about issues of sex and contraception, to which AIDS was intricately tied. Makenete, who had also served as head of the Lesotho Family Planning Association, said he often clashed with the military council over the issue of family planning, which he believed was central to reducing poverty in Lesotho. In those days, he admits, he saw family size as a far greater threat to Lesotho's future than AIDS but believed that the two messages could be combined, especially when it came to the promotion of condoms.

"The church wasn't very vocal, but they tried to discourage people from using condoms," Makenete said. "The mere fact that the Roman Catholics were in the majority made it difficult to talk about AIDS."

After those first, tentative, and misdirected AIDS prevention efforts, almost nothing was done for the next decade. The first major HIV survey wasn't conducted until 2000 and, although a test for HIV became available in 1985, the year before Makenete became health minister, the first free testing center in Lesotho didn't open until 2003. Meanwhile, in tiny Lesotho, the virus spread from a handful of initial patients, to hundreds, then thousands, then tens of thousands.

It was a missed opportunity. Makenete shook his head and gestured to his waiting room, where several fat old ladies were waiting with young children who must have been their grandchildren. The generation in between was dying of AIDS.

"In the late 1990s, I used to see one case a month. Now I see one new case a day."

IT WAS NOT UNTIL late 1988 or early 1989 that the first person from Lesotho fell sick from AIDS, or at least was known to have become ill from the virus. Even then, the patient had contracted the virus elsewhere, in Zambia.

Although the details of the case have since been lost to memory, Makenete and others recall that the patient had lived in the Zambian capital, Lusaka, almost a thousand miles north of Lesotho. Makenete remembers she was in her late thirties or early forties and believes she was married to a South African, an African National Congress activist who went into exile in Zambia. Another former health ministry worker, though, thought she was a nurse who had married a Zambian teacher who had worked in Lesotho and then returned with him to his home. What everyone I spoke to about the case agreed on, however, was that while in Zambia, the woman's husband died and she fell ill. On discovering that she was HIV-positive, the Zambian government deported her to Lesotho, where she ended up at Queen Elizabeth II Hospital, commonly known as Queen II.

There was, in those days, no sense yet of confidentiality and privacy, although it would not be long before the international community imposed those ideas on Lesotho. So the country's medical professionals paraded through the dying woman's hospital room to see this Basotho who had contracted this new killer disease.

Adeline, though, knew nothing of all this. She was too young to have heard about the first cases of AIDS in her country or to hear the warnings about foreign men. By the time she came of age, the issue had been veiled in silence. She learned nothing of the epidemic in high school, though it was there that she and her schoolmates first began to take boyfriends.

It wasn't until years later, as a young adult, that she learned about AIDS. By then, of course, it was too late.

3

A MAN IS A PUMPKIN

A FEW DAYS AFTER we first met, I offered
to drive Adeline to her home village, where she planned to spend the
weekend with her son, Bokang. I picked her up at In 'n' Out Catering after she finished work, and we headed out of the city in the late
afternoon bustle toward Ha'Senekane, which lies about half an hour
outside Maseru.

To get there from Maseru, you drive northeast past Ts'enola and
up a steep, winding road that passes into a natural break in the cliffs
called Lancer's Gap. Below, the sprawling, dust-colored suburbs of
Maseru stretch for miles. Above, on the Berea Plateau, a potholed,
two-lane road passes through small villages of tidy brick houses,
pastureland, and fields of corn. Young men and boys, wrapped to
their necks in heavy blankets, herd cows and goats, and women till
the land. Here, in the founding days of the Basotho nation more
than 150 years ago, five thousand mounted Basotho warriors
defeated a British invasion in one of the rare victories by Africans
over European troops.

The setting of Ha'Senekane itself is spectacular: the village sits at
the edge of the plateau, looking over the grassy lowlands, while distant mountains form a jutting natural barrier. On a clear day, the
blue sky seems to stretch forever. The village, which is home to

about three hundred families, rambles along the main road with no real center or core; most of the buildings near the road are made of sturdy brick or stone, a sign of the community's relative prosperity, although there are also a few round huts of mud and thatch.

Ha'Senekane is hardly the most remote or rustic of Lesotho's villages. Located on a main road not far from the capital, it benefits economically from easy access to the city's markets and jobs. Some residents, like Adeline's mother, even commute daily in minibus taxis to Maseru. Yet it seems a long way from the modern bustle of the capital. Local chiefs still allocate land and negotiate disputes between families, and many households rely, at least in part, on what they can grow. There is no electricity, and night descends with inky blackness, broken only by the occasional glow of flickering candles or paraffin lamps in windows. As we drove out of Maseru in the fading light, Adeline told me she found rural life boring, with nothing to do at night but go to sleep with the setting sun. "I like the city now," she said.

Adeline's mother was a seamstress who sewed traditional dresses in a room in Maseru's commercial district that she shared with seven other women and a makeshift hair salon. She carried pictures of her designs, modeled by Adeline and her cousins, to show to prospective customers on taxis and as she walked through town. Adeline dropped by to see her on most days. That day, though, as on many nights, her mother had slept in her office, locking herself in for safety and working late into the evening to finish a commission. Adeline's father usually returned to Ha'Senekane one weekend a month from the South African mine where he worked.

We found Bokang, nicknamed Bongy, at the house of Adeline's aunt. It was nearly dark, and the house was lit with paraffin lamps that cast a soft, flickering light on the well-apportioned home. Adeline's uncle, like her father, was a miner who spent much of his time away but provided well for his family. The rooms of the small house were overstuffed with formal and uncomfortable furniture of the type sold in the installment shops in Maseru: sofas with wooden frames and attached velour cushions, oversized wooden wall units for displaying little treasures. A rarely used television sat in a corner, attached with wires to a car battery, and crocheted doilies decorated the tables.

Bongy hid in the shadows while the rest of the family greeted me. Adeline's aunt, a plump, smiling woman with youthfully smooth skin the color of melted chocolate, clapped her hands before leading me into the sitting room and offering me tea. I sipped my tea, milky and sweet, while Adeline's cousins stared at me wide-eyed, as if an alien had landed in their living room. Finally, one of them, a young woman who worked in a textile factory, exclaimed: "There's a white person sitting in our house drinking tea. And she drinks tea just like a Basotho!"

Adeline laughed. She seemed amused by her cousins' excitement. She had a serenity about her that made her seem older than her twenty-three years; I often wondered if coping with being HIV-positive had matured her or whether it was just her nature. I suspected the latter played the more powerful role and that the strong support and love of her parents had given her a great deal of self-confidence.

I liked this about her. She welcomed me almost immediately as a friend to whom she was eager to show Basotho life and from whom she could learn more about the rest of the world. She never showed me the undue deference, a legacy of apartheid and colonialism, that so often taints relationships between Africans and Westerners. In the months that followed, I would sometimes treat her to dinner at a local restaurant or take a bucket of Kentucky Fried Chicken to her house, but she took pride in being able to show hospitality to me as well. Often when I was visiting Lesotho, she would cook me dinner, and once she presented me with a gift, a cloth bag her mother had sewn for me with an image of a hut and the word *Lesotho* screen-printed in blue ink on one side. I never felt with Adeline that she wanted or expected anything from me, except perhaps information, which I was happy to provide.

As we sipped our tea, Bongy finally emerged from hiding. He was big for his age, with a lower lip that stuck out in a permanent pout. When he overcame his shyness, he was curious and self-confident. He looked healthy, although Adeline had told me that he was often sick and she worried that she may have infected him during labor or while breast-feeding. She wanted to take him to be tested, but her mother had refused, and Adeline, despite her independent spirit, was a traditional girl who obeyed the wishes of her parents.

Bongy was clearly doted on by Adeline and the rest of the family and used to getting his own way. He had, Adeline told me earlier, recently decided that he didn't want to go to school anymore. He attended the local equivalent of a preschool, called a crèche, but he fought with the other children and had decided, sulkily, that he would boycott it. Bongy also quickly decided that I was his special friend. Although we couldn't exchange a word—he spoke only Sesotho and I only English—weeks later Adeline told me he demanded to know why I never called to speak to him on his grandmother's cell phone. (Ha'Senekane has no electricity and no post office—mail is picked up from a larger village for a fee by a local shopkeeper—but like an increasing number of places in Africa, it has good cell phone coverage.)

Although Bongy knew Adeline was his real mother, he called his grandmother *'me,* the Sesotho word for "mother." He called Adeline "Mofu" because he couldn't pronounce her name. Although fostering by grandparents is not uncommon in Basotho culture—Adeline herself was raised primarily by her grandmother—she told me it sometimes made her sad that she was missing so much of his childhood. "He's the only child I'll ever have," she had told me in the car. She had a boyfriend, George, whom she soon hoped to marry. Because of her infection, though, which he knew about, they were uncertain whether they could have children.

There was much staring and giggling during that first visit and not much talk. I left Ha'Senekane about an hour later carrying, despite my protestations, a large, lumpy green pumpkin, a glass jar of canned peaches in a sweet sugary sauce—both from the garden of Adeline's aunt—and a traditional broom made from grass.

LIKE MOST HIV-POSITIVE PEOPLE, Adeline cannot date with precision the moment HIV entered her body and began multiplying in her blood, although she is certain of the man who infected her. She had had only one long-term relationship, with Bongy's father. In this, she represents the silent majority. Today, 59 percent of Africans with AIDS are women. For many of these women, marriage may in fact be the largest risk factor for contracting AIDS, and some studies indicate that the majority of HIV-positive women in Africa may have had only one or two sexual partners in their entire lives.[1]

When exactly she was infected, and whether her partner was infected prior to meeting her or during the course of his relationship with her, she will likely never know. Adeline might have slept with Bongy's father dozens, even hundreds, of times before he passed the virus to her. Or perhaps she was infected on her very first sexual encounter, when the physical trauma of losing her virginity—the breaking of the hymen, which often causes bleeding—offered the virus a door into her body. Contrary to popular belief, HIV is not a particularly infectious agent, although research has shown that it is more easily transmitted from a man to a woman than from a woman to a man. Without aggravating circumstances, such as an existing sexually transmitted disease, it is believed that a man will pass the virus to a woman during unprotected vaginal intercourse in only one or two sexual encounters out of a thousand; a woman is even less likely to pass the infection on to her partner.[2] Young women are believed to be particularly vulnerable, though it is not known exactly why. Some researchers have speculated that their reproductive tracts are not fully developed; others think it may simply be because many young women first become sexually active not by choice, but through force or violence, and often with men who are much older and therefore much more likely to be already infected.[3]

Many Africans—indeed many people around the world—believe that if they have had sex once with an infected person they are doomed. They have been encouraged in this belief by AIDS prevention messages that are intended to shock or scare. In fact, one of the great mysteries of the African AIDS epidemic is how it has reached such terrifying proportions so quickly considering the low rate of heterosexual transmission. In the United States, the early AIDS epidemic among gay men was amplified by the gay sexual revolution, with its doctrines of free and frequent love, as well as the increased chance that the virus can be transmitted through anal as opposed to vaginal sex. Although AIDS is becoming a heterosexual epidemic even in America, especially among people of color, nowhere else in the world did it burst into the mainstream as quickly, and with as devastating effect, as in Africa. While not all African countries have been stricken by this new plague, the continent is home to almost two-thirds of the world's HIV-positive people, although it has only 10 percent of the world's population.[4]

There have been all sorts of theories about why Africa has been so uniquely cursed, ranging from the bizarre to the mundane. Some have pointed to sexual customs such as the use of vaginal drying agents or sexual cleansing practices. Others have put the blame on prostitution, multiple sexual partnerships, or the prevalence of untreated sexually transmitted diseases.

A number of these theories, or at least the way they have been commonly expressed by Western researchers, have deepened the gulf of mistrust between Africa and the West. Many African leaders and scientists are deeply offended by what they see as an unnecessary focus on the bizarre, which, they believe, feeds into racist stereotypes of Africans as oversexed and primitive. For example, a man named Abraham Karpas wrote two letters to scientific journals in the early years of the epidemic in which he recalled an anthropological study that claimed men and women in the Rift Valley in East Africa smeared themselves with the blood of monkeys to increase sexual stimulation.[5] This, he postulated, would have been an ideal vector for the initial transmission of the virus from monkey to man.

Any discussion of AIDS by necessity trespasses into the uncomfortable area of sexuality. Given the difficult history between Africa and the West, it is no surprise that this is such a loaded issue, and Western researchers have made many mistakes in the way they have approached AIDS and sexuality in Africa. Still, there are elements of truth in many of these hypotheses. The use of drying agents, for example, may indeed make women more vulnerable to the spread of AIDS. But while I have met African women who claim to practice dry sex, as well as men who believe that a woman who becomes too wet during sex is promiscuous, dry sex is by no means practiced in all the communities where AIDS has cut a swath. The same is true for wife inheritance or sexual cleansing practices, in which a recently widowed woman is expected to sleep with a close relative or community elder; each of these may indeed contribute to the spread of AIDS, but none of them provide anything near the full answer.

Scientists may one day find a biomedical reason for the rapid spread of AIDS across Africa. I would not be at all surprised if it were discovered that some people are simply genetically predisposed to infection and that whatever causes this predisposition is more common in Africa than elsewhere. It often struck me that certain families seemed to be hit disproportionately hard. A woman I knew in Johannesburg, Hlengiwe Leocardia Mchunu, had eight siblings, seven of whom were infected with HIV and six of whom have died. That seems to be a disproportionate amount of sorrow for a single family, too much to be explained by bad luck.[6]

If there is a single, underlying cultural cause for the African AIDS epidemic, it is more likely to be found in the broader, calamitous social changes experienced by Africans in recent times, first through the process of colonialism and later as they were thrust unprepared into the modern, postcolonial world. In recent decades, Adeline's world, and that of millions of young Africans across the continent, has been in transition. The quiet of Ha'Senekane is giving way to the bustle of Maseru, Basotho blankets to hipster jeans, and traditional responsibilities to a new individualism. Many of these changes may be necessary to help the continent compete in an increasingly globalized world: few African leaders honestly believe that Africa's future lies in subsistence farming. Yet these changes are nonetheless deeply unsettling and, in the era of AIDS, even deadly. It is probably not traditional African sexual customs that are causing the spread of AIDS, but rather the breakdown of what was once a coherent moral and sexual system—what social scientists call social cohesion—as African societies struggle to adapt to a new world.

Such questions were for Adeline, however, academic. She only knows that at some point in the past few years, a single particle of HIV, a speck thousands of times smaller than a single human cell, entered into her blood. Once inside, it invaded one of her blood cells and began to replicate, sending copies of itself out into her bloodstream to invade and kill other healthy cells.

Although HIV can build homes in several types of cells, it usually attacks a specific type of white blood cell, called T-helper cells, whose function is to help the body fight off infection. As more and more virus particles replicate, killing more and more of the cells that the body depends on to fight disease, the infected person becomes increasingly susceptible to other bacteria, fungi, and viruses. AIDS does not itself kill its host; it merely strips away the protections that keep a person safe in a world teeming with potentially lethal infectious agents. Eventually, as the body is bombarded by microbes in an increasingly hostile world, it simply gives up.[7]

In those first few days after exposure, Adeline may have experienced flulike symptoms as her body struggled to fight off this new invader. Many newly infected people experience high fever, swollen lymph glands, a sore throat, and even skin rashes. If Adeline did fall temporarily sick then, she did not note the significance of the symptoms and has long forgotten them. Eventually, though, her body won a temporary battle over the virus and brought the infection under a degree of control.

For years, the virus quietly multiplied in her blood, slowly stripping away her body's defenses like a colony of termites eating away at the foundations of a building. A small percentage of infected people—known as long-term nonprogressors—stay healthy for fifteen or more years, perhaps forever. No one knows why. For most, though, it is only a matter of time. Eventually Adeline's body began to lose its ability to fight off other infections, and normal, everyday microbes that her blood would have normally easily defeated began to plague her. None of these in themselves were life-threatening, but like the foundations of that house, she was weakening.

ADELINE WAS STILL a high school student when she met Peter, a handsome, serious-looking man nearly a decade her senior. In the photo album she still keeps at her mother's house, and which she showed me on another trip to Ha'Senekane, he is dressed in American, urban-influenced clothes, his muscled arms peeking out of shiny shirts adorned with athletic logos. The pictures reinforced the image I had formed of him from my conversations with Adeline—as that of a city boy, cut adrift from his cultural roots, afloat on the turbulent sea of African modernity. He was, I thought, not a man who would be caught dead in a traditional Basotho blanket and hat.

Peter was the friend of one of her schoolmates and came from Teyateyaneng, called TY by most Basotho, a small town about a half hour's drive from Maseru. Adeline had studied there at one of Lesotho's better high schools; it was one of her teachers in TY who inspired her to become an accountant.

Adeline was better educated than Peter, who like many Basotho men had abandoned education early in favor of the mines. In Lesotho, the only country in Africa that has a higher literacy rate among women than men, such gender disparities are not uncommon. Nor was an age difference of ten or more years between partners.[8] This age disparity has both traditional and modern roots. In earlier days, a young man often could not marry until he had proved himself and saved for the bride-price. Today, older men are attractive to Basotho women like Adeline for many of the same reasons that Western ones frequently are to Western women: they are often more mature and have greater earning power. I once heard Adeline berate a younger cousin who was staying with her for having a boyfriend ten years older: the girl had been fifteen when they met, he was twenty-five. "Be careful of older men," she warned. Then she sighed, realizing her own hypocrisy. "I like older men too."

Peter was the first serious boyfriend Adeline had ever had. Her album is filled with scribbled hearts and with photographs of him, or the two of them together, surrounded with colored decorative borders. Some of the photographs look like the kind of snapshot you might get at a carnival or amusement park, with romantic settings as backgrounds. Around the pictures were words cut from magazines, phrases in colorful letters, sayings like "True Love" and "Forever." The album, I thought as we flipped through the pages, belonged to a girl who had yet to taste the bitterness of love gone sour.

In the Lesotho of old, a girl would have passed from her father's home to her husband's, with little interlude in between. There were clear markers between childhood and adulthood, rites of passage such as initiation and marriage. But in the 1990s, as old ways were rapidly giving way to new, Adeline found herself navigating that strange and terrifying new phase of life: adolescence. She had a kind of freedom women her mother's age had never had but, like many girls of her generation, little guidance on how to experience that freedom gracefully. When she met Peter, Adeline fell in love with him with the passion of first romance and with all the expectations of a teenager whose ideas of love were culled from South African soaps, American sitcoms, and pop music.

"He was irresistible," she explained to me wryly, long after they had separated. "And I fell into his trap."

Peter spent much of his time in Rustenburg, a South African platinum-mining city a few hours' drive away. When he returned to Lesotho he would bring Adeline presents or pay for the special, expensive photographs. Unlike many young women in Lesotho who depend on presents from boyfriends to survive, Adeline didn't need the presents. Her family was not rich, but they provided for her comfortably. But it is part of an unspoken code in Lesotho that men will woo girls with gifts and presents. Women, even educated, self-sufficient ones like Adeline, expect this, and it is one of the reasons so many young women enter relationships with older men and are infected with AIDS so young.[9]

In September 2000, at the age of nineteen, Adeline became pregnant. She was afraid of what her parents, who had sacrificed so much to send her to school, would say. So she hid the fact from her mother, avoiding her as much as possible. A few months earlier, before Adeline got pregnant, Peter had asked her family for permission to marry her, but they had refused, saying she was too young. With Bongy growing in Adeline's womb, the couple decided to elope.

Although many of her classmates from her village had already had children, often outside of marriage, Adeline feared her parents would be angry at her. She was an only child, her family's great hope, and they were, in many ways, a traditional family who wanted things done according to custom.

Marriage, in Basotho culture, is more than the joining of two people; it is also the joining of two families. Today, even Christian Basotho who want to be married in the church usually uphold many traditional customs, especially the payment of a bride-price, known in Sesotho as *bohali,* but sometimes also called *lobola,* from the name used by another Southern African people, the Zulu. Traditionally paid in cows, *bohali* is negotiated between the families of the bride and groom. Today it is often paid in cash, though still negotiated in cows, with the exchange rate—how much money per cow— also part of the negotiations.

Some women's rights activists in Africa oppose the practice of *bohali,* arguing that it leads to increased abuse of women. Many men, they argue, believe that once they have paid *bohali,* they have "bought" their wives and can therefore do anything to them. The payment of *bohali,* they argue, also makes it difficult for women to divorce their husbands, since under custom, they cannot be divorced unless their family repays the *bohali,* something that many families are unwilling or unable to do.

Traditionalists argue that the custom is intended to honor women, not to disgrace them. The bride-price is evidence of the woman's value, and its payment ensures that a woman is valued in her new family.

Adeline's beliefs, on this subject and others, are a curious mixture of modern and traditional; she wanted *bohali* and a church wedding. Yet she is nevertheless a bit of a feminist, although she would never call herself such. She believes a woman should work to keep her independence and, following her mother's example, says that she would run the household finances. She did not, however, want to give birth outside of wedlock.

So, on a warm December Thursday, Adeline and Peter went to TY, to the house of Peter's family, where a sheep was slaughtered to welcome her into the family. From that point on, she considered herself married, although she learned years later that according to customary law she was not considered a full wife because *bohali* had never been paid.

Adeline's mother accepted the relationship, although Adeline said her mother never really liked Peter. He was, she thought, too much of a city slicker, an urban boy who had no respect for traditional ways or for the responsibilities of fatherhood. And she worried that Adeline would not finish her education.

Still, she helped Adeline through the pregnancy and welcomed Bongy into the family when he was born. Although traditional Basotho culture frowns on premarital pregnancies, it also places a high value on fertility. Women are expected, and expect, to marry and bear children young. Growing poverty and urbanization have reduced the number of early marriages, in part because men increasingly have difficultly paying *bohali,* and in part because traditional sanctions against premarital sex and pregnancy have fallen away. According to tradition, for example, the family of a man or boy who impregnated a girl before marriage would pay a fine, usually one cow, to her family. Such sanctions, though, are rarely enforced, although many young women are today becoming pregnant without being married.

Although she had worried about her parents' reaction, Adeline did not think that she was too young to get married. There may have been an element of teenage rebellion in her behavior, but she was also upholding a broader cultural belief in early marriage and motherhood. By the age of twenty-four, more than half of Basotho girls have children; by thirty-two almost all do.[10] A woman without a husband is accepted; a woman without a child is considered strange or even tragically unlucky.

Adeline would often tease me and ask me when I was going to get married and have children. By Basotho standards, I was an old maid. It was strange for a woman of my age, in her late twenties, not to be a mother. I explained to Adeline that in my culture—in our conversations about such issues, "her culture" and "my culture" became shorthand for talking about differences between Lesotho and the West—it was not uncommon for women to wait until their thirties to marry and have children. Many women I knew delayed motherhood, I told her, because they enjoyed the freedom of being single and wanted to focus first on their careers. And, I told her, many choose not to have children at all. Adeline would always just shake her head and laugh at the strange ways of Westerners.

"But don't you *want* to have a baby?"

Adeline was ambitious and goal-oriented, "on her way to the top." Yet in her world being a mother was no impediment to upward mobility. The extended family provided a way to care for children, even when their parents were working in the cities or the mines. It was, in many ways, a far more effective system than the modern nuclear family.

I met many educated, successful women in Lesotho who had chosen not to get married because they worried about losing their freedom and independence. Under Basotho law, all women are legal minors, subject to the will of their fathers, husbands, and sons. But in practice, it is primarily married women who give up many of their rights.

"Women, especially women who are educated, just want to have children, but want to be independent," a woman named Selloane Pitikoe, who worked for the American nongovernmental organization CARE, told me. "During the old days to fall pregnant without marriage was a bad thing. Now there is no stigma attached to being pregnant."

She was speaking for her friends, as well as many of the women she worked with in Lesotho's textile industry. But she was also speaking for herself. She was an unmarried mother and planned to stay that way.

Adeline, though, perhaps because she herself came from a loving family or perhaps because she was by nature a romantic, wanted motherhood and marriage. Things, though, didn't turn out quite the way she had planned.

When she went into labor with Bongy, Adeline was living alone in Maseru. Peter was away in South Africa, where he worked, and her mother was home in Ha'Senekane. Adeline knocked on the door of a neighbor, an old woman, who helped her to the Catholic hospital in Roma, a nearby town where Lesotho's national university is located. Queen II in Maseru was considered Lesotho's top government hospital, but Adeline considered Roma a better facility. It was a lonely way to welcome a new life into the world, and a sign of changing times. It is only now, with thousands of women living alone in cities, far from their families, that a young woman like Adeline would have to call on the help of a near stranger at such a time.

Adeline's mother joined her later in the day, and, as was customary, Adeline returned after the birth to her mother's home for a period of seclusion lasting several months. She shaved her head—also in accordance with custom—and learned to nurse her son. At the end of that period, Peter came to visit, and Adeline's photo album displays photographs of the three of them as a happy family: Adeline sits in a chair, cradling a tiny infant, her shaved hair just beginning to grow back, while Peter stands behind her, his hand on her shoulder proprietarily. This image of the happy family Adeline had longed for would last for only a short time. Not long after those pictures were taken, everything fell apart.

When Bongy was a few months old, Adeline took him to Rustenburg to stay with Peter and her in-laws, who lived in a house provided by the platinum-mining company for which many of the men in the family worked. The mining quarters that serve Rustenburg's platinum mines are windswept, barren neighborhoods filled with row after row of small, cookie-cutter houses. They are, however, a vast improvement on the old days of migrant mine labor in South Africa, when foreign mine workers lived almost exclusively in single-sex hostels, often packed up to sixteen to a room.

Still, Adeline found Rustenburg a lonely place. "It was boring there. There was nothing to do. There were no jobs for women, so we just stayed at home." To top it all off, she complained, the weather was bad. "It was too hot."

Her in-laws treated her kindly enough, but Peter was a changed man. No longer the tender lover, he drank heavily and often failed to come home at night. Then he began to beat her. He would come home drunk and begin to hit her. More than once, she ended up in the hospital and the police were called. But Peter seemed only to get worse. "I didn't recognize him," she said sadly.

Adeline's father-in-law despaired of what to do with his son and tried to rein in his behavior. Peter's father, Adeline said, was a gentle man. Father and son often fought over the son's behavior, and at least once, Peter was kicked out of the family home. Bewildered at the changes in the man whom she had loved, after a few months Adeline eventually packed up her bags and took Bongy home to her mother in Lesotho. It must have been hard to leave the father of her son and her young love, I suggested.

"Not after what he did to me," she responded, tears in her eyes.

More than two years later, Adeline remained angry with Peter; she had refused to speak to him since she left Rustenburg or to let him see Bongy, despite efforts by his parents to initiate a reconciliation. But after her diagnosis she felt she needed to speak to him, to tell him that she was HIV-positive and he probably was too.

IN ADELINE'S WORLD, marrying a miner did not seem an extraordinary act or one that carried particular risk. While miners spent much of their time away, such long separations between husband and wife had become accepted as part of life. Her father was a miner, and her uncles and cousins were miners. For generations, the women of her family had built lives in Lesotho while their husbands were far away. There were, many found, even certain advantages to the arrangement, a degree of autonomy that rural women might not otherwise have had. The wives of miners ran their homes with little interference from their husbands and, if their husbands brought their salaries home, as Adeline's father did, lived comparatively prosperous lives.

But the migrant labor system also created the perfect breeding ground for an AIDS epidemic. The men who left for the mines lived dual lives, with one foot in the slow, seasonal rhythms of their rural homes and the other in the fast-paced world of South Africa's rough-and-tumble mining communities. In the cities, they lived crowded together with men from other places, listened to jazz, and drank beer in makeshift bars, known as *shebeens,* that teemed with prostitutes. Far from their families, many miners paid for love or took local girlfriends. Some men even found companionship and sexual release in the arms of fellow miners, though most Africans will claim stridently that homosexuality is unknown on the continent.[11] That few miners remained celibate during their long absences from home was a known and accepted part of life, but also one that was shrouded in secrecy.

I once asked Adeline if she thought her father had other women in Virginia, the South African gold mining town where he worked.

"Of course," she responded without much hesitation. "But he's careful not to let my mother know."

To be fair, it wasn't only men who strayed from the marital bed. Many women told me that in Basotho culture, it had become acceptable for women to take other sexual partners while their husbands were far away, as long as it was done discreetly. Men, more than one person told me, were even expected to quietly accept children borne by their wives who could not possibly be theirs.

"People had been in these extramarital relationships for so long that it had become traditional," a National University of Lesotho sociologist, Itumeleng Kimane, told me. "But there was no HIV/AIDS then."

While there is no doubt that the migrant labor system contributed to the development of a culture that accepted the existence of multiple sexual partners, there is sometimes a tendency in Lesotho to ignore the system's deeper cultural roots and the ways in which traditional beliefs have adapted to Christianity and urbanization. Polygamy was once a common feature of Basotho life, though white missionaries—both Catholic and Protestant—who arrived in the mid-nineteenth century worked hard to stamp out the practice. Women converts were told to leave their polygamous husbands and men with multiple wives to cease having sexual relations with all but one, although the missionaries realized that additional wives could not simply be abandoned.

Official polygamy, however, operated under its own strict rules: a man could take more than one wife, but he had to be able to support all of them equally, providing each with her own house and fields. For a man, having many wives was a sign of prosperity; he must be able not only to support such a large family, but also to pay *bohali* for each new wife. Traditional polygamy also existed within a relatively closed geographic area; most marriages occurred between men and women who lived within walking distance of each other. Often, according to anthropologists, it even occurred within families. Marriages between first cousins, for example, were widely encouraged.[12]

Today, official polygamy has all but disappeared. In its place, an informal system has developed in which men have a single wife but are allowed, quietly, to take other partners outside marriage. Men, and some women, will defend this arrangement as traditional, saying that Basotho men have always had many women. According to a contemporary Sotho saying, "A man is a pumpkin," with many vines stretching out in different directions. A woman, in contrast, is a cabbage: she stays closed up, waiting for her man to come home.

These new relationships, however, are more volatile and provide fewer protections for women than traditional polygamy. While women may receive gifts and financial support from non-marital partners as long as the relationship continues, they have no socially accepted claim on the man or his family at the end of such a relationship. A wife cannot be easily discarded; a mistress can. This system, which many Basotho men will claim is "part of their culture," is actually a corruption of traditional ways that gives all the power to men and leaves women powerless. Men get all the advantages of polygamy with none of the responsibilities. With things so tilted in their favor, it's no wonder that few men are willing to speak out against the status quo. In the many trips I made to Lesotho over a period of nearly two years, I spoke to various people involved in the country's AIDS fight. The women I spoke to nearly always mentioned culture—though what they meant by culture was in fact this relatively new system of multiple, informal sexual partners—as the biggest barrier to tackling the rising number of new infections.

"The Basotho are very culture-bound," I was told by a spry,

grandmotherly woman named Agnes Lephoto, who is the AIDS coordinator of the Christian Health Association of Lesotho, an organization that acts as an intermediary between the government and the country's many mission hospitals and clinics. "They believe that having multiple partners is the right of men and that he shows his manhood by having many partners. In a country that is 99.9 percent Christian this is still the way they believe. Culture is stronger than religion."

Women, she said, were willing to change their behavior because they were seeing the impact of AIDS in their own communities every day. They were the ones who nursed the sick and cared for the orphans. But the men of Lesotho, she said, were "blinded by culture" and were the ones who dictated the rules of sexual relationships. I asked her how the attitudes of men could be changed.

"Ah," she said, drawing the word out with a shake of her head, "it's so entrenched. It outpaces even education."

"If you could have a minister of the church or a cabinet member," she finally added after a little thought, "or someone who is prominent say, 'I am positive and this is why,' perhaps men would listen. But our men don't want to say such things. Until we get prominent men to come out, especially ones who are positive, nothing will change."

It was true that Lesotho's men, even those who had begun to speak about AIDS, generally refused to confront the issue of multiple partners. With the exception of Dr. Makenete, none of the prominent men I spoke to in Lesotho would readily acknowledge the need to address "culture" as part of prevention efforts; they preferred to talk about condoms or testing or antiretroviral drugs.

Certainly none of them were using their positions of power to encourage people to change their ways. Even the churches tread warily on the issue, fearful of alienating adherents or being accused of promoting a "colonialist agenda." When I asked the local Catholic archbishop, Bernard Mohlalisi, whether the church was promoting fidelity as part of their anti-AIDS efforts, he told me they were focusing on care rather than on prevention. "We're not focusing on the sexual transmission of AIDS," he told me. In Lesotho, even the

Catholic Church—called the Roman Church in Lesotho—will not stand up and tell men they need to stop screwing around.

I wish I could say I was surprised by Mohlalisi's answer. The churches in Lesotho, and across Africa, have largely failed in regards to the AIDS epidemic. The Catholic Church's well-publicized and long-standing resistance to condoms is part of that failure, but perhaps more significant has been its broader failure to address the issue of sexual behavior. The pulpits of Africa should have been ringing with calls for changes in sexual behavior for the past two decades, yet even today many religious leaders are hesitant to confront the issue.

Finally, more than twenty-five years into the epidemic, churches are beginning to address the growing problem of orphans, to speak out against stigma, and to help care for the sick and dying. That's a start, but it won't help keep alive those who are still uninfected. Many Catholics working at the grassroots level in AIDS-stricken African countries are increasingly uncomfortable with the church's persistent stance against condoms—especially its refusal to allow their use between married partners when one is infected and the other uninfected. Some have even gone so far as to quietly hand out condoms or to encourage their use in certain cases. Even Mohlalisi does not condemn outright the use of condoms in all cases, saying only that it was a "matter of conscience" for the individual priest and parishioner.[13]

Condoms, though, are only part of the solution, especially considering that most women are infected within marriage, where their use is less likely. Married couples in Africa, as elsewhere in the world, want children. There is growing awareness among both African and Western AIDS experts that issues of sexual behavior must be addressed. Too often, however, the prevention debate has been polarized between secular liberals, who focus too much on condoms, and religious conservatives who emphasize abstinence.[14] Writer Helen Epstein makes a persuasive case that it is the fidelity prong of the widely accepted though rarely implemented prevention mantra "ABC"—Abstain, Be Faithful, or Condomize—that is most important and has been most neglected in AIDS prevention efforts.[15]

Promoting fidelity seems like a perfect, and uncontroversial, role for churches in the AIDS fight. The Catholic Church is Africa's largest, most organized faith: in Lesotho, more than half the population is Catholic, along with the king and many of the country's important chiefs. They have a voice, but continue to do nothing even as their own fall ill and die from AIDS. Dr. Makenete told me that some of the first cases of AIDS in Lesotho were among priests, a claim that Mohlalisi denied but others in the church confirmed. The sick priests were sent to South Africa for treatment, but the church stayed silent about the larger issue.

4

AIDS STRIKES CLOSE TO HOME

ONE COLD WINTER EVENING, Adeline and I sat in a makeshift hair salon on a threadbare sofa amid chemical fumes and posters advertising American beauty products for blacks. It was the end of the month and she wanted to get her hair relaxed. I thought Adeline seemed in good spirits, though she admitted to being tired and her skin had broken out in small pimples. Later that evening I would learn that she had been putting on a brave face.

The salon, really just half a room with a mirror and a few plastic chairs, was located on the second floor of a decrepit sandstone building, just down the hall from where Adeline's mother sewed her traditional dresses, in a chaotic neighborhood in central Maseru known as the Bus Stop. Outside, the street was bustling with end-of-month commerce as people restocked their shelves after being paid. Inside, there was a splurge of activity. While we waited, a man in the back of the room was making counterfeit Puma products, applying slick screen prints in red and blue of the company's signature cat to white T-shirts and hats. The effect was quite realistic.

Adeline moved to a plastic chair in the middle of the room and donned a plastic apron. The stylist smeared pungent chemicals on her hair that burned the inside of my nostrils. "George's uncles," Adeline informed me, "are coming to pay *lobola* at Easter."

When she tested HIV-positive, Adeline assumed her romantic life was over. No man, she thought, would want a woman fated to suffer a slow and agonizing death, who carried in her blood a deadly virus. Such thoughts must have been a hard blow for Adeline the romantic, who still harbored dreams of happy ever after.

Her fears were not unrealistic. Single HIV-positive women, especially ones like Adeline who are open about their status or responsible enough not to begin a relationship without disclosing it, often say finding love after the virus is difficult. Many complained that no men will date them, even HIV-positive ones. A few women I knew had met boyfriends through AIDS organizations—at least one couple, both of them widowed, met through Positive Action—but even many HIV-positive men say they want uninfected partners.

Women I met, in contrast, were often far more willing to accept the risks involved in dating someone who is HIV-positive. As Adeline's HIV-positive friend Koali had put it, "Women have more love inside them than men." He himself, he admitted, wanted to marry a woman who wasn't HIV-positive. Another Positive Action member I heard about, though never met, was even rumored to use his public appearances—where he spoke about being HIV-positive—to pick up women. He had impregnated at least one girl, I was told, and had ordered her to refuse an HIV test if it was offered at the hospital when she gave birth, even if they offered her a single-dose of an antiretroviral that could dramatically reduce the chance that she would transmit the virus to her child. Such treatment was not available in Lesotho when Adeline gave birth to Bongy.

Just when Adeline had reconciled herself to a life without love, though, an extraordinary man walked into her life. His name was George, and like Peter, he was about ten years older than Adeline. According to custom, which traces ethnic heritage through the father's line, George is a Xhosa, one of the people who inhabit South Africa's southeastern coast. But his grandfather, a powerful traditional healer—or witch doctor, in George's words—had moved to

Lesotho, where he impressed the Basotho with his powers, became a rich man, and married a local woman. George himself had grown up in a township outside Johannesburg, and his urban family was now a mixture of Zulu, Xhosa, and Sotho. He often visited relatives in Ha'Senekane, though, where he had inherited a house, and said he felt closer to his Sotho heritage than his Xhosa.

The Christmas following Adeline's HIV test, George came to Ha'Senekane. His marriage, to a girl from the village who had been a classmate of Adeline's, had recently fallen apart, and he was looking for love. The two met and became friends. Adeline saw it as a harmless flirtation: he would return to Johannesburg and nothing more would come of it. She would never have to tell him she was HIV-positive because it would never go that far.

But George was not so easily dissuaded. He continued to pursue her after he left, calling her on her cell phone from Johannesburg and professing his love. Adeline, still recovering from the disintegration of her relationship to Peter, was flattered by the attention. But eventually, when he began telling her he would come to visit, she told him he didn't want to be with her because she was HIV-positive.

"He said at first he didn't believe. But then he said, uh-ah, that is not a problem. His sister had been infected and her daughter too. He said it felt like something he had already lived with," she told me. He told her that he respected her for telling him and that if he found another woman, she might be HIV-positive too but wouldn't know or have the courage to tell him.

George often visited on weekends after work, arriving in a minibus taxi from Johannesburg late at night, and would take her out to restaurants. Or she would cook for him in her small room, using food that he brought from Johannesburg. I asked her once if he ever cooked for her. She laughed hard at that. "George, he knows how to cook, but he does not like to." She asked me if men in my culture cooked, and when I told her that I insisted my partner do his share of the cooking, her only response was, "Wow." It was her common expression of amazement, drawn out into two syllables: "Wo-ow."

George worked as a mechanic in a suburb of Johannesburg, in a workshop that specialized in high-end German cars. He made a good salary—nearly twice what Adeline earned—although like Peter, he had far less education than Adeline. George had never finished high school and had at first struggled to find a job in an economy that had a dwindling need for unskilled labor. He eventually found work in the normal way, through a friend who already had a job in the shop. He was lucky to have stumbled on an increasingly rare thing in South Africa: an unskilled job that came with job security and benefits.

As we sat in the hair salon in the dimming light, Adeline told me that she and George were planning to get married. She had recently learned from village elders that although she had considered herself married to Peter, under traditional law—a set of unwritten rules that can be fluid and changing—the marriage had never been completed since he had never paid *lobola*. The elopement ceremony, she learned, sealed their engagement, but not their marriage. In a way, though, it made it easier to end the relationship. Peter's family would have to come and pay a fine for his impregnating her before she could be free to marry George, but there was no *lobola* to return.

George had also quickly become an important father figure to her son, Bokang. Bongy, Adeline said, had not seen Peter in years and barely remembered him. So George filled an empty space, providing a male role model in a world otherwise composed largely of women.

"Bongy is his son. He loves Bongy." Adeline assured me. "And Bongy loves him like a father. He is the only father Bongy has." On a recent trip, he had brought Bongy a heavy winter pea coat. Bongy loved it, although it was still several sizes too large.

I asked her if George wanted to have more children and whether they had discussed the issue.

"Maybe, but there are tests to be done," she said quietly. There in the hair salon, she did not elaborate. Adeline did not actively hide her status, but she did not openly advertise it either. She had never been the victim of discrimination based on her HIV status, but many other members of Positive Action had told her stories about their negative experiences, so she told only those people whom she trusted. Most of her family knew, though she had told no one at her work. Nor did Adeline tell the girl, a former student, who was now living with her while she finished her studies and who cooked and cleaned in return for food and a place to sleep.

Such talk was certainly not for the hair salon, especially when so many people around knew Adeline and her mother. It was not the first or last time we danced around the issue in the presence of others. "But he says if we cannot have more children he is happy just to have Bongy."

George, I later learned, did not know his own HIV status. He was afraid to get tested, despite Adeline's encouragement. And although he and Adeline used protection, he worried he could have been infected by a previous partner.

When her hair was shiny and straight, Adeline and I headed to The Good Times Café, a new restaurant that had recently opened in Maseru. The restaurant was shiny and new, glittering with metallic chairs and the colors of the American flag. It served cocktails and whiskeys at a high bar, along with what in Lesotho passes as American food. Although the prices—for food at least—were modest by Western standards, this was clearly the realm of Lesotho's elite. We even ran into one of Adeline's former accounting lecturers.

We sat down and I began to scan the menu, which was laminated like the kind you might get at an American sit-down chain restaurant. The menu featured hamburgers and chicken burgers and something they called a California burger. I asked Adeline what she wanted and she burst into tears. There was something she had been waiting to tell me all day, she said. "Bongy has tested positive."

Adeline sobbed silently into her hands, her body heaving with each silent cry. I had never seen Adeline cry for herself, but now she was racked with grief. I was not prepared for this and didn't know what to say. This was still an open wound, raw and painful. Anything I could say seemed inadequate, so I handed her a napkin and asked her to tell me what happened. She dried her eyes and took a few gulping breaths.

Adeline, I knew, had long worried that she had passed the virus on to her son. For months she had known enough about the virus and how it was transmitted to worry that she might have infected him during birth or while breast-feeding, even though she had stopped a few months after he was born once the sores appeared under her arms. "I wanted to get him tested, but my mother refused," she had told me many times. I too had worried about the boy and encouraged her to have him tested. But Adeline didn't want to disobey her mother.

Recently, though, Bongy's visits to the doctor had become increasingly frequent. "He never seemed completely well," she explained. By 2004, he was visiting the doctor nearly every month. Finally, the special pediatrician that Adeline's mother took him to, one of the only specialists in children's medicine in Lesotho, recommended that he be tested for HIV. Relieved, Adeline gave her permission. The test, like her own a year earlier, had told her what deep down she had already suspected. Bongy too was sick. "It is a double pain," she said, tapping her chest over her heart, "to know that it came from me."

Without intervention, 30 to 45 percent of babies born to HIV-positive mothers will themselves become infected. Infection can happen before birth, during the process of birth itself, or through breast-feeding. The likelihood depends in part on how far the mother's disease has progressed; the more virus in her blood, the greater the chance that she will pass it on to her baby.[1] In developed countries, doctors had known since 1994 that antiretroviral drugs given to pregnant women could greatly reduce the transmission of HIV to infants, and by the time Adeline gave birth to Bongy, America and Europe had all but stopped the transmission of the virus from mothers to their children. But few African women had access to such drugs.

In the late 1990s researchers in the developing world began experimenting with shorter courses of antiretroviral therapy that, in the absence of full-fledged treatment for pregnant women, might still reduce the likelihood of transmission. Researchers in Thailand found that a four-week course of zidovudine, also known as AZT, the first antiretroviral drug approved for the treatment of HIV, could reduce transmission rates by 50 percent. But the drugs still cost about $89, far more than most people in the countries hardest hit by AIDS could afford, and researchers worried that the logistics of putting women on a four-week course of drugs might prove difficult in countries with underdeveloped prenatal care.[2] Later, researchers in Uganda, South Africa, and Tanzania discovered that just two doses of the antiretroviral drug Nevirapine, one given to the mother just before birth and the other to the baby just after, had similar results.[3]

Here was a cheap way to save thousands of babies that could be implemented even in countries with relatively poor medical facilities. The doses of Nevirapine cost only a few dollars (later its maker, the pharmaceutical company Boehringer Ingelheim, offered to give the drug free to any country with a program to prevent mother-to-child transmission), although there were also costs for testing, counseling, and formula milk.

When Adeline gave birth to Bongy in 2001, no hospital in Lesotho routinely offered HIV tests to pregnant women, much less antiretroviral drugs. The use of antiretroviral drugs to prevent the transmission of the virus from mother to child was well proven by 2001 when Bongy was born, but only a tiny number of HIV-positive pregnant women on the continent had access to it. In neighboring South Africa, around the same time, AIDS activists were taking their government to court to force them to offer the lifesaving drug. In Lesotho, which was poorer and less politically organized, the debate had not yet even begun. That year alone, thousands of HIV-positive women in Lesotho, like Adeline, passed the deadly virus on to their children when the technology existed to prevent this. The world had simply decided that it was too difficult or too expensive to save Basotho children like Bongy.

Adeline dried her eyes and went to the bathroom to wash her face. I felt tired and helpless, uncertain how to comfort her. I knew she had told me, in part, because she hoped that there was something that I could do to help.

When she returned from the bathroom, eyes red and puffy, Adeline asked me what could be done for her son, the only child she was likely to ever have. The doctor had given him an antibiotic, called

Bactrim, to help fight infection, along with a vitamin supplement and medicine for his persistent cold symptoms. But she knew that would not be enough to fight off the virus forever.

I had little good news to give her. While the treatment situation for adults was changing, for children the picture remained bleak. Antiretroviral drugs for children were still expensive and were made by only a few companies, and there were no generic versions of the drugs. In Lesotho, at that time, antiretrovirals for children were almost impossible to get. Baylor College of Medicine, the Lesotho government, and the drug company Bristol-Myers Squibb planned to build a pediatric AIDS clinic, but it would not open for at least a year. Without treatment, half of infected children die before the age of two, and most will not reach their fifth birthdays.[4] Bongy had lived longer than most, in part probably because he got regular medical care and had good nutrition. But he was already beginning to show symptoms. It was, I knew, a race against time.

Adeline said she had been feeling tired and worn out, but was otherwise feeling fine. She was also taking vitamin supplements but told me that many days she was too tired to cook and simply ate bread and tea. I chided her gently and told her she needed to eat well to keep her body strong. I also asked her if she had reconsidered her own decision not to seek treatment, which was beginning to become available for adults in Lesotho. She replied that for the time being, she was still feeling well, but that George wanted to take her to a special doctor in South Africa the next time she visited him in Johannesburg. She planned to get another CD4 count done and to reevaluate then. I reminded her she could get the same tests almost free from the government which had just opened the country's first antiretroviral clinic, called Senkatana, but she seemed to distrust the government medical care.

"Besides," she said, pushing her food around her plate, "if anyone should get ARVs, it should be Bongy."

THAT SATURDAY, I drove Adeline home to Ha'Senekane, where she planned to spend the weekend. I was heading back to Johannesburg the next day and intended just to make a quick visit to say hello to her family. I also hoped to meet Adeline's father, who was home for his monthly visit from the Beatrix gold mine where he worked in South Africa.

It was a cold and blustery afternoon, and the wind had a bite that made spring seem a long way away. As we arrived, it began to rain softly. We dashed inside from the car, our arms wrapped around ourselves for warmth, and were greeted by Bongy, who demanded to know if we had brought him KFC. He loves Kentucky Fried Chicken, which has become popular in many parts of Africa, but to his disappointment we hadn't brought any. He was mollified by a bag of Nik Naks, a cheese-flavored corn chip that resemble Cheetos.

While Bongy ate his chips, we sat down in the kitchen for tea steamed in a pot and slices of homemade bread with Adeline's father. The kitchen was painted pale green and outfitted with a large wooden table, a gas stove, and a long bench against one wall. It had the feel of a country cabin, rustic but cozy. As we ate, a skinny old woman in a long skirt tumbled through the door. She was Adeline's Aunt Tsidi, the eldest sister of her father.

Tsidi was rail thin, with a deeply lined face, and was clearly very poor. She looked more like Adeline's elderly grandmother than her aunt; Adeline told me Tsidi was twenty years older than her father and lived in a small house on the other side of the village. Her clothes, though clean and well-tended, were worn, and her thinness had a hungry edge to it.

Still, she had a cheerful disposition, and she greeted Adeline with a gap-toothed smile and asked who I was. The girl whom Adeline's family hired to care for Bongy during the day handed Tsidi a large slice of bread and a metal mug of sweet tea, which she dipped into heartily. It was a long time before she came to the point of her visit. Her only son, Zachariah, was sick and she had come to ask for help.

It was bitterly cold outside. Since Adeline wanted to see her cousin Zachariah, who was the age of her father, in his fifties, we drove Tsidi to her small home, a crumbling, one-room brick house on the ridge of a hill overlooking a patchwork of small fields. The relative wealth of Adeline's branch of the family became glaringly obvious.

We stepped inside and waited for our eyes to adjust to the dim light. The rectangular house had a mud floor and ochre-colored walls. On one side, in a pit in the center of the floor, were the smoldering remains of a small fire with a kettle, where Tsidi obviously cooked, and a small pile of dried corn kernels next to a stone mortar. It was the only food in the house.

On the other side, to the right of the door, stood two single beds. One, neatly made, must have been Tsidi's. In the other, on a rough sack placed directly on the sagging wires of the bed frame, lay Zachariah.

He was wrapped tightly in blankets, with only his head exposed. His face, illuminated by a ray of light from the house's single window, was skeletal. Yellowed eyes jutted out from his skull and his gums had receded, leaving the long roots of his teeth exposed. Zachariah made no sound, except for an occasional hiccup. He was clearly dying, and in a quick glance, I realized Adeline knew it too.

She was shocked, both at Zachariah's state and at the desperate poverty of her aunt. She asked her aunt if he had been to a doctor and whether they had any food. The answer to both was no. A few months earlier, Tsidi said she had taken him to a local man. But he wasn't really a doctor, just a man who had once worked in the pharmacy of a hospital and knew a little bit about drugs. Tsidi wanted to take him to the hospital in Maseru, but he was too sick now to ride in a taxi. She would have to hire a private car to take him, at a cost of perhaps 150 maloti or more—nearly $25—and she had no money even for food. She worried too that if she took him to Maseru and he died, she would have no way to bring him home for burial.

Adeline and I stepped outside to speak, although her aunt spoke no English.

"He has AIDS," she said, fear in her eyes. She was clearly frightened. In his pain and suffering, I think, she saw her future.

I asked her if Tsidi still wanted to take Zachariah to the hospital. If she did, I would drive him there. I had doubts about whether they would be able to do anything to save him; he was clearly close to death, and Tsidi didn't have enough money to take him to a private hospital. We would have to go to Queen II, which I had yet to visit but had heard bad things about. But I thought they might be able to do something to ease the pain and make his last days more comfortable.

We went back inside and Adeline relayed my offer to her aunt. She clapped her hands with gratefulness and asked if we could come back in half an hour, to give her time to wash her son before we went to Maseru.

We returned to Adeline's house to tell her family what we planned to do. Her mother had returned from Maseru, and she and Adeline discussed Zachariah. She had known he was sick, but not how badly, and agreed that we should take him to Maseru. But it was Saturday night, and graduation day at the University of Lesotho. Adeline's mother worried that there would be no doctor staffing the hospital that night. I agreed to delay my return to Johannesburg, and we made plans to come back the next morning. We would have to start early, in order to get there before the line at the hospital got too long.

Adeline and I drove back to Maseru, this time with Bongy in the backseat chattering about how he was going to be a driver when he grew up, while Adeline's mother returned to Tsidi's with food and a spare mattress to tell her the new plan.

I PICKED ADELINE and Bongy up at 6:15, and we drove to Ha'Senekane in the early-morning mist. The haze gave everything a dreamlike feel; we passed sleeping villages and riders on horses, who appeared like apparitions from the semidarkness, their bodies shrouded in heavy blankets.

We left Bongy with his grandmother. Tsidi was waiting for us when we arrived around seven. She had washed and dressed Zachariah, who was sitting up on his bed, wrapped tightly in blankets. Adeline's father had come to help, and he and Adeline carried Zachariah to the car. Adeline's cousin was waiflike, his skin ash-colored and as translucent as parchment; it flaked off in small pieces every time he moved. Zachariah's clothes sagged loosely on him, and his yellow-striped pants, which looked like they had walked out of another decade, nearly fell off as they moved him into the car. I was terrified he would die on the way.

Adeline sat in the front, with her father, aunt, and cousin squeezed into the back of my small car. Zachariah said nothing the whole trip, but his mother chattered away in Sesotho, laughing and joking. She would learn English, she told Adeline, so she could come to Johannesburg and work for me. She practiced a few words in English and Adeline teased her about her pronunciation. I was surprised at first that Tsidi was not more somber, given that we were driving her dying son to the hospital. It was not that she was insensitive to her son's plight; Tsidi clearly cared deeply for Zachariah and had devoted herself to his care. Perhaps it was simply her way of coping with the tragedy, or perhaps the trip, as desperate as it seemed to me, had given her a sliver of hope.

Queen II, the country's flagship hospital, lies in the center of Maseru. It is a cluster of low, brick buildings painted white and capped with green, sheet-metal roofing. The entrance is a narrow road, suitable only for a single car, that serves as both entrance and exit.

When we arrived, I waited in the car with Zachariah and Tsidi while Adeline and her father went inside to fetch someone to help. They returned with a metal gurney, and together we helped Zachariah onto it and then rolled him up the ramp into the emergency room, which was already half full.

The emergency room didn't look too bad at first. There were beds and intravenous bags filled with clear fluid. The linens were ripped but clean, and there were at least basic medical supplies. But the nurses were a disgrace. They barely looked up as we rolled Zachariah inside and made no move to assess his condition, much less to comfort him. One of the two nurses sat covering a clipboard with white surgical tape. Another, plump from inactivity, sat behind a desk. Her job, it appeared, was to ring a bell when it was time for a new patient to enter the emergency room. We spent hours there and she never moved an inch. Later, an even fatter nurse arrived. This one sat behind a counter at the entrance of the room, stuffing her face with food. Her job was to collect the 10 maloti fee, about $1.50, from patients before they could enter.

We waited for more than an hour before the doctor arrived, and the whole time Zachariah lay on the cold metal trolley. Tsidi had to fetch and then empty a bedpan for him. When the doctor, a South Asian woman, finally came to begin her examination, she told Adeline and her father to move Zachariah onto one of the beds. The nurses just watched, offering no help. The doctor was clearly hesitant to touch Zachariah and asked Adeline to unbutton and pull back her cousin's shirt. In English—our only common language—she told us that she suspected tuberculosis and that Zachariah probably didn't have long to live.

"TB and something else," Adeline whispered to me. "She doesn't want to say."

The doctor wanted to admit him, but she didn't think there was a free bed in the ward, so she sent him for a chest X-ray. Adeline and her father rolled Zachariah through the hospital corridors, which were outside but covered, to the X-ray room but were told there that there was something wrong with the machine, so only people with stab or bullet wounds were allowed to get X-rays. Everyone else was supposed to go to the military hospital across town. Somehow, I'm not sure how, Adeline and her father managed to get one anyway.

By the time they returned, the South Asian doctor had disappeared. A nurse eyed Adeline suspiciously and asked her where she had gotten the X-ray, which she was then carrying in a brown envelope. Adeline told the nurse that they had gone home to fetch them.

"If she knows we got them here, she might make a fuss," Adeline said to me, still whispering.

A long line had formed in the waiting room and now snaked out the door. There was a woman whose middle finger had turned green, a small boy with a tubercular cough, and a young man with a bandaged head who had gotten into a car accident the night before. Like us, he had assumed there would be no doctor on duty during the night and had waited until the morning to go to the hospital. One young woman with an injured foot was carried in on the back of an older woman, probably her mother. Later, two women were rolled in on metal gurneys. Like Zachariah, they were thin and wasted.

"AIDS," pronounced Adeline.

Adeline and her father went off in search of the doctor, leaving me with Zachariah. I didn't know what to say to him or even if he could understand English. Uncertain what to say, I patted his hands, hoping to offer him a little of the human comfort the nurses seemed unwilling to provide. Tears began rolling from his eyes, but he was too weak to even brush them away. I don't know if they were tears of pain, gratitude, or embarrassment.

Finally another doctor, this time a man who looked East Asian, came to look at the X-ray.

"Abnormal pneumonia," he pronounced in a heavy accent. He told Adeline that he wanted to admit Zachariah—as the best English speaker in the family, Adeline had become their spokesperson—and began to prepare an IV drip. The doctor told Adeline to ask Zachariah to make a fist, but he was too weak. The doctor had to make the fist for him and squeeze it in his own hand. He stabbed Zachariah several times before he found a vein. Adeline and I both cringed.

The IV in, the doctor scribbled some notes on Zachariah's medical card and sent us to Ward 5, the men's ward. Again, we rolled him ourselves. Inside the ward, we were greeted by a harried nurse in a surgical mask who told us there was no bed for him. I looked around and every bed was filled with a man who looked much like Zachariah, and the air was hot and sticky with disease and death. It seemed impossible that anyone could get well there, and I recalled the words of a local aid worker who had told me the day before, "They say at Queen II, you go in the front door and out the back—through the morgue."

The nurse was sympathetic but waved her hands at the overflowing beds with a shrug. There was nothing she could do.

We discussed various options. No private doctors were open on a Sunday. We could try taking him to another government hospital in a different city, but the situation there might be the same, and even if he did receive care, it meant that he would be alone. Tsidi didn't have enough money to visit him or to stay nearby. And if he died there, it would be difficult for her to take the body home for burial. The family had no money to pay for a private hospital and those too were far away in any case. I could offer to pay, but money was only part of the problem; he was dying of a disease that this country still had no capacity to effectively treat. I did not offer to pay, although I would have if they had asked, for fear that I would be imposing my desire to save him on the family, perhaps raising unwarranted hope and causing unnecessary suffering. I worried that by taking him to the hospital, I had already made things worse.

After consulting with her aunt, Adeline said we would take him home to be cared for there. He would die, we all knew. But that was the family's choice, and they seemed to accept it as inevitable. Adeline went to the hospital's pharmacy to fill the prescription the doctor had scribbled, some over-the-counter painkillers and antibiotics. They only had the painkillers.

On the way back to Ha'Senekane, we stopped at a grocery store. I went inside and bought some cornmeal, broth, eggs, peanut butter, pumpkin, and butternut, all things that could be mashed into soft, "baby" food. I didn't know if Zachariah could even eat that, but it would be better than dried corn kernels, the only food they had at home.

We were silent in the car. Tsidi was no longer laughing. I wondered whether my assistance had made things worse. Perhaps we simply had caused Zachariah additional discomfort by moving him, and prolonged what we all knew was inevitable. Then again, perhaps the IV and pills and food eased his last days. I will never know. Tsidi called me an angel. I didn't feel much like one.

I still wonder whether there was more that I could have done. In the end, though, I think I made the right decision. It was not my place to try to "save" him, and it is a conceit to think that I could. In the United States, we fight death until the bitter end, using extraordinary means to steal a few more days or even a few more hours, no matter what the cost. We don't want to give up, even in the face of the inevitable.

Zachariah's mother had accepted his fate and decided it was better for him to die at home than alone in a strange hospital bed, where it is unlikely much could have been done for him anyway. Even if he had pulled through temporarily, the virus was already strong. No one in the family, except Adeline, had even acknowledged what truly ailed him.

Adeline and her father moved Zachariah back into the house—now he at least had a proper mattress to lie on. When he was tucked back into bed, I leaned over to say good-bye. As I did, he tried to stifle a hiccup and vomited blood and clear liquid. Before I could stop myself, I started back. Tsidi rushed to his side to clean him up, and once again, fat tears trickled from his eyes. This time, I'm sure it was embarrassment. I left, ashamed.

That afternoon I left for Johannesburg. Within the week, Zachariah was dead.

5

CRUMBLING SUPPORT

I was in the United States by the time Zachariah died and unable to attend his funeral. I had gone home in part to visit my grandfather, whose cancer had recently relapsed. I went with him to the Scott and White Memorial Hospital in Central Texas for his chemotherapy treatment. I was struck, as we waited in the air-conditioned lobby with its plush couches and piles of magazines, by the contrast between that hospital and the ones I had seen in Lesotho. The vast majority of people at Scott and White were old. The barren, overcrowded waiting room at Queen II where I had been just weeks earlier had been filled with children, teenagers, and middle-aged people. In the small Texas city of Temple, a backwater by American standards, my elderly grandfather was receiving state-of-the-art treatment for cancer. Queen II, supposedly Lesotho's premier hospital, didn't even have antibiotics. Much later I would learn that our experience there was far from abnormal. A report by the government ombudsman later that year found Queen II as we had, with drug shortages, too few nurses and doctors, and buildings in disrepair. There was still no working X-ray, although a new machine sat unused on the floor, waiting for installation because of unpaid bills.[1]

When I spoke to Adeline on the telephone after I had returned to South Africa a few weeks later, she told me that Tsidi had fallen into a depression. Zachariah was her only son and she was having trouble dealing with his death. There was no one now to look after her in her old age. She had gone to stay with relatives in a nearby village; this was somehow customary, a way of officially mourning, although I didn't quite understand the intricacies of the tradition.

Adeline had spent a few days at home over Christmas, although not as long as she would have liked. The catering business was kept busy with seasonal parties until December 23, and then she'd had to return to work ten days later. "I just rested," she told me over the phone. "I've been so tired."

Bongy was doing well, and the vitamins and antibiotics the doctor had given him seemed to be helping. He hadn't been sick since. Adeline seemed cheered by this news and by the fact that she had been able to spend some time with him. I thought about how difficult it must be to know your child was ill but not be able to see him.

George, her boyfriend, had come for part of the holidays, but he had not paid *bohali* as planned. He'd been unable to save enough but said that he had paid off some of his debts and now hoped to be able to save more.

Peter's family had come to speak to her parents as well. They were supposed to come to pay a penalty for impregnating her without marriage. Instead, they came to ask if Adeline and Bongy would return to him. Adeline's father refused. She had not spoken to Peter since December 2002, nine months after she left in him Rustenburg, when she went to the funeral of her sister-in-law. Peter's brother, the family told her parents, was now sick too. Adeline suspected that the cause was AIDS.

I PICKED ADELINE UP after class a few months later, and we headed to the nearby Maseru Sun, one of the two big hotels in town, for dinner. To her, it was the most luxurious thing Lesotho had to offer and a symbol of the world she hoped one day to enter. Adeline had only been to the Maseru Sun once, in 1997, when she went with her classmates to play the slot machines in the hotel's small casino. "We spent everything, even the transport money," she laughed. "I had to call my mother for money to go home."

We sat down at the nearly empty buffet and Adeline served herself a heaping plate of salads. Her eldest uncle, she told me, wanted to take Tsidi's house from her and turn it into something for the tourists, maybe a restaurant.

There weren't many tourists in Ha'Senekane, nor could I imagine them lining up to eat in her ramshackle house. But as a woman, under traditional law, Tsidi had no claim to her own home, except through a male family member. Her only son was dead and she had no husband. The seizure of property from widows and orphans is a growing problem in many communities, and one that is driven by the clash between tradition and modernity. While it's true that customary law is patriarchal, custom also dictated the young and the elderly were to be cared for by the extended family and community.

Adeline pointed this out to her father and convinced him that the family could not take Tsidi's house from her. Together, they eventually convinced the majority of her uncles, except the eldest, who would have inherited the house. At Adeline's instigation, the family also decided to help Tsidi fix the house, each contributing some materials or labor. Adeline donated new doors. She lamented, though, the neglect of old women in her culture.

"The Basotho, they think that a woman should die first, and if she doesn't they think she is a witch," she said as she moved on to a plate heaped high with meat and vegetables.

"Basotho men, they like to marry younger girls so they get respect," she continued. What about your parents, I asked? Adeline laughed and said that it hadn't worked out for her father. Her mother, she said, ran the household finances.

"If he doesn't bring the pay slip, eish, then he will be in trouble. He will have to explain where the money went!" she said. I asked her what would happen when she and George married. She said she would keep hold of the bank card. "I have Bongy at home, so I have to."

When she lived in Rustenburg, Peter never gave her money, so she depended on her in-laws. She doesn't know what he did with his salary, but thinks he spent it on drink. She never wanted to be in that situation again.

One of her cousins, she told me, had faced the prospect of raising a child on her own with no support from the child's father. Desperate, she tried to secure an abortion in a country where the practice is still illegal, although it can be obtained across the border in South Africa. Marie Stopes, the international family planning organization, has even placed a large advertisement at the border. But Adeline's cousin didn't have enough money to go to South Africa or didn't know she could. The family doesn't know who performed the procedure, but something went wrong and the girl died. Adeline shuddered at the memory.

POSITIVE ACTION, the group Adeline turned to when she first discovered she was HIV-positive, was founded by an eccentric German businessman named Ingo Seifert, who first came to Lesotho in 1983 as a backpacker. Ingo had been bumming around the world for some time, working odd jobs, when he impregnated a Basotho woman. He decided to stay, opened a television repair business, and has been in Lesotho ever since.

Plump and balding, with the leathery, reddish skin of a white man who has spent too much time under the African sun, Ingo was a bit dodgy, but he had boyish charm and a disarming, almost innocent honesty that was hard not to like. He helped found Positive Action after a close friend, a fellow German who also lived in Lesotho, died from the virus. He told me that for a while he thought he too was infected, though it turned out that he had experienced a false positive test.

In its first years, Positive Action was quite active. It solicited money to put up the country's first AIDS-awareness billboards, recruited new HIV-positive members, and even got a few enrolled in antiretroviral drug trials in South Africa long before such drugs became available in Lesotho. This was in a period when no one else was doing much about the growing problem.

Around the time I began visiting Lesotho, however, the organization had begun to fall into disarray. Several of the more dynamic original members, including Koali, had recently been hired as peer counselors by a deep-pocketed international nongovernmental organization (NGO), Population Services International, or PSI, which was opening voluntary counseling and testing centers around the country; they no longer had time to volunteer at Positive Action. The members left in charge were, in general, less well-educated, less articulate, and, it seemed to me, less compassionate than those who had moved on. They also didn't get along with Ingo and quickly voted him off the organization's board, though he said he had already planned to leave. His management of the organization had sometimes been controversial, and he had been accused of failing to keep his business interests completely separate; some members of the organization felt he—a non-HIV-positive white man—was profiting from their despair.

In 2004, the United Nations was also pushing hard for Lesotho's various organizations of people living with AIDS—several others had popped up since 1999—to form a network. That suggestion, I quickly learned, had led to much infighting between the different organizations, each worried that cooperation would dilute its influence.

One of my first visits to Lesotho for this book coincided with the visit of Stephen Lewis, the United Nations Secretary-General's outspoken special envoy on AIDS in Africa. Lewis, who has done much to bring attention to the epidemic, had arranged to meet with representatives of organizations of people living with AIDS. The attendees were agitated, so Lewis evicted me from the meeting in order to protect the privacy of the people and encourage them to speak openly about their experiences. I later learned they were agitated not by the presence of a journalist in the room, but over UN efforts to form a network.

Being openly HIV-positive had become a good way to earn money, and many of the people living openly with AIDS in Lesotho had turned it into a full-time profession. By around 2002, Lesotho was under pressure from the international community and beginning to feel the impact of a rising death rate; there was suddenly more discussion about AIDS from the government, the United Nations, and community organizations. For a long time, though, there was lots of talk and not much action. Several Peace Corps volunteers, many of whom had been assigned to help implement government AIDS programs, told me they often joked that the only thing Lesotho did about AIDS was to hold workshops.

Members of organizations of people living with AIDS began receiving stipends from the government, NGOs, or the United Nations to speak at these meetings. Such engagements were jealously guarded and much fought over. Once, before I realized how bad things had become, I made the mistake of referring a man who had recently tested HIV-positive—I had met him at the offices of a local doctor—to Positive Action and several other groups.

A driver for a government ministry, he had asked me where he could meet other HIV-positive people and even expressed an interest in sharing his experiences, something that few Basotho men had so far been willing to do. When I spoke to him a few weeks later, he said he had called the numbers I had given him, including the contacts at Positive Action, who all turned him away, some of them, he hinted, quite nastily. I was horrified. A year earlier Positive Action had provided a major lifeline for Adeline, yet by the time I arrived, it had become little more than a money-making enterprise for a handful of people.

Ingo attributed this to cultural differences, though he really seemed to be blaming it on poverty. "The mentality of the people here is not an NGO mentality," Ingo said. "The notion that you volunteer because you really want to help—we have the luxury of doing that because we have the time for it. Here that mentality doesn't exist. People want money. They have needs and they want to fill those needs."

Many people living with AIDS in Lesotho are desperately poor. There is almost no social welfare system (in 2005, Lesotho began for the first time to provide tiny pensions of less than twenty-five dollars a month to elderly people) and no free health care. If you are poor and sick in Lesotho, life is a daily struggle to feed your family, access health care, and stay alive. In this context, I understood the slightly mercenary behavior of many of Lesotho's openly HIV-positive people and why the government, NGOs, and the United Nations had made a policy of paying them for their time.

At the same time, I was disheartened by the way in which poverty and misfortune seemed to have hardened many of them to the plight of others. I asked Adeline once about this problem. "It's difficult," she replied. "Many of the members have no jobs, so this is the only way they can get money. But still, there should be a sense of volunteerism—of helping your community without profit."

I worried too what this failure of leadership portended for the future of Lesotho: there seemed to be no natural leader among the HIV-positive people I met, someone whom I could envision spearheading a grassroots movement to demand better care and treatment for people with AIDS. Many people spoke highly of a woman named Ntilo Matela—including Adeline, who had met her at a conference. The founder of another organization called People Living Openly with AIDS, Ntilo died on Good Friday 2005, before I had a chance to meet her. She had begun taking antiretrovirals and her health seemed to be improving. But one day she began feeling sick and the next day she was dead.

ONE MORNING, not long after Ingo had been ousted from the organization, I dropped by the offices of Positive Action, which were then located in the back room of a house on the edge of the Bus Stop. Most expatriates I knew refused to go there, claiming that it was too dangerous. But it was my favorite part of the city. It had an aggressive, frenetic edge that I loved. Much of Maseru is sprawling and dully suburban, but the Bus Stop thumps with life.

After Ingo's departure, Positive Action hired Tebatso, a thin young man with short braids and a hint of a beard, to be the organization's coordinator, using money from an international donor. I asked Tebatso what had happened with Ingo.

"He was using the members. He was profiting from Positive Health, which should have been benefiting the organization as a whole," Tebatso said, referring to a side business Ingo had started selling vitamins and supplements.

There may have been some truth to this, yet I thought there was a certain hypocrisy as well. Ingo certainly wasn't the only one at Positive Action making money from people with AIDS. Two of the new board members weren't openly HIV-positive. Tebatso, who was drawing a decent salary from the organization, said he knew his status but wasn't ready yet to disclose it. Unusually, I suspected that the reason he didn't want anyone to know was because he was not HIV-positive and didn't want to be accused of exploitation. Yet these same people were complaining about others exploiting the HIV-positive. Their real objection, I thought, was that Ingo was a white man—and therefore, by definition, rich—making money from people with AIDS.

When I explained my project, Tebatso demanded to know how it would help people living with AIDS. "There is all this research going on, but not a lot of it helps local people," he said. I told him I was trying to help people in other parts of the world understand what was happening in Lesotho. That satisfied him almost too easily, as if he had only halfheartedly been asking the question.

I asked Tebatso if Positive Action planned to recruit new members. He looked nervously at a few of the board members, who were sitting on a couch on the other side of the room, and said they wanted to straighten out the organization first. The issue of recruiting new members would remain a point of major contention for months to come; the existing members had an entrenched interest in keeping the organization small. Tebatso tried to imply that people didn't want to join Positive Action because there was a lack of volunteer spirit in Lesotho.

"We're poor and we have no jobs," he said by way of explanation. I responded that I had visited other African communities that were even poorer where people did volunteer. He thought about this for a while and then said, "It's because we haven't suffered enough yet."

Tebatso was articulate and informed, yet he had a nervous quality that made him seem slightly anxious. Adeline was initially impressed by him and the things he claimed to have done. He had worked previously for an NGO that did conflict resolution and had studied in Europe and South Africa. He was impressed by Adeline as well and told her he thought he could help her get a scholarship to study abroad. She was excited by the idea and talked about it at great length for several weeks. Then, suddenly, she stopped mentioning it.

Early in 2005, a Peace Corps volunteer named Chuck Quehn arrived at Positive Action. Chuck, who was in his midfifties, had run AIDS organizations in Florida and Seattle. He had assumed when he was posted to Lesotho that his skills would be put to use. Instead, the Peace Corps sent him to a remote corner of the country and assigned him to do agricultural work. Unhappy there, he lobbied to move to Maseru and was eventually allowed to transfer to Positive Action on the condition that he live outside the city, which the Peace Corps considered too dangerous. Each day he commuted to Maseru by minibus taxi from a village about ten miles away. Chuck helped Positive Action apply for a big grant from Ireland that would allow them to start some new projects and hire more staff.

Chuck told me he often struggled with what his role should be in the organization. As an American with far better formal education than any of the members and long experience in fund-raising and running nonprofits, it would have been easy for him to assume a leadership role. He was frustrated with many aspects of Positive Action, especially in financial areas, but he also quickly realized that it was not his place to impose his values on the organization.

"I came in with all these ideas about how I was going to change things, like eliminating payments for members who came to meetings, but then I realized there wouldn't be any members left," he said. Chuck said he did try to stress the importance of spending money that had been donated for specific projects on those projects, arguing that more money would not be forthcoming if previous funds had been misspent. Even that, however, was a battle.

The members didn't see anything wrong with paying themselves large sums to attend meetings or spending money that had been donated for a computer on a television. In their minds, the purpose of the organization was to help people with AIDS, so anything that helped them was a fair use of money.

NOT LONG AFTER she was confirmed to be HIV positive, Adeline made the journey to Maluti Adventist Hospital, the mission hospital associated with the small health clinic where she had been tested. It was located about forty miles from Maseru in the picturesque village of Mapoteng. The nurse at the small clinic had counseled her that they might be able to help.

At the time, in late 2003, although an estimated 350,000 Basotho were infected with HIV, Maluti was the only hospital in Lesotho to have a dedicated HIV/AIDS clinic. Every health facility in the country was feeling the impact of the disease, but with the exception of Maluti and a few private doctors, the majority of clinics and hospitals simply treated opportunistic infections while ignoring the underlying infection.

More often than not, doctors never voiced their suspicion that AIDS was the underlying cause. Over the last two decades, this is the way AIDS has almost always been treated in Africa. Patients come in with tuberculosis or pneumonia or herpes or one of a dozen other common, AIDS-related opportunistic infections, are given their pills (if the health location they are sent to is lucky enough to stock them), and sent home.

I understand why many doctors hesitated to tell their patients that they carried a fatal disease, yet in the end this contributed to the veil of silence surrounding AIDS. But the situation also reflected a larger failure by doctors and the medical community to explore other treatment options. In the West, we do not give up on a patient simply because a full cure for his disease does not yet exist. Yet, for many years, Africans with AIDS were seen as a lost cause. While it's true that until recently no real treatment for AIDS existed, there were several relatively inexpensive interventions that could have helped prolong many lives and had been used in the wealthy world before the development of effective antiretroviral therapy. Doctors could have recommended lifestyle changes—such as eating well and stopping drinking and smoking—or prescribed prophylactic antibiotics, which can help prevent a number of opportunistic infections and were widely used in the United States, especially before the development of the new drugs. Even vitamin supplements, which some new research has shown can help delay the progression of the disease in poor countries, might have helped.[2] Yet there was very little research in these areas and, until recently, almost no guidance from the international community about how such low-tech interventions might have been used. "No disease in history has been so talked about and so little treated," one doctor who had spent his career working in Lesotho told me with frustration, though he said things are beginning to change now with improved access to antiretroviral treatment.

The continued existence of church-affiliated clinics and hospitals is a legacy of Lesotho's long mission history. These days, most mission health facilities receive the bulk of their funding from the government and only a small amount, if any, from the churches with which they are affiliated. Less than 10 percent of the budget at Maluti, for example, comes from outside donors and only a small fraction of that from Seventh-day Adventist organizations. Yet they retain the reputation of providing better care than government facilities, and many Basotho will travel long distances to receive help at such facilities, if they can afford the cost. As independently run facilities, mission hospitals are allowed to charge higher fees than government hospitals; it is this extra income, which supplements their meager government funding, that enables them to maintain higher standards. However, since the patients they serve are inevitably poor, many mission health facilities are still run on a shoestring budget; things at Maluti were sometimes so bad, I was told, that at times staff were forced to hold patients, or their bodies, hostage until their families paid their debts. That practice, though, had recently been abandoned.

"What the administration is increasingly realizing," a Peace Corps volunteer named Dick Nystrom, who, along with his wife, Pam, was finishing a two-year posting at the hospital, told me, "is that these people have nothing to negotiate with. So the hospital is trying to absorb an increasing amount of the costs." He continued: "Hospitals are having to try to figure out how to provide quality services with no money. It's an impossible task."

Still, most Basotho who could afford the fees (but could not afford to travel to neighboring South Africa for top-quality care) went to mission hospitals or clinics, and if they could, they came to Maluti, which had a reputation as the best hospital in Lesotho. Although the hospital's primary charge was to care for patients in the surrounding area, I knew many Maseru residents who went there for treatment.

Doctors at Maluti were among the first to begin responding to the threat posed by AIDS in Lesotho. They began offering HIV tests in 1991, long before such tests were widely available at government hospitals and more than a decade before the first center dedicated to voluntary counseling and testing would open. Four years later, under the direction of a young pastor and former mine worker named Mokhotu Makhalanyane, the hospital opened the country's first dedicated HIV/AIDS center.

In those days, there were no drugs to treat the disease, or at least none available for the poor of Lesotho. The triple cocktail of anti-retroviral drugs that is now the standard treatment for AIDS in wealthy countries first became available in the United States in 1996 but remained, for another five years, far too expensive for all but a handful of rich African patients who could afford to travel abroad for treatment. For many, all Maluti could offer then was a more comfortable death. The hospital started a home-based care program to help teach nearby communities and families to provide better care for the dying.

Perhaps Maluti's most significant contribution, however, was simply its acknowledgment of the epidemic. The hospital began offering AIDS tests and kept track of how many patients tested positive and how many of those later died. These statistics show the dramatic and rapid growth of the epidemic in the 1990s and provide a rough idea of what was happening across the country, although there were certainly regional variations in infection and death rates.

In 1994, the hospital had 5,905 admissions, of which 140 died during their stay (many more patients died after going home, but no accurate record of how many exists). Only seven of those deaths, about 5 percent, were known to be HIV-related. A decade later, in 2004, nearly eight thousand patients were admitted to the hospital, of whom nearly seven hundred died. Most striking, however, is that a staggering 52 percent of those deaths were *known* to be AIDS-related. The hospital was not only seeing more patients per year, stretching its resources, but an increasing number of those who did come were dying while in its care. For the health workers at Maluti, those were dark days.

A few months before Adeline went to Maluti, in late 2003, the hospital had received a donation of a machine that could measure CD4 counts, the first privately held machine of its kind in the country. The new machine, combined with a recent, and dramatic, fall in the price of antiretroviral drugs—due in part to the new availability of generic versions made in India—meant the hospital had begun to prescribe the life-prolonging drug regimes to those who could afford them, although the prices were still out of reach for most of the patients who tested positive at the hospital.

It was a brutal calculus. Those with money would live; those without would die. Maluti Adventist was a fee-for-service hospital that relied on income from patients to stay operational, and the staff often faced difficult choices about the rationing of care. Yet no disease laid out so starkly the divergent fates of the poor versus the rich, or at least the comparatively rich. Of course, in a global context, it had long been the case that rich AIDS patients lived and poor ones died, but then the rich and poor had lived on different continents. Now they lived next to each other in the same villages and shared the same hospital wards.

Adeline's CD4 count indicated that she had progressed into full-blown AIDS, and the Nigerian doctor who staffed the health clinic—almost all Lesotho's practicing doctors are foreigners—suggested that she begin antiretroviral treatment immediately, if she could pay. Adeline went home to think about it. She could probably afford to pay for the drugs out of her teaching salary, which was then 800 maloti a month, but it might consume half her income or more, leaving a very thin margin for the rest of life's expenses. And it left no cushion if she fell ill and needed to see a doctor or check into a hospital. For the time being, she was feeling well—better, in fact, than she had before she tested positive a few months earlier. In the back of her head, she admitted later, she worried about her son. Who would pay for his drugs when he began to need them? So despite the fact that her body was perilously undefended, Adeline decided to wait. "It was the stress," she said, convinced that her CD4 count would rebound now that she had come to terms with her infection. She would turn to antiretrovirals when she began getting noticeably sick.

I often worried about the wisdom of this decision; Adeline had still not started treatment when I met her in mid-2004. Nor had she gone back for another CD4 count, so she had no way of knowing whether her theory about the relationship between stress and the progression of the disease was true or merely wishful thinking. I had met enough HIV-positive people who seemingly healthy one day were dead days or weeks later. It was true that she hadn't fallen seriously sick since her test, but I feared that a powerful infection might sweep her suddenly into severe illness. Then Adeline might well die. Treating sudden, life-threatening diseases was not one of the strong points of Lesotho's hospitals, even good ones like Maluti Adventist.

In the months I spent visiting Lesotho, Adeline's reluctance to seek treatment posed, for me, a difficult ethical and moral dilemma. My role as a journalist was to try to understand, not influence her choices. And yet I felt that her decision was based on a lack of information and was potentially putting her at dire risk. When I hadn't spoken to her in a few weeks, I would pick up the phone to call with apprehension. What if she had died? I couldn't force her to seek treatment, but I did encourage her to get another CD4 count and seek further medical advice.

Around the time I began visiting Lesotho, Senkatana, the country's first antiretroviral clinic, opened in an old leper hospital on the edge of the city of Maseru. It was not quite free—patients had to pay the same ten-maloti fee they paid to visit other government hospitals—but it was dramatically cheaper than Maluti or the other private doctors who offered antiretrovirals. I visited the clinic several times and always relayed my observations to Adeline. I even offered to drive her there, but still she hesitated.

Yet, Adeline's choice was, perhaps, not so irrational, especially given her situation. Antiretroviral drugs contain potent chemicals and, like many modern pharmaceutical miracles, have physical side effects, some of which can themselves be life-threatening. Problems such as weight gain, anemia, adult-onset diabetes, sharply elevated cholesterol levels, and rashes are seen in many patients, and although most of these are not serious, they can be uncomfortable.[3] Once begun, the drugs must also be taken for life. I know many Americans and rich South Africans who choose to delay taking antiretroviral drugs for as long as possible, trying, as Adeline was doing, to keep themselves healthy through good nutrition, homeopathic remedies, and treatment of opportunistic infections. Judge Edwin Cameron, one of the first South Africans to make his HIV-positive status public, writes in his memoir *Witness to AIDS* that he resisted his doctor's advice to begin antiretroviral drugs for a long time.[4] At the same time, Cameron had doctors monitoring his progress. If he fell suddenly ill, he would have had all the benefits of a first-world health system to nurse him back to health. The health-care system in Lesotho offered no such safety net.

Nevertheless, had Adeline begun treatment through Maluti Adventist, it would have put her in a precarious economic position. Traveling to the Maluti hospital was a long and expensive trip, and one she would likely have had to make each month since it is unlikely she would have been able to pay for more than a month's prescription at a time. Also, although Maluti's decision to offer antiretroviral drugs to those who could afford them was done with the best of intentions, born of a sincere desire to help those who otherwise faced a death sentence, I also had my reservations about the quality of AIDS care there.

I had met another woman, a round-faced factory worker with a girlish voice, whose name was Charlotte. She earned a similar salary to Adeline as the leader of a sewing line in one of Maseru's Chinese-run factories. Her husband had died in April 2003 and soon afterward she tested HIV-positive. The same doctor at Maluti whom Adeline would later see suggested that Charlotte begin antiretroviral drugs. She took his advice, but although the doctor told her not to stop taking the drugs, even for a short time, she didn't truly understand the risk. Perhaps because he was concerned that she could not afford the entire three-drug cocktail, the doctor also prescribed her only two of the three drugs that are part of the normal AIDS treatment regime, which also increased the likelihood she would develop resistance to the medications.

HIV is an unusually adaptable virus, and there is a high risk of mutation in patients who take the wrong regime of drugs or fail to take their drugs faithfully and at prescribed times of day; such lapses are potentially deadly for the patient, who might no longer respond to available treatments. It is also worrying for public health experts, whose greatest fear is that HIV will mutate into something even more deadly than it is now. Imagine a virus with the lethality of AIDS combined, for example, with the virulence of Ebola or the transmissibility of the common flu. Or, in a less dramatic example, consider the threat posed by a common variety of AIDS that is simply resistant to the treatments developed over the last decade. We would be back at ground zero, back in the dark days of no hope. The threat was more than hypothetical, both because of the unique characteristics of HIV and Africa's poor history of drug management. Malaria remains one of the continent's biggest killers, in part because many of the drugs used to control the disease no longer work.

The most common reason for the misuse of drugs in Africa is poverty. Charlotte struggled to pay for her drugs, which cost more than half her normal monthly salary of around $100 (650 maloti). She had also borrowed 1,800 maloti from an old woman to pay for her husband's funeral. The old woman took Charlotte's bank card and withdrew 500 maloti each month for more than a year, long after the debt and any interest had been paid off. For the first few months after Charlotte began taking the drugs, family members—especially her husband's grandfather, who earned a pension in South Africa—helped her pay for them while she and her son lived almost exclusively on cornmeal. She grew thin and her skin lost its luster. Because she wasn't eating, the drugs made her sick. But her family too were poor and after a while said they could no longer help. Charlotte had to decide between food and medicine, so she stopped taking her drugs.

Charlotte's story was not unique. A Tanzanian doctor named Tonny Mwabury who had special training in HIV treatment and had recently opened his own clinic told me that he was seeing a large number of patients who had been improperly prescribed antiretroviral drugs by private doctors. He worried that doctors were casually prescribing the drugs without understanding the risks. If a patient couldn't afford all three drugs in the cocktail, they would prescribe one or two. And they made little effort to follow up with patients who began treatment to ensure that they continued. He had one patient who had been given just ten doses of an antiretroviral called Nevirapine. She later died. I wrote a story for an American newspaper quoting Dr. Mwabury, which was later followed up by the BBC.[5]

Although neither piece directly criticized the Lesotho government, and both pointed out that the problem was not limited to Lesotho, Dr. Mwabury—who also worked part-time at Maluti—was promptly dragged before a government committee and threatened with the withdrawal of his license to practice medicine in Lesotho. He was eventually given a warning and allowed to continue working.

It was a chilling reminder that Lesotho's democracy remained paper thin. When I later confronted the health minister, Dr. Motloheloa Phooka, about the case, he admitted that the uncontrolled proliferation of antiretroviral drugs was a problem and that the stories had brought the government's attention to the issue. But in the next breath, he complained about how much damage the stories had done to people's faith in the drugs—the BBC is carried on Lesotho TV and on an FM radio station—and the audacity of the foreign doctor who had criticized his host government.

6

ADELINE'S THING

For some reason, I had pictured George as a thin, serious man. Peter's look and image, on the other hand, was inspired by *tsotsi* culture, South Africa's tough, urban equivalent of American gangsta rap style. Though George too lived in the townships and was nearly the same age, Adeline described him as a traditional man and said he had gone through the disappearing Basotho initiation process that marked the transition from childhood to adulthood. For six months he lived in the wilderness with other young men his age, learning what it meant to be a man. Before that, he had used drugs and flirted briefly with crime. The initiation experience, he would later tell me, had helped him to become a real man.

Women once participated in something similar, but Adeline's family had abandoned such practices when they embraced Christianity. Neither Adeline nor her mother had been initiated, though her grandmother had been. Few young urban people these days go through traditional initiation, and I assumed George's conservatism would manifest itself in his dress and manner as well as his beliefs.

My mental image of George was reinforced by his voice, which on the phone was deep and soft. His English was slightly hesitant and peppered with township slang. Adeline, in contrast, spoke school English rather than street English, slowly and with her consonants enunciated, but with the ease and familiarity of a fluent, though not native, speaker. In the end, George was nothing like I had imagined him.

When I finally met him, it was in a South African township on the outskirts of Johannesburg, not far from my home. George's niece was having a twenty-first birthday party, a celebration that in South Africa marks the passage between childhood and adulthood, although turning twenty-one confers no special legal rights. Like their American counterparts, young South Africans today become legal adults at eighteen: they can vote, fight for their country in war, and drink legally. But twenty-one has become the symbolic moment of adulthood in modern South Africa and is usually celebrated with a rowdy party and copious supplies of booze. Perhaps "twenty-firsts," as they are called in South Africa, were originally celebrated largely by white South Africans who inherited the tradition from the British, but as traditional initiation ceremonies have slowly disappeared, they are increasingly being embraced by South Africans of all colors. George's relatives had been planning the event for months. Adeline had also been looking forward to it.

The youngest of eight children, George lived with his extended family. Their township of Wattville was on the edge of a white, working-class city known as Benoni, located about fifteen miles east of Johannesburg in an area today called the East Rand. Although Benoni is technically a separate city, a decade of boom times and urban sprawl have erased the dividing lines and it has become simply part of the endless tumble of neighborhoods that comprises Johannesburg. It is on the poorer, less fashionable side of the sprawl, far from Johannesburg's staid, middle-class, white suburbs or the glitz of its northern neighborhoods, where rich whites and South Africa's postapartheid black elite strike deals over cigars and fine whiskeys before heading home in their high-end BMWs. To Adeline, though, there was no difference—it was all just Johannesburg: city of big lights, big dreams, and big dangers.

By the time we made our way to Wattville on the Saturday morning of the party, Adeline was struggling to hide her annoyance with George. We had driven to Johannesburg from Maseru the night before, after Adeline finished work, but didn't arrive until after ten. George had promised to come pick her up at my house but couldn't find someone with a car. I had a car but didn't know how to get to Wattville—which was not even on my map—and George didn't know how to give me directions. We tried to find a place where we could meet, but there was no place we both knew and which he could reach at night by public transport.

We lived in the same city, but in different worlds: I behind high walls in a neat, green neighborhood in one of Johannesburg's largely white northern suburbs, and he in a poor, little-known township on the fringes of the metropolis. Well past midnight, he was still trying to find someone with a car; exhausted, we made arrangements to meet the next morning at a mall in Benoni that was shaped like an old Mississippi riverboat. The next day, we waited there for more than an hour before he called my cell phone and said he could not make it. Instead, he gave us directions from the mall to his sister Dora's house, where the party was being held. Predictably, we got lost—there are no maps of Wattville and only a few street signs— and Dora had to walk several blocks to come find us. Adeline was not pleased.

At the house, party preparations were in full swing. Women were stirring stew and rice in gigantic cast-iron pots over open fires under the overhang that served as a garage, while in the kitchen huge mounds of carrots, onions, and potatoes were being chopped with enthusiasm amid rapid chatter that blended English and several African languages. The men were in charge of brewing traditional beer outside; in the spacious kitchen women cooked and chatted.

We were greeted like long-absent family members and dished up plates of pap and tripe—stiff white corn gruel and boiled intestines—before being ushered into the comfortable living room, crowded with furniture. A local favorite, tripe has a strong, pungent smell and a chewy consistency. When you eat it with your fingers, in the traditional way, the smell sticks to your hands for hours.

Wattville—which Adeline pronounced "Wardville"—is the oldest surviving township in the East Rand, having been founded in 1941; in geography and design it is a legacy of apartheid policies that tried to control the migration of Africans to the cities. Townships, located on the fringes of white cities, were intended to be temporary holding places for the black labor that whites needed but didn't want living too close by. More like poor workers' housing than slums, the townships are architecturally soulless, though many families have labored hard to add a personal touch to their homes.

In the old part of the township, where George lives, the houses are neat brick buildings, almost all alike from the outside, lining wide streets. The houses all have electricity and running water, and many have been improved by their owners. Inside, each is unique, reflecting the tastes of the family who lives there and often the era in which it was upgraded. Almost all of George's immediate family still lives in Wattville. The house he shares with a sister and her children was clearly decorated in the 1970s. The entrance to one of the bedrooms, used by George's nieces, is an arch covered in rust orange tiles, and some of the windows are made of opaque glass. The house where the party was being held, which belonged to another sister, was more modern in décor, but similar in size and shape.

Like many Johannesburg townships, Wattville has a reputation for violent crime and when I later looked it up in the archives of several Johannesburg newspapers, the only references I found were about the recently arrested criminals—murderers, hijackers, robbers, and rapists—who called Wattville home. In one salacious case that hit the headlines a few months after my visit, a local minister and his wife were arrested for abusing foster children. They were receiving government grants for taking care of the children, one of whom, a five-year-old boy, was found locked in a shed, without food or water, and covered in his own feces.

The Wattville I saw that day, though, was a friendly place. On Saturday morning, when we arrived, the streets were buzzing with activity. Children played on the streets and young men lovingly washed and polished beat-up old cars. Neighbors greeted each other from front yards and barked reprimands at errant children. There was, much more than in my own neighborhood on the other side of the city, a sense of community. Wattville felt like a small town, where extended families live in close proximity and everyone knows each other and their secrets.

George finally arrived as I was struggling to finish my tripe with Adeline in the living room. He walked in with a slightly loping gait, hands in pockets, and stuck out his hand in greeting. At first, I didn't realize who he was because when he introduced himself, hand extended, he used his last name, which I didn't immediately recognize. Adeline laughed and told him to stop joking.

"Tell her your first name," she ordered.

"George. I'm George," he grinned. The man looking down at me was plump and had a baby face. His clothes were preppy, but worn with a slight sloppiness; he was dressed in navy blue pants, hung low to expose the band of his underwear, a polo-style shirt, and a baseball cap. Everything, except the hat, appeared a size too large. It was a look American skateboarders worked hard to cultivate, but I couldn't figure out if it was intentional or accidental on George's part.

George, I quickly discovered, was a jokester. As we walked through Wattville to his house, he asked me how old I was. I was younger than he. He asked if I was married. When I said no, he told me I was the perfect age for him. I looked at him and his face was straight, but there was a twinkle in his eye. Adeline, he continued, would be his first wife, but he wanted to have at least one other: she would live in his house in Lesotho, the other would live in Wattville.

"In our culture," George declared, "a man should have at least two wives. My grandfather had two wives." He was joking, I was pretty sure. At least Adeline kept laughing. I had seen a dried brown palm frond shaped in a cross hanging on the wall of his room—of the type handed out in Catholic churches on Palm Sunday—so I asked him what his church would think of his taking more than one wife. He just laughed.

We spent the day chopping and cooking in preparation for the party, to which more than a hundred people had been invited. To appease Adeline, who was still annoyed with him, George washed my car, which was covered in dirt from Maseru's muddy roads, in the driveway of the house. His family was friendly and welcoming, if at first a little amused by the presence of a pale-skinned American. His niece, in whose honor the party was being held, was thrilled that I had come. "I'm going to be famous!" she shrieked as we stuck toothpicks loaded with pieces of hot dogs and cheese into large breads baked in the shape of crocodiles. "I'm the only girl in Wattville who is going to have a white girl at her party!" She also confided to me: "No black girl has ever bought these," she said, gesturing at the crocodiles.

George's older relatives were equally friendly, if more curious about exactly who I was and how I knew Adeline. She hadn't told George's family about her HIV status yet, and it wasn't my place to disclose it for her, so I told them part of the truth, that I was writing a book about women in Africa and that Adeline was going to be in the book. One of his sisters, Dora's twin, looked at me thoughtfully when I told her this.

"We women, especially we women in Africa, we suffer too much," she said slowly, drawing out the word *too*. "Our husbands, they tell us that we cannot do things. When I was young, I used to think that it was just our culture, but now that I am older, I am not sure."

GEORGE ASKED ME if I could go with him to collect some ice at a nearby store. We climbed into my newly cleaned car, along with a little girl with long braids—she was a relative of George's whose relationship I couldn't quite work out—who wanted to ride in the car. It was early afternoon, but George had been drinking steadily all morning and there was beer on his breath.

"At first I wasn't happy that you were Adeline's friend," George told me as he directed me through the maze of streets in Wattville. He meant, I knew, that he wasn't happy that I would be writing about Adeline. "But then I decided that it was okay." He paused. "I have a white friend too. He came to Ha'Senekane to stay with my family."

It was a sad statement about the persistent racial and economic divides in South Africa that although George lived in the country's most integrated city, he could call only one person of another race a friend. That friend, he told me, was German.

We continued our earlier conversation about gender relations, this time more seriously. George is less educated than Adeline, a fact that he is clearly aware of and somewhat apprehensive about. He had been taught that it is a man's job to take care of his wife and children, yet he was facing the prospect of marrying a woman whose earning capacity was far higher than his own. He seemed to be struggling with what it means to be a man in a changing world.

George had been married once before, to one of Adeline's class-mates, a girl she later told me she did not much like. The woman had come with George to Johannesburg, where he supported her and helped her finish high school. They had even had a child who had died as an infant. But once she finished high school, George said, she got a job, started seeing another man, and eventually left him. He let her go. "A man's strength is not only in his arm," he said. "It is here too." He tapped his chest, just above his heart. He was telling me that he was not a violent man and that he showed his manhood by letting her go.

Clearly, though, George blamed his wife's departure on her new-found financial independence. He told me he didn't want Adeline to work, but that she was determined. He shrugged when he told me this, as if to say, "Women!"

I often worried that the class divide between Adeline and George yawned far greater than either of them realized. While they came from similar backgrounds—both were raised in stable, two-parent, working-class families—their ambitions for life seemed dramati-cally different. Adeline clearly expected to enter the middle class and had the education and drive to make that possible, although loom-ing over all her plans was the virus that was quickly multiplying in her blood. She rarely talked about her infection and her plans for the future in the same breath; it was as if they were two separate realities, like nonconcentric circles.

In the months I spent visiting Adeline, she would talk often about the life she wanted to have, and which she expected would be available to her when she had passed her accounting exams. When I told her once that I was getting rid of my car, a ten-year-old Opel that was groaning increasingly loudly on my long cross-country trips, she asked me what it would cost and discussed the merits of the cars she would one day like to own. My car was okay, she clearly thought, but nothing spectacular. When I would pick her up after her classes, it was often the oldest and least flashy car waiting outside: her classmates, many of whom worked for the government or international companies with offices in Lesotho, could afford fancy cars, and so, she thought, one day she would as well.

Cars weren't the only Western luxury Adeline coveted. Earlier that Saturday, as we waited for George at the mall, she stopped to look in the window of a jewelry story to admire the various engagement rings. Like an American girl, she wanted a diamond. But she also wanted *bohali*. I pitied the African man who had to save for both and wondered silently how George would ever afford a diamond ring.

When Adeline pictured her future, she saw a big house in the suburbs, a flashy car, and fine restaurants. I could see her in that world, sitting behind a fancy desk at a big company. George had more modest ambitions. Once I asked Adeline if she wanted to live in Wattville after she and George were married. She cringed and confided that she did not; it was too close to George's family and, I guessed, not quite what she had imagined in her white-picket-fence dreams. When I asked the same question of George, he looked surprised. "Of course we will stay in Wattville," he said. "My family is here. I have a house here." Months later, she told me they talked about the issue and he had agreed, grudgingly, that they could live somewhere else if they could afford it.

I wasn't quite sure how to broach the subject of AIDS with George; how do you ask someone how he feels about the fact that his loved one carries a deadly disease, a disease which he, himself, might be infected by? We were preparing for a party, not a funeral, and it seemed the wrong time for this discussion. George, however, turned the conversation to that topic without my prompting, although he pointedly refused to name the enemy. He called it "this thing" or "Adeline's thing." Nevertheless, there was no doubt what he was talking about.

"In a way, I think I am lucky," he told me, as we drove through the winding streets of Wattville. "I could be with another girl and maybe she would know but she would not tell me. Not every girl will just tell you."

It seemed an incredibly wise statement from a man who had spent his entire life in an environment, we are continually told, where AIDS is so stigmatized that people fear for their lives if their status is revealed. It also, I thought, revealed the extent to which the virus had invaded the lives of ordinary Africans.

George assumed that any woman he entered into a relationship with had a good chance of being infected. Although many AIDS education campaigns still focus on teaching people about the existence of the virus and convincing them that they are vulnerable, my experience has been that there are few people who are still unaware of the disease, especially in urban areas. That is not to say that people are fully informed or that their knowledge isn't defined more by rumor and urban myth than by fact. Yet, I found that like George, many men in communities like Wattville and Maseru not only know about AIDS and fear it, but assume that they are or will be infected. Out of fear that such information might be confusing, or might serve as a disincentive for behavior change, AIDS messages have largely failed to inform Africans that the virus is not transmitted in every sexual encounter and that even if they have had unprotected sex with someone who is infected, they may still be uninfected themselves.

Living as they do under the ever-present shadow of death, many young Africans, particularly young African men, have adopted a fatalistic attitude. Assuming they will die, they live as if there is nothing that can be done about it. In the townships of Johannesburg, one common name for the disease is "Lotto."

George, fortunately for Adeline, had taken a more pragmatic view of his situation. When I asked him if he worried that he might become infected himself, he shrugged. "We are careful," he said.

"Does that mean you use condoms?" I asked. He laughed. It was not the kind of question that, in Africa, a woman would directly put to a man. But I was an outsider, and a guest, who could be excused for impertinence. He mumbled something that sounded like yes and changed the subject.

"Adeline doesn't like it when I drink," George told me as he pried the lid off an extra-large bottle of beer that he had bought at the store where we picked up the ice. We were still in my car and, having been raised in a place where an open bottle of alcohol in the car could land you in jail, I eyed the beer nervously. I was sure it was illegal in South Africa too, but said nothing. "But she must accept. I am a man."

Didn't he think that his drinking worried Adeline because of her past experience, I asked delicately, alluding to Peter and his booze-soaked abuse. Adeline had told me that George didn't like to be reminded of her former partner. "He doesn't want to hear anything about that family." George frowned and was quiet for a while.

"Maybe you are right," he said. "But I am a man."

TODAY THE NUMBERS of men and women infected worldwide with HIV are about equal, yet in the early years of the epidemic most researchers focused largely on the epidemic's impact on homosexual men. Many Western researchers, particularly American researchers, struggled to accept that women too could fall victim to this new virus and that it could be spread through heterosexual as well as homosexual sex.

In the United States, the Centers for Disease Control first reported a case of the new illness in a woman in August 1981, just two months after the first reports of *Pneumocystis carinii* pneumonia among a cluster of gay men. That first case, however, was in a female intravenous drug user, prompting many researchers to continue to ignore women as a significant risk group.[1] Although other women fell victim to the disease in both Europe and America in the first years of the epidemic, it wasn't until June 1983 that the research organization recorded the first definitive case of heterosexual transmission. The patient was a seventy-three-year-old woman whose only risk factor was that she was married to a hemophiliac who had been using factor VIII, a clotting agent created from the blood of thousands of donors. Despite their advanced age, she and her husband reported regular sex.[2]

It would be years before American researchers would generally accept that the new disease could be transmitted through heterosexual sex and that women, as well as men, were at risk of being infected. As late as April 1985, at the first international conference on AIDS, held in Atlanta, where a flood of papers positing apocalyptic scenarios in Africa were presented, many American researchers still doubted that there could be an AIDS epidemic driven by heterosexual sex.[3]

In contrast, many European scientists agreed from very early on that the disease could be transmitted heterosexually. Although the first identified cases in Europe were among homosexual men, researchers there quickly diagnosed a number of cases, both contemporary and retrospective, among women. The only possible cause seemed to be an infectious disease, originating in Africa, and spread through heterosexual sex.

Indeed, many European doctors found the Americans' preoccupation with the homosexual connection rather bizarre. As Jacques Leibowitch, the French doctor, wrote in *A Strange Virus of Unknown Origin,* looking back on the early history of the epidemic with the hindsight of only a few years: "AIDS is not a disease specifically linked to the homosexual condition—and never has been. Viruses, even in 1984, cannot recognize homosexual victims as such and no one in biology has ever regarded such a thing as conceivable."[4] Scientists had long known that other sexually transmitted viruses, like hepatitis B, which had also ravaged America's gay community, could also be transmitted heterosexually. Yet there seemed to be a kind of tunnel vision among many academics in America, who saw AIDS as largely, if not exclusively, a gay problem.

In looking for a source of the new disease, American scientists also quickly got off on the wrong track. When a number of Haitians living in the United States fell ill with symptoms similar to those of the gay men, researchers hypothesized that the small island nation might be the original source of the disease and that gay American men who vacationed there had brought the virus to American shores. In retrospect, it is not clear whether AIDS first came to Haiti or America. The first cases in each country occurred too close in time to one another to make a reliable determination. One possible scenario is that Haitians were infected by African expatriate workers from Zaire and then passed the virus to visiting Americans.[5] Equally possible, however, is that American homosexuals brought the disease to Haiti. What is now clear, however, is that neither America nor Haiti was the birthplace of the virus.

Haiti's experience as an early scapegoat in the war on AIDS served as a warning to African nations, which would soon face similar claims. When, at the 1985 Atlanta conference, Western researchers presented wild claims—later to be disproved—of astronomically high infection rates in countries like Kenya and Rwanda, and suggested that the continent where humanity first emerged might also be the birthplace of AIDS, a simmering storm erupted.[6]

African leaders and researchers quickly denounced as racist any suggestion that the continent was the source of AIDS. The first cases of AIDS appeared in America, they argued, so why point the finger at Africa? Tragically, this debate over the origin of the disease— purely scientific in the eyes of Western researchers, deeply symbolic to Africans struggling to define themselves in the era after colonialism—would delay the response to the growing epidemic for many years.

These cultural tensions hung heavily over early efforts to measure the impact of AIDS on the continent, as did doubt about the potential dangers AIDS posed for women. Early reports from Europe indicated that the epidemic might already be well entrenched in several Central African countries, and that women might be at risk, but from Africa itself there was virtual silence. So in 1983 two separate teams of Western scientists independently began laying the groundwork for investigative trips to what would very soon be dubbed the "AIDS belt" of Africa.

One group, which included Dr. Nathan Clumeck, from the Saint-Pierre University Hospital in Brussels, who had previously reported on the treatment of African patients in Belgium for symptoms of AIDS, went to the Rwandan capital, Kigali. During the course of four weeks working with doctors there, they found twenty-six patients suffering from what appeared to be AIDS. A second team, consisting of Belgian and American researchers from the Centers for Disease Control, spent three weeks at the Mama Yemo Hospital in Kinshasa, the populous capital of Zaire. They too found numerous cases of suspected AIDS, indicating the disease was already well entrenched. In both places, women comprised significant numbers of the sick. In Kinshasa, the ratio of men to women was almost one to one, and the researchers found two clusters of patients who seemed to have infected each other heterosexually.[7]

The two groups, who both published in the same edition of the British journal *The Lancet,* were unequivocal in their findings: AIDS could be transmitted heterosexually and could affect women. "No patient had a history of homosexuality, intravenous drug abuse, or transfusion in the previous 5 years," the authors of the Rwandan study concluded. "An association of an urban environment, a relatively high income, and heterosexual promiscuity could be a risk factor for AIDS in Africa."

The research put African AIDS on the scientific map and marked the beginning of a flood of Western scientists to Africa that continues to this day. Although African scientists collaborated on both studies and are named as coauthors on both, they would rapidly fade into obscurity even as many of their Western colleagues became giants in what would become the largest global battle against a disease in history.

THE TWENTY-FIRST was quite an affair. In a small tent that had been erected in the yard, close family and other guests of honor, including me and Adeline, were seated at tables covered in brightly colored cloths and sprinkled with shiny confetti shaped in little "21s." The birthday girl was thoroughly embarrassed by stories told in English, or in Zulu or Sesotho, two of South Africa's eleven official languages.

It wasn't all lighthearted though. The master of ceremonies for the evening, an elegantly dressed, middle-aged cousin of the birth-day girl, seized her moment on the stage to lecture the young party-goers about the growing dangers of their world.

"My generation fought the struggle against apartheid," she told the guests as they squirmed uncomfortably in their seats. "But everything will be lost if your generation does not win the fight against AIDS." She particularly admonished the girls. "You want to have fun, but you must not go with any boy. You must respect your-selves."

The girls giggled and the boys rolled their eyes. Besides family, most of the guests were young, near the age of the birthday girl: some of them were probably already infected. But they were young and tragically complacent and seemed to think this was all rather dreary talk for a party.

In the growing darkness, the family celebration transformed into a teenage party. Dance music blared from speakers and the birthday girl's aunts began dishing overflowing mounds of food onto plates: chicken, beef, rice, pap, chakalaka (a spicy salad made of cooked vegetables), mashed beetroots, mashed potatoes. In the shadows, I saw young girls and boys dancing close.

7

AWAKENING

NINETEEN-EIGHTY-SIX, the year Lesotho marked its first AIDS case, proved to be a turning point in the global fight against the virus. That year, for the first time, new attention turned to the threat of AIDS in Africa. The reports in 1984, from Rwanda and Zaire, sparked interest in the Western academic community, which saw in Africa's older, more entrenched epidemic a chance to study the disease's origins and natural progression. They also saw in Africa a terrifying glimpse of the future for other parts of the world. If Africa had a generalized epidemic transmitted through heterosexual sex, perhaps one day America and Europe would too.

Western researchers began streaming into the continent, and several important AIDS research projects were begun in Africa, the most famous of which was Project SIDA in Kinshasa, named after the French acronym for the disease; it involved many of the Belgian, American, and Zairian scientists involved in the original *Lancet* paper whose results had so shocked the world. Headquartered at the Mama Yemo Hospital, Zaire's flagship hospital, in specially built, air-conditioned laboratories, and funded largely by the American government, the project received the full support of the Zairian government, under one condition: that the researchers stay quiet about their findings.

Researchers told visiting journalists that they were not allowed to speak about their work and that the government did little to inform its own people about the dangers of the new disease. "Whenever anybody talks about AIDS here, it's like this," an American health worker told Associated Press reporter Paul Raeburn, cupping her hand over her mouth. A Western doctor working on the project even refused to tell the reporter in which medical journals research from the project had been published.[1]

Nevertheless, during the seven years the project ran—it ended abruptly when expatriate staff were evacuated in mid-1991 during unrest caused by Zairian soldiers angry that they hadn't been paid—a total of 120 articles were published and 1,000 abstracts presented at international conferences. Much of our early knowledge, indeed much of what we still know about the epidemiology of AIDS, was learned in those early years at Project SIDA: that the risk of transmission through casual contact is almost nonexistent, that mosquitoes can't transmit the disease, and that untreated sexually transmitted diseases increased the probability of infection.[2] The researchers were able to follow thousands of infected patients over long periods, something that would have cost a prohibitive amount in a developed country.

Evidence from Project SIDA and other research projects in Africa finally prompted the World Health Organization to launch, in November 1986, the Special Program on AIDS, the predecessor to the current UNAIDS. Announcing the new program at a 1985 meeting of AIDS researchers held in Bangui, the capital of the Central African Republic, Dr. Fakhry Assaad, the World Health Organization official in charge of communicable diseases, said the focus would be on prevention: "We have nothing to combat AIDS except education," he said.[3]

It would be an uphill battle. Through most of the 1980s, with a few exceptions like Uganda's rebel-turned-president Yoweri Museveni, African political leaders largely ignored the threat posed by AIDS to their own people, seeing it as a disease of Western decadence.

Assaad chose as the program's head Jonathan Mann, a lanky,

outspoken American who had formerly headed Project SIDA. Mann was given the near impossible task of halting the march of AIDS with a part-time secretary, no budget, and no full-time staff. Beginning with those modest resources, he would, over the next few years cajole, warn, and pound his fist until the world began to take note of the epidemic under way in Africa.[4]

In the four years before he resigned after falling out with the new head of the World Health Organization in 1990, Mann raised millions of dollars for global AIDS, made great strides in the collection of data on the epidemic, and prompted many countries to take their first, fledgling steps toward combating the disease with the writing of national AIDS plans.

He would also help to entrench a human-rights-based approach to the disease, which has stood virtually unchallenged for almost two decades. Mann genuinely believed that the epidemic could be controlled only by convincing people to change their behavior and that any attempt to coerce people—by forcing them to be tested or to reveal their status or by restricting their movements—constituted a violation of human rights that would only drive the epidemic further underground.

There was a sound basis to his concern. By 1986, when the Special Program on AIDS was founded, countries around the world had begun passing discriminatory laws targeting HIV-positive people— and those suspected of being infected by the virus. By 1991, twenty-three countries had even passed laws allowing for the surveillance, hospitalization, or isolation of people with AIDS, although only Cuba actually implemented a large-scale quarantine program.[5] "We are witnessing a rising wave of stigmatization: against Westerners in Asia, against Africans in Europe, of homosexuals, of prostitutes, of hemophiliacs, of recipients of blood transfusions," Mann warned delegates of the Third International Conference on AIDS in Washington, D.C., in June 1987.[6]

Years later, Peter Piot, who had been one of Mann's colleagues in Kinshasa and would later become the first head of UNAIDS, credited Mann for leading the world away from a punitive, fear-based response to AIDS. For that he certainly deserves credit. And yet, in the hardest-hit countries, like Lesotho, many people are increasingly asking whether the overarching emphasis on individual rights, while well intentioned, may have hindered efforts to combat the disease and even contributed to the stigma against the infected. Concerned about the rising tide of discrimination against people with AIDS, Mann and others emphasized the right of HIV-positive people to keep their status confidential.

Five years after the new epidemic was first identified, most African countries were still unwilling to publicly admit the presence of AIDS. Countries refused to issue visas to journalists hoping to report on the issue and denied permission to researchers to study the extent of the problem. But that denial was becoming harder to sustain.

Uganda became the first African country to acknowledge the scope of the crisis. In the early 1980s, people in a rural district near the border with Tanzania called Rakai began dying of a strange wasting disease that people called "slim." Local doctors suspected that the cause might be AIDS, but the country's then-president, Milton Obote, refused to acknowledge that "slim" might in fact be the same disease that was killing gay Americans on the other side of the Atlantic.

Then in January 1986, the same month Lesotho experienced its first coup, a rebel army swept into Uganda's capital, Kampala, and toppled the government. At the head of this army was a military man named Yoweri Museveni, who, unlike his predecessor in the presidency, took AIDS seriously.

Museveni—who saw the disease as a security threat as well as a potential humanitarian disaster—soon ordered his generals to get tested, founded Africa's first National AIDS Committee, and began speaking about the disease at every opportunity. The country's response was generally low-tech and locally designed, featuring slogans inspired by local slang such as "Zero Grazing," which encouraged men to stay faithful. In 1993, the nation's HIV prevalence rate began to fall, making the country the first in Africa to stem the spread of the virus.[7]

Despite its comparative openness, Uganda often rankled at

international press coverage of the epidemic there, as well as the insinuations by scientists that it was the source of the virus. Still, compared to the near silence of its neighbors, its response to the epidemic is largely considered one of the few successful efforts to slow the spread of the disease, although the source of its success is still much debated. Some researchers argue that the introduction of condoms helped stem the tide; while others believe that other behavior changes, such as a delay in the age of first sexual intercourse and reductions in the number of partners, are the primary cause of the fall in infection rates. All agree, however, that Museveni's leadership on the issue played a vital role.[8]

A few months after coming to power in 1986, Museveni also sent his new health minister, Dr. Ruhakana Rugunda, to Geneva for an annual summit of the World Health Organization. There, Rugunda announced that Uganda was facing a serious AIDS epidemic and asked for international help;[9] his speech would inspire another new health minister, Dr. Makenete of Lesotho, to return home and take steps in his own country.

DESPITE LESOTHO's early action on AIDS, it wasn't until 2003 or 2004 that the country began to awake to the magnitude of the crisis. During the tumultuous 1990s, while the virus burrowed its way into the fabric of Basotho life, most of the country's political leaders were consumed by a battle to control Lesotho's paltry resources. While a handful of dedicated, hardworking civil servants continued to labor quietly in the background to slow the epidemic's spread, AIDS largely disappeared from the political radar.

The 1986 coup did not herald the end of political instability in Lesotho and instead marked the beginning of a long and troubled period in the country's history. Even Dr. Makenete, who still defends the seizure of power in 1986, acknowledges that it set off a vicious cycle. "You know what they say," he said, "once a coup, always a coup."

In 1990, four years after Moshoeshoe II returned to power and installed Major General Justin Lekhanya as the country's military leader, another coup took place. Tension between the king and the major general over who actually controlled Lesotho had simmered for years, but in 1990 it reached a boiling point. Lekhanya purged the military council and cabinet of royalists—including Dr. Makenete—and stripped the king of his powers. Moshoeshoe once again went into exile and was later deposed, replaced by his son, who was sworn in as King Letsie III.

Less than a year later, in May 1991, Lekhanya himself was toppled by a group of military officers, angry about the size of their pay raises; they marched into the offices of the state radio network and announced that he had been replaced.[10] The country's new leaders did, as promised, organize national elections and a transition to civilian rule in 1993, but true political stability would remain elusive for another decade. The military, still bloated for such a tiny country, continued to threaten rebellion while the king and the parliament continued to jockey for power.

No ruling government was secure in its position until 2002, when a proportional representational system that gave opposition parties a greater stake in parliament was adopted by Lesotho. Before that point was reached, AIDS would weave its way, unhindered, into villages and homes across the country.

In 1986, the year Dr. Makenete took office, there was one reported case of full-blown AIDS. By 1990, there were twenty-three. By the end of 2000, a total of 14,640 cases of AIDS had been reported. And those, of course, were only the people who sought medical attention. Thousands more died without ever seeing a doctor, while hundreds of thousands more were infected but remained asymptomatic. By the time the country began to awake, a major epidemic was under way; an estimated 25 percent of adults were infected with the virus.[11]

It is unfair, of course, to blame Lesotho's AIDS epidemic entirely on its tumultuous political environment. Many more stable countries across the continent also failed to adequately confront the epidemic during the early years when prevention efforts might have been most effective, and it is perhaps the nature of politics everywhere to be reactive rather than proactive. There are few success stories anywhere in AIDS prevention, and those that do exist are hotly debated.

Yet there is little doubt that the instability in Lesotho—and in neighboring South Africa, whose troubles affected the entire region—created a political environment in which it was nearly impossible to take decisive action against the new threat. During this period, many government functions crumbled, though it is difficult to determine how substantial the decline in services really was since many departments ceased issuing annual reports and their budgets were no longer audited to determine whether money was being spent appropriately.

The situation at the Ministry of Health and Social Welfare during this period was particularly dire. Lesotho had once been praised for the quality of its basic health care, but by the end of the 1990s the health system was in disarray. Many clinics and hospitals were suffering from severe staff and medicine shortages, and increases in the price of health care meant many people, like Tsidi and Zachariah, could no longer afford to access Western medicine. Basic indicators of the community's health, such as the number of mothers who died while giving birth and the overall rate of malnutrition among children, began to worsen after decades of slow improvement.[12]

Amid this chaos, early efforts at HIV surveillance also collapsed, leaving the department with almost no information about the growing epidemic. Lesotho had begun tracking the epidemic in 1991, through anonymous surveys conducted at a handful of prenatal and sexually transmitted infection clinics, but stopped after 1994. In 1996 surveillance was restarted, but for several crucial years the country lacked the technical resources to analyze the data that had been collected.

When AIDS surveillance stopped, infection rates were still lower than 10 percent. By the time the data was analyzed in 2000, infection rates among pregnant women at the five sites that were tested ranged from 19.8 percent in one rural area to a staggering 42.2 percent in Maseru. Among patients at clinics for sexually transmitted infections, 65.2 percent were infected. In the years during which Lesotho had let down its guard, AIDS had mushroomed into a health crisis of massive proportions.[13]

Even without the statistics, though, workers at the Ministry of

Health and Social Welfare began to realize that AIDS had become a major crisis. Dr. Thabelo Ramatlapeng, who was director-general of the ministry from 1995 to 2002 and now heads the Lesotho Red Cross, says she began to realize the scope of the epidemic when reported cases of tuberculosis began shooting up. For many years, the annual number of cases had remained stable at around a thousand a year. Then, in the mid-1990s, something changed.

"All of a sudden the number of cases tripled," she said. "The health sector couldn't cope."

As the number of TB cases rose, the cure rate began to fall. Some of this, Ramatlapeng admits, may have been due to a decline in the quality of care and a switch in the way TB patients were treated. Prior to 1986, all tuberculosis patients were hospitalized for two months. After that year most were treated at home through a program called Directly Observed Treatment Shortcourse (DOTS), in which patients are given free drugs and monitored in their treatment by a health worker. But the real reason more people were dying of TB, Dr. Ramatlapeng and her colleagues soon realized, was AIDS.

But the wheels of government turned slowly in those days, and it wasn't until 2000 that the ministry finally commissioned a study to examine the extent of the epidemic thus far. Data had been collected, but never analyzed.

The results of the study were shocking, even to those in the health department who suspected that AIDS was growing quickly: in the mid-1990s, the number of AIDS cases had suddenly ballooned, in line with the rise in tuberculosis cases. In 1995, there were 341 newly identified cases. The next year, there were 936. By 2000, the number had risen to 3,760. These, of course, were new cases of full-blown AIDS, reflecting a much larger underlying epidemic.

The report also found that more women than men had been stricken: 55 percent of the cases in 2000 were women, and the highest-risk profession appeared to be "housewife," followed closely by "unemployed" and then "miner/former miners."[14]

In response to these startling statistics, along with pressure from the international community, King Letsie III declared AIDS a national disaster. The government developed a national plan to fight AIDS, which called for the foundation of the Lesotho AIDS Program Coordinating Authority (LAPCA) in the office of the prime minister to spearhead efforts against the epidemic. AIDS suddenly became a serious political issue. But the organization had an unclear mandate, little money, and no power. It took several years for the government to even appoint a director and hire staff. There still seemed to be no real sense of urgency.

After the 2002 elections, the sense of alarm increased, although even then there was still more talk than action. Prime Minister Pakalitha Mosisili convened a cabinet meeting on the issue and the next year hosted a regional meeting on AIDS. The first lady, his wife, gave some money to orphans. Despite the increased talk, though, real action came more slowly, and then only when international funds began flowing into the country in large amounts. Suddenly, there was a jumble of new initiatives and programs, not all coordinated or well run. But finally something was being done.

LESOTHO'S FIRST real movement on AIDS came when the government, pushed heavily by the United Nations, launched an initiative to encourage people to get tested. In June 2003, the country's first voluntary counseling and testing center was opened in Maseru. Nine months later, Mosisili and the Catholic archbishop Bernard Mohlalisi were publicly tested for HIV. The prime minister encouraged all Basotho to get tested: "Knowing one's status will help stop the pandemic from spreading to those who have not yet been infected at the same time as assisting those who are already infected to live longer, and better quality lives." [15] It was an admirable step by the politician, and one few other African leaders have yet emulated. Still, looking back, many Basotho are now asking why it took eighteen years for the government to embrace testing as a tool in fighting the epidemic.

Although a few mission hospitals and clinics, like Maluti, had been offering the service for nearly a decade, only a tiny percentage of people in Lesotho knew their HIV status. Government hospitals sometimes did tests, at the request of doctors or as part of broader HIV surveillance, but these results were rarely shared with patients. When people did request AIDS tests at one of the few facilities that could offer them, such as Queen II, rules about confidentiality and consent—rules that local doctors say were imposed by international experts from outside Lesotho—cast a heavy shadow of secrecy over the disease.

Dr. Pearl Ntsekhe, who now runs Senkatana, recalls that when she was a doctor at Queen II the emphasis on confidentiality reached absurd levels. Counselors who tested patients couldn't tell the doctors who were treating them the results of the test without getting permission from the patient.

"The counselor had to talk the patient into letting the doctor know. Then they would say, okay, you can tell the doctor but not the nurses," she said. "From the beginning it was emphasized that we had to treat this disease with confidentiality. But these are things that came from the outside. We never sat down as Basotho and said we need to have confidentiality."

In retrospect, Dr. Ntsekhe now believes, this approach to the epidemic contributed to the fear and silence that continues to surround the epidemic today: "There was something wrong with the way we approached AIDS from the onset. It should have been normalized. New diseases should never be hushed up. They should be transparent. It's a disease like any other and we should have treated it that way."

Dr. Ramatlapeng, the former director-general, also believes that more should have been done earlier to encourage people to learn their status so that they could have taken steps to prevent spreading the disease to other people. Testing should have been more widely available, she believes, and even when there was no treatment, people should have been told when they tested positive during government surveillance programs.

"If you are going to test someone, tell them. Otherwise they might infect someone else. I think people should have been told. Even before antiretrovirals they could have taken steps to address the issue," she said. "For Lesotho, the approach wasn't the right one.

People don't understand if you ask for consent. They think it's something special, and that contributed to the fear and stigma."

Skeptical at first, I was eventually convinced by the arguments by people like Dr. Ramatlapeng and Dr. Ntsekhe, who now believe that the human rights approach to AIDS, which has come to mean an emphasis on the right of people with AIDS to privacy and confidentiality, was not appropriate in Lesotho. Illness in the West is often a private affair, between the patient and his doctors. Many of the first AIDS patients in America chose to battle the disease without the help of their families, who either didn't know or didn't approve of the fact that they were gay. Such an individualistic approach to AIDS is entirely foreign to Africa, where most basic nursing is performed by family members. Even many hospitals rely on family members to feed and bathe patients—in Lesotho, as across much of the continent, illness is a family affair, not a private one.

Like Dr. Ramatlapeng, I also fear the approach to AIDS in Africa has unwittingly contributed to the very thing it was intended to combat: stigma. For almost two decades, until recently, the system gave people a disincentive to learn their HIV status. International standard practice for HIV testing requires that the test be given in a private room, by a specially trained counselor who can give pre- and post-test counseling. Often the testing is done at a special site, separate from where other health services are offered, and the results must be kept confidential.

Usually the counseling includes information about the stigma that people with AIDS are likely to face. Often women are encouraged not to disclose a positive diagnosis to their spouses for fear of abuse. As in the case of Queen II, special permission must be obtained before even the doctors and nurses treating the patient are informed of the patient's condition. Many doctors I spoke to also said the secrecy became so great that they felt unable to offer HIV tests to patients they believed to be suffering from AIDS-related infections.

Why, I often wondered, had no doctor told Adeline's former husband, Peter, that he was likely suffering from AIDS? He had been to the doctor and to the hospital many times, and those treating him must surely have suspected he was infected. If a doctor thought he might have cancer or cholera or tuberculosis, the doctor would simply have tested him for that disease and told him the results. Yet with AIDS, somehow, that has become impossible.

Even as AIDS activists have bemoaned the lack of good HIV-positive role models in Africa, the subtle, underlying message has been that it's better not to tell. I began to feel that our entire response had been built around the belief that people are basically judgmental, selfish, hateful, and prejudiced, that families will turn out sick relatives, husbands will beat wives who disclose that they are HIV-positive (even if, as is usually the case, it is the man who brought the infection into the home), and communities will scorn those stricken by this terrifying illness.

There is no doubt that this is sometimes the case, and yet it seems to me that there is something fundamentally wrong, even racist, about the assumption that most or all Africans will respond in this way. Most HIV-positive people I met had, like Adeline, received enormous support from their families, if not always from strangers. Often those who did not came from families that were already dysfunctional or abusive. And I met many good men who, on discovering that they were HIV-positive, had taken steps to prevent passing on the disease to their wives and children. If their situations had been reversed, I believe George would not have wanted to infect Adeline and would still have worn a condom.

Lesotho's recent campaign to encourage all Basotho to be tested has encouraged many people to take steps to learn their HIV status. Yet the fear and suspicion surrounding AIDS is now deeply entrenched, and many people still refuse. The day Adeline told me Bongy had tested positive, her company had catered an event for a local teacher's union to launch their HIV-testing campaign. Afterward, teachers were asked if anyone wanted to get tested. No one volunteered.

8

SOMETHING HAS TURNED

For HIV-POSITIVE PEOPLE in Lesotho, the picture suddenly became more hopeful in the years immediately after Adeline tested positive. AIDS in Africa became a major international issue and, after years of declining foreign assistance, money began pouring in. NGOs wanted to open offices there, donors clamored to fund HIV-related projects, and Britain's Prince Harry spent part of his gap year—a year many British students take off between high school and college to work and/or travel—in Lesotho working at an AIDS orphanage.[1] International pharmaceutical companies, battered by bad press over the high cost of antiretroviral drugs in Africa, wanted to prove their social conscience by funding treatment programs on the continent, and American president George Bush had pledged $15 billion to fight global AIDS, much of it for treatment. The World Health Organization declared that by 2005, three million people in poor countries would be able to access antiretroviral treatment.

Lesotho's health minister said that, as part of this program, twenty-eight thousand Basotho would be given antiretroviral treatment.[2] In June 2004, the country's first AIDS treatment center opened, under the able management of Dr. Ntsekhe. The center was funded by Bristol-Myers Squibb in cooperation with the government. The pharmaceutical company provided the drugs and technical assistance; while the government provided the site, in a former leper hospital, and paid the salaries of the staff.

The center was dubbed Senkatana, after a boy in a Basotho myth who saved the nation by slaying a monster who had swallowed the Basotho people. Mosisili, the prime minister, had by this time begun to call the epidemic "the Monster" in speeches. It was an apt metaphor; AIDS was indeed swallowing the nation. Whether Senkatana and antiretroviral drugs could save it, however, remains uncertain.

Many of the first patients were already taking antiretrovirals but had been buying their drugs from private doctors. Others who were seeking help for the first time were in the late stages of the disease. Dr. Ntsekhe told me some of the first patients were rolled in on wheelbarrows or driven to the center in neighbors' cars. Several members of Positive Action were among the first to enroll, but Adeline still hesitated. Within a few months, the program had exceeded its capacity; Bristol-Myers Squibb had promised to provide enough drugs for only five hundred patients.

In a very short period, other programs funded by the government or NGOs were rolled out at Queen II, Maseru's military hospital, and hospitals in other parts of the country. At Maluti hospital, however, doctors complained that although they already had a functioning program, the government still hadn't provided them with free drugs. Since many of the patients were factory workers who were laid off at the end of 2004 when Lesotho's clothing industry took a major hit, the hospital was desperate to get the free drugs to keep the women on treatment. Instead it was offered eight counselors for its testing program.

Despite fears that no one would come forward for treatment, the new centers were quickly flooded and struggled to keep up with demand. By the end of 2005, an estimated eight thousand patients were being treated, far short of the twenty-eight thousand the health minister had promised but progress nonetheless. The doctors, nurses, and pharmacists, though, struggled to keep pace with the growing numbers. There were promises to hire more staff, but there were none to hire. Lesotho was chronically short of medical personnel. "These foreign recruiters come and set up an office at the Lesotho Sun and hire away more nurses in a single day than we train in a year," Phooka, the health minister, complained to me in an early-morning meeting. At Queen II, by the end of the year, a thousand patients on ARVs were being cared for by a single harassed doctor. And still the wards were full of the sick and dying.

For children the picture was even less optimistic. Over the course of 2005, however, a building was rising near Senkatana for a new children's AIDS clinic, also sponsored by Bristol-Myers Squibb. And a children's clinic was planned for Queen II; but for Bongy time was running out.

IN JUNE 2005, Bongy fell sick with tuberculosis, one of the most common AIDS-related opportunistic infections and one of the most dangerous. The expensive Maseru pediatrician the family had been taking him to was away, so Adeline's mother took him to the local clinic in Ha'Senekane, which prescribed him medication for TB. By the time I next visited, a month later, he was feeling better. But it was an ominous sign.

That same month, Adeline saw Peter again for the first time in several years. She went to see him in TY, where his family lived, to tell him that he should give up hope for a reconciliation. "I'm finished with him," she told me. He was skinny and looked tired, although he had returned to work on a contract basis. His brother had died, and Adeline had no doubt the cause was AIDS.

Adeline also told Peter that she and Bongy had both tested HIV-positive. When she broke the news, he was silent. He said nothing at all, just stared into space. She pressed him to get tested, but he refused. "Most of the men, they still refuse," she told me when she related the story. She shook her head. "I don't want to see him again."

Adeline was also desperately looking for a new job. She had applied for work at the post office, but there was a problem with her accounting certificate. The program had changed somehow since she had finished it and now they said she wasn't qualified. Adeline had also applied for several positions at Positive Action, and she had high hopes.

Tebatso's six-month term at Positive Action ended badly. Cell phones started disappearing from the office, then some petty cash. Tebatso was suspected, but there was no proof. Eventually he disappeared with money belonging to the World Food Program, which had been given to Positive Action to start a food-for-work program for HIV-positive people.

Adeline's opinion of Tebatso had changed too, even before she heard about the accusations of theft. He promised her things he couldn't deliver, raising her hopes and then dashing them. His promises of a foreign scholarship, for example, never materialized. Much later, after Tebatso disappeared, Adeline spoke dismissively of him. "He didn't even have a degree," she said, meaning a high school diploma.

With Chuck Quehn's help, the organization had received funding to hire three new staff members. Adeline applied for two of the jobs, coordinator and bookkeeper. She told me she had not run for a position on the board at the end of the previous year in part because she had hoped to get a paid position with the organization when it received more funding. She seemed more enthusiastic about the prospect of working for Positive Action than I had seen her in a long time, if ever.

"I want to work to get ARVs for children," she said. "I have plans."

Previously, Adeline had seemed to me curiously uninterested in politics and activism. She didn't vote during the country's first local elections, which occurred one week while I was in town, although she supported the idea of taking more power from the traditional chiefs, who she said were often corrupt, and giving it to elected officials. In general, she seemed to lack faith that politics had much effect on her own life—it seemed to her mainly to be about power—and feared that involvement could be potentially dangerous.

This lesson was likely reinforced by her own family's experience; one of her grandfathers had been killed in political violence during the 1970s. It had happened long before Adeline was born, and she knew little about how he had died or why, except that he had come home after working in South Africa (she thinks in a factory), became involved in local politics, and was killed. The issue of getting antiretrovirals for Bongy, however, seemed to galvanize her even more than her own situation. She wanted to use Positive Action as a forum for making that case.

But she faced stiff competition: almost 250 people had applied for the three jobs the organization had advertised, most for the bookkeeping job. Adeline hoped that her previous work with the organization would help her. "Most of the other applications are not from openly HIV-positive people," she told me.

In fact, it probably worked against her. The other women were jealous of Adeline, who was better educated than they were, and often made sniping comments about her behind her back, even accusing her of trying to seduce their boyfriends and other male members of Positive Action. This I had a hard time believing. I worried that they were also jealous of my relationship with her—not because they wanted to be the subject of a book but because they assumed that she was benefiting in some way from it. Although she was called in for an interview, she didn't get the job; and, while she hesitated to admit it, Adeline was deeply disappointed.

It might have been luck in disguise. The new staff quarreled endlessly with the board members, especially four women who camped out daily in one of Positive Action's two rooms. The grant included money to create several new jobs manning a call and drop-in center. The idea, according to Chuck, was to spread the jobs, which included daily shifts, out among a number of people, giving each a small, but regular, monthly income. The four women assigned all the jobs to themselves. When donations came in, they wanted to divide them among themselves as well. Every time I came for a visit, they would harass me endlessly about when I was going to buy them lunch. Finally I brought them a bucket of Kentucky Fried Chicken as a peace offering, and after that they were always friendly.

The board members were furious too when the staff succeeded in recruiting new members. They accused the staff of stealing printer ribbons and refused to sign checks for office supplies. After a while, it was open war: the board members stayed in the back room, watching videos all day (the grant had also included money to buy a television, VCR, and DVD player), while the staff worked in the front room. Every little thing became a battle.

ADELINE SENT ME a text message in September, saying that she had found a new job as the bookkeeper and administrator of a small NGO with an impossibly long acronym: LNLVIP, the Lesotho National League for Visually Impaired Persons. The job didn't pay much more than her work at In 'n' Out Catering, but at least she was working in an office and she hoped the experience she gained there might open other doors with international NGOs or the United Nations.

"I think something has turned," she told me brightly when I called to hear more. Her luck, she said, was back. If she could only pass her exams at the end of the year, the third and most difficult year of her chartered accountancy course.

"Sharp," she said, wishing me farewell in South African slang.

I visited Lesotho one last time a few weeks later. We had arranged to meet for lunch, but when I called, Adeline told me she had the flu—a fever and sore throat—and asked me to take her to the health clinic. When we arrived, there was miraculously no line and the nurses saw Adeline right away. Later we learned that they had closed for lunch but treated Adeline because she was with me; a visit by a foreign person, they assumed, must be important.

The nurses gave her a shot and a few bottles of thick, darkly colored syrup. With no laboratory or medical books, the nurses treated symptoms, not diseases; patients with the flu and strep throat received the same treatment. The medicines and consultation together cost 50 maloti, about $8. Only if symptoms became more serious and the patient sought treatment from a doctor would they get a more thorough examination. And even then, it was often the doctor's best guess.

A few days later, Adeline felt better. Again I encouraged her to go for another CD4 count and to consider starting treatment for herself and Bongy. A children's clinic had opened at Queen II with drugs from the Clinton Foundation and support from the UN Children's Fund, UNICEF. On July 18, 2005, Bill Clinton himself had come to dedicate it. The Bristol-Myers Squibb children's center was scheduled to open soon on World AIDS Day.

"Maybe it's time," she said.

PART II
DESPAIR

INGWAVUMA, SOUTH AFRICA

9

UMBULALAZWA

MANTOMBI NYWAO doesn't know how old she is or in what year, in our calendar, she was born. In her childhood, lifetimes were not counted in that way. Her small, green, government-issued identification book says she was born in 1941, but that date is little more than a guess based on events she can remember from her youth. The identity book of her husband, Obed, says he is a year younger than she, but Mantombi dismisses this with a laugh.

"It is not possible," she says, "that a husband could be younger than his wife."

Everyone in her family, including her husband, calls the old woman Gogo, which means "grandmother" in the local language of Zulu. She is a fat, jolly woman with very dark skin and a wide, flat nose. Gogo dresses haphazardly, as if still unused to Western clothes. Often she wears a towel wrapped around her waist as a skirt or a man's shirt over her heavy breasts, with the buttons askew. On each of her cheeks there are three horizontal ceremonial scars, each about an inch long. The soles of her feet are dry and cracked and as thick as leather; she wears shoes only when going to church or to a government office. These days she is wearing them often as she fights to get a grant to help support her five orphaned grandchildren.

In 2002, Gogo's eldest daughter, Lungile, came home with her five children, ages seven to nineteen. Lungile's second husband had died that year, and she and her children were turned away by her husband's people in a village called Manyiseni. The husband's family claimed their house and land. Her in-laws said they would give a home to Makhisi, the only one of Lungile's children that they were related to, but the others would have to go.

So Lungile brought her family home to Gogo, in the mountain area of Machobeni, near the town of Ingwavuma in South Africa's KwaZulu-Natal province. They arrived in a minibus taxi, carrying only a few meager belongings. Lungile's eldest child, Nozipho, had already left to make her own way in the world. But five children remained: Nokukhanya, Phumlani, Sbuka, Mfundo, and little Makhisi, whose name means "Christmas," the day of her birth. The family took with them only what they could carry, just some clothes and blankets and a few treasured valuables, like a photograph of their late father. Machobeni was not far away, in the grand scheme of things, but it would be years before they would return to Manyiseni. The next time the children would see their relatives would be at their mother's funeral, in Machobeni.

For more than a year, Lungile and her children, who used the last name Mathenjwa, lived with Gogo and Obed, crowded into a few small huts shared by a dozen other relatives. The whole family survived on Gogo's old-age pension from the government, the chickens that pecked their way through the yard, and the bananas and corn she grew on her small piece of land.

Later, Lungile and her children moved into a small, three-room house that had been built by her brother on a neighboring plot of land bordered by tiny purple *ibozane* flowers. It was a modest place, constructed of stones held together with concrete and chicken wire and topped with slats of sheet metal.

In Machobeni, the kind of house a family lived in was one indicator of wealth, but not always an entirely reliable one. Families that lived in houses of stick and mud were invariably poor, but ones that lived in sturdier structures were not always rich. The Mathenjwas' new house was a step up from a hut, but they were as poor as any family in the neighborhood. The roof was sturdy and kept the rain out, though the sea blue walls were infested with mice. There was no electricity or running water in the area to be bought at any price, yet rich families had indoor kitchens with stoves and refrigerators that ran off gas canisters. The Mathenjwas, though, like almost everyone else they knew, cooked on wood fires in an outdoor structure of wood and metal that leaned against the house. Often, however, there was little to cook. School fees went unpaid and the house contained little more than three beds and a few pots. Without Gogo's pension, there would have been nothing at all.

Still, the family survived. Then, Lungile fell ill. Her mysterious symptoms were the same as the ones that had taken her husband. She was racked by vomiting and diarrhea, and sores erupted all over her body. She became painfully thin. Gogo nursed her daughter in the old way, as she had been taught by her parents and grandparents long ago. She rubbed salt into Lungile's sores and used her finger to clean her anus, rubbing it clean until it bled. The blood, Gogo believed, would wash away the evil things inside her daughter's body. Nothing, though, seemed to work. Even the white doctors at the government hospital in the nearby town of Ingwavuma could do nothing.

While Lungile lay dying, her eldest daughter, Nozipho, came home from the city of Ulundi—once the capital of the apartheid-era independent homeland of the Zulu people—bringing with her a daughter of her own. Nozipho too was burdened with mysterious ailments. She had blisters all over her body and had grown thin from vomiting.

Mother and daughter shared the same room. Two generations of Mathenjwa women lay together, both withering away from an unnamed illness. When Lungile finally died in February 2003, she gave her children to her mother. "Look after them for me," she begged.

Gogo and her grandchildren buried Lungile in the yard under a guava tree, next to the child-sized grave of a cousin who had died some years before. They covered her coffin with dirt and piled small stones around the edges of the burial mound. There was no head-stone to mark the spot, but the grave itself rose from the ground. It was the first thing the children saw each morning as they emerged from their house and the last thing they saw before they went to bed. For Nozipho, it was a constant reminder of the fate that lay ahead. In her last months, after her mother died, the young woman set aside money for her own coffin. She was twenty-six.

Gogo bore the loss of her child with the stoicism of her generation. Lungile was not the first child she had lost; the old woman had been born in a time when women expected that not all their children would outlive them. One child, half of a set of twins, had been stillborn, and another of her children had died in an accident as an adult. But this new disease was something different, Gogo thought. Nor was her family the only one to be struck by this strange illness that made adults as helpless as babies. Everyone seemed to know someone who had died mysteriously. At first, she had no name for this new plague, so she began to call it *umbulalazwa:* the disease that is killing the whole world.

It was only after Lungile's death, when she was caring for her granddaughter Nozipho, that Gogo acquired a name for the evil that had struck her family. Three times she used some of her pension money to hire a car to take Nozipho to Mosvold Hospital, more than two miles away in the town of Ingwavuma. They told her that Nozipho had a new disease, AIDS, which could not be cured and always killed. They said it was spread by blood and through sex, and that Gogo must be careful when she nursed her granddaughter. Gogo went to the hospital to learn how to take care of Nozipho. They gave her plastic gloves and told her that if a person has problems, like vomiting or diarrhea, that would not go away, that person would not live long.

"Only then did I realize what my child had died of, what my granddaughter was sick with," Gogo said. The old woman thought about how she had cared for her daughter Lungile and feared that she too had caught AIDS. She also worried about nursing Nozipho, but the girl was her blood and it was her duty. So great was her fear that once she even went to the hospital intending to have an HIV test, but she worried that someone might see her and decided in the end not to have the test done.

Gogo thought that if the white doctors could not save Nozipho, maybe traditional medicine could. She had no knowledge of modern science, and viruses were to her as magical and inexplicable as demons or spirits. When the doctors said they could not cure Nozipho, she thought they meant only that they did not have the power to cure her. So she bought Nozipho some medicine from a herbalist who lived near her brother in the flatlands below Machobeni. Her brother's son had suffered from the same symptoms, and the woman's medicine had seemed to help. Gogo thought it might help Nozipho too.

But Nozipho refused to take the medicine and poured it out from the yellowed plastic coke bottles onto the dirt yard. Gogo was angry and the two women fought.

As the white doctors had predicted, within a few months Nozipho too was dead.

ON A CRISP DAY in June 2004, I went to the Mathenjwas' house with a soft-spoken young man named Thando Mbhamali, who worked for a local charity organization. We drove as close as we could in his big, white pickup and, when we could go no farther, parked and walked the last bit along a narrow footpath.

By local standards, the Mathenjwas did not live in a particularly remote area, and the roads leading to their house, though made of dirt, were well maintained. The town of Ingwavuma, with its shops, schools, and hospital, lay just a few miles away. The family's homestead sat just below a grassy airstrip, which was still occasionally used by the hospital to bring in supplies, although it had decreased in importance since the paved road to Ingwavuma was finished in 2001. The Zulu royal family also had a little-used palace nearby. It was one of their minor residences, really little more than a cluster of houses that looked like a cross between a Lego castle and a modern African homestead.

Three months had passed since Nozipho's death, and the family was preparing for a traditional cleansing ceremony, which was held to free the spirit of the dead from its bonds to the living. The

Mathenjwas were one of several thousand recently orphaned families identified by a local organization called Ingwavuma Orphan Care as having recently lost relatives to AIDS. For several days, I had been tagging along with workers from the organization—which had been founded a few years earlier by a British doctor, Ann Barnard—as they delivered food and checked on the status of families with whom they had been working.

When we arrived, the family lined up outside the children's house and Thando introduced me. Gogo hobbled down from her own house, which was up a short hill. The smaller children huddled in her skirts, while the older ones fidgeted and kept their eyes down. They answered my questions quietly and politely, but warily too.

That first meeting was formal and awkward as we sized each other up across the vast cultural and economic divides that separated my world from theirs. Thando explained I was a journalist and that I was writing a book, but such details meant little to them. Unlike Adeline, who often commented when we were together that something would be good for my book, the Mathenjwas had little familiarity with literature. Gogo could not read at all, and the only books the family owned were a few picture books for children that Nozipho had acquired for her daughter. In their minds, at least at first, I'm sure I was simply a rich outsider who had come to collect information on their plight, and who might, if they were lucky, be able to offer some help in the end.

It had been more than a year since their mother had died, they told me. During that time, the family had partially scattered. Nozipho's daughter went to live with her father's family. Makhisi, the youngest, had gone to live with her paternal uncle, not far from Gogo's home village in the flatlands that lay at the foot of the Lebombo mountains. And the eldest surviving girl, Nokukhanya—who was usually called Khanya—had taken her son and moved in with her boyfriend in Ndumo, another low-lying village near the border with Mozambique. Her boyfriend, a teacher, was the son of a neighboring family. Khanya had become pregnant by him when she was seventeen and was a student in his school.

By the time I met them, three months after their sister's death, only three of Lungile's children still lived in the small house next to Gogo. Phumlani, a handsome, serious boy of twenty-one, had become the family's young head, although he had not yet finished high school. He shared a room with Mfundo, a wiry twelve-year-old who stood awkwardly on the boundary between childhood and adolescence and dreamed of becoming a soccer player. The wall above Mfundo's bed was papered with pictures of soccer stars cut from magazines. Of the girls, only Sbuka remained. She, perhaps, felt the loss of her mother and sisters most acutely. At sixteen she was sleeping in a room by herself for the first time in her life. It was the same room where Nozipho and Lungile had died.

After the death of Lungile, Thando, from Ophan Care, had helped Nozipho apply for a grant from the government to care for her younger siblings. South Africa offered monthly grants of 560 rand, about $85, for each child (up to a maximum of five) being cared for by someone other than their parents. Although the grants had not been designed specifically in response to the growing AIDS-related orphan problem, many local nongovernmental organizations like Ingwavuma Orphan Care had seized on this as a practical way to provide long-term financial help to families affected by the epidemic. The grants were a generous social welfare provision that almost no other African country could offer, but one that was also tangled in a thick web of bureaucracy and infiltrated with corruption.

In recent years, government grants for the sick, elderly, and orphaned had become the main source of income for many families in the area. In the cash-poor economy of Ingwavuma, some of the wealthiest families were those who received several different grants. Only Sbuka and Mfundo were young enough to qualify for the foster-care grant—and even Sbuka would soon be too old—but the almost $175 a month the two grants eventually brought in was a huge sum in the area. Gogo also received an old-age pension of just over $100 a month. Her husband, Obed, also received a disability grant for his asthma, but could not always be relied upon to share it with the rest of the family. When I came to visit after pension day, he would sometimes show me some new possession he had recently acquired. Once it was a cell phone, another time a pair of jeans and a shirt more appropriate for a teenager than an old man. Sometimes he contributed a bit of meat or some vegetables to the family table, but the task of feeding and clothing the family fell largely to Gogo.

Nozipho, I later learned, had not told her grandparents that she was applying for the grant. When it came through she bought a white Formica table and four chairs for the previously empty living room of the house and put a down payment on a gas-operated refrigerator. The grant, though, took nine months to process, and Nozipho died a few months after it came through, long before the payments for the refrigerator could be completed. When she died, the monthly grant payments stopped immediately, sending the Mathenjwas, who had been momentarily wealthy, back to desperate poverty. The day I came with Thando, he had come to update them on the process of having the grants transferred to Gogo's name.

The Mathenjwas were, in many ways, quite typical of the families I met in the Ingwavuma area, although they had suffered the double blow of losing their parents and eldest sister. Like the Mathenjwas, most orphans in the area were assisted in some way by relatives, usually a grandmother, but also often an aunt or uncle. In the traditional and closely knit communities of the area, there were few orphans who were entirely abandoned by their families. Households headed by children did exist, but they were the exception rather than the rule, and most of these were in fact headed by teenagers or young adults who preferred to stay in their parents' home. Sometimes the assistance from family members was grudging or exploitative; more often it was extended by generally well-meaning relatives who themselves were already struggling to survive.

Phumlani, Sbuka, and Mfundo, the three of Lungile's children still at her house, lived in semi-independence. Their grandparents, along with an ever-changing number of aunts and uncles and cousins, lived in a larger homestead up a short, overgrown path. Each month after she received her pension, Gogo bought them a large bag of finely ground white cornmeal, called mealie meal, which was cooked into a stiff porridge called pap. The bag had to last until the next pension day. Sometimes during the month she would give them some chicken or a few vegetables, but most days they had to find their own *shembo*, the meat or vegetable topping for the pap, or go without. And since they lived in their own house, with no adults to supervise them, there was no one to ensure that they went to school or kept the house clean.

Still, the children were remarkably disciplined. Most days they rose before dawn to make the long walk to school, staying at home only when they had no soap to wash their uniforms. Much of the household work fell to Sbuka, as the only girl, although each child did his or her own washing, even Mfundo. Sbuka kept the house neatly swept and the beds made as her mother had taught her, but other things had begun to lapse. No one cared for the vegetable garden, which had become tangled and overgrown with weeds. Often, too, they were too tired or lazy to collect firewood to cook. The wooden kitchen that their mother had built next to the house slowly disappeared into the fire until there was nothing left but the metal roof, which they propped up against the wall of the house to make a small shelter against the wind.

Over time, I learned that the relationship between the Mathenjwa children and their grandmother was often fraught, though never, I think, due to intentional malice on either side. Between Gogo and her grandchildren, though, lay an enormous gap that seemed to have been wrenched even wider by the loss of the intermediary generation. Gogo was a traditional woman who had been raised in a day when young men still wooed their wives with beaded love letters. She had never gone to school or traveled farther than the plains of Maputaland below Ingwavuma, where she had been born. I asked her once what was the most distant place she had ever traveled to. "Far, so far I don't even know," she replied. "It's too far to even measure." After a few more questions, I determined that she had never been farther away than Jozini, a slightly larger town about forty miles from Ingwavuma. Her entire world could be seen from the edge of the low mountains in which they lived.

Although they had all been born before the fall of apartheid, Gogo's grandchildren had the expectations of "born frees." They did not see their future in a life of subsistence farming, but in the modern South Africa outside Ingwavuma's borders. They had no television, and the schools in the area were, by and large, doing an appalling job training young people for the modern employment market. Yet they had had just enough of a taste of the broader world to know what they were missing. Unlike Gogo, they had played in the nearby ocean and visited the big city. The cruelty of modern South Africa for their generation was that they were promised much that would never be. What had become possible had not necessarily become feasible. Gogo's grandchildren were coming of age in a far bigger, more complicated world, filled with temptations and dangers Gogo could only begin to understand.

Like most people in the area, the family spoke very little English. Gogo and Obed, whom everyone called Mkhulu, which means "grandfather," spoke none at all, and the children, though they all attended English-language schools, spoke and understood surprisingly little. Over time, as they became more comfortable with me, they gained confidence in their English, and by the end we could carry on conversations of relative sophistication. Phumlani, who was by nature shy and soft-spoken, grew most eloquent when describing his love of Michael Jackson and could sing quite a few of the pop star's most famous lyrics. He was surprised, though, when I told him of Jackson's recent troubles, not to mention the change in his skin color. Phumlani did not think such things were possible and wanted to see a photograph as proof.

Clearly, though, English was not the ideal form of communication, so I hired a young woman—a volunteer at the local Women's Center—to help translate for me. In the end, Zethu became for me more than just a translator of language; she helped me to understand much about Zulu culture and the local community. Many times too she helped me avoid embarrassing faux pas.

INGWAVUMA, which is the largest settlement near where the Mathenjwas live, sits in the northernmost part of the South African province of KwaZulu-Natal in an area known as Zululand. Tucked in amid the rolling hills of the Lebombo range, it is sandwiched between the mountains and the sea, near where three nations meet, in one of South Africa's most remote, and poorest, corners.

Although Ingwavuma, named after the nearby Ngwavuma river, is only about 350 miles from Maseru, as the crow flies, the two places could be continents away. While Lesotho's landscape is sparse and rugged, the Lebombo mountains are lush and verdant. Although subtropical, the climate is warm and wet. The temperature rarely falls below freezing and in the summer months the air is thick and wet with humidity. Even after several years of drought, which struck the area at the beginning of the new millennium, the landscape was green and heavily vegetated.

In the distance, across the miles of flat plains below, lay the endless, sandy, white beaches that line the Indian Ocean. Not far to the north is Mozambique, a vast, former Portuguese colony still struggling to rebuild after sixteen years of brutal civil war. To the west, on the other side of the mountains, is Swaziland, Africa's last absolute monarchy, where each year the young king chooses a new wife from the kingdom's maidens, who come to dance bare-breasted for his mother.

Modern Zululand has only a handful of towns and few paved roads. Most houses, like the Mathenjwas', still lack running water and electricity. There are few jobs, and the vast majority of families depend largely on government grants or on remittances from family members working in the city. Although most families also grow vegetables and corn, the staple crop, and keep some livestock, it is a rare family that has enough land and labor, not to mention money for seeds and fertilizer, to grow enough to feed their entire family for the whole year. Like the Mathenjwas, most people in the area live with one foot in subsistence agriculture and the other in a modern cash economy.

The small towns that lie scattered through the region are, like Ingwavuma, little more than modern trading posts. Founded in 1895 as a colonial judicial center, Ingwavuma was connected to the outside world by a paved road in 2001; before that, the only way to get there was on a treacherous, winding dirt thoroughfare that passed through the mountains. Even now, the pavement ends abruptly just beyond the town center, as if you have reached the last outpost on the edge of some great wilderness. Locals say they have been promised that the road will one day be extended into Swaziland, but until then, it goes to Ingwavuma and no farther.

The town has a grocery store—nicknamed the Boxer, after the company that used to run it—with everything from meat to coffins. The town also has a hospital, a few Chinese-run clothing stores, a gas station, some schools, and a few government offices. There aren't neighborhoods or even streets, except for the main paved road, and the buildings are spread out over a considerable distance.

My first visit to the area coincided closely with a celebration of a decade of multiracial, democratic rule in South Africa. On April 27, 1994, Nelson Mandela was elected as the country's first black president, ushering in a miraculously peaceful transition from a racial regime to a modern democracy.

Although most people in Ingwavuma did not support Nelson Mandela's African National Congress (ANC)—the area has usually voted predominately for the Zulu nationalist party, the Inkhata Freedom Party—expectations were high that life in the new South Africa would be better than under apartheid. A decade after those first elections, many of those expectations remained unfulfilled. Life had improved in some ways, but more than a century of underdevelopment is not easily wiped away.

After its annexation by the British, the Ingwavuma area was set aside as part of a "native reserve" where whites were forbidden from owning land. Under a system similar to the indirect rule used by the British in West Africa, the people there continued to be governed by their traditional chiefs and headmen, who were under the authority of a British magistrate and, ultimately, the governor of the colony.[1] Ingwavuma itself was founded as the site of the area's magistrate; its first buildings were a prison and a courthouse. Later, Catholic and Protestant missionaries arrived to build schools and a hospital.

The British policy, however, was less enlightened than it first appeared. Although it prevented Africans from being entirely disenfranchised, the amount of land set aside for them was not large enough to sustain the entire population, and the creation of the "native reserve" in Zululand marked the beginning of an overpopulation problem that continues to this day. Africans were also heavily taxed by the British government, through the imposition of hut taxes, custom duties, and fees to register marriages and divorces.

These taxes, which fell more heavily on Africans than on whites, subsidized the development of nearby white areas. They paid the salaries of white government officials, funded the building of roads and hospitals in white areas, and subsidized white schools.[2] The taxes also helped to push Zulus into the wage labor system, providing much-needed manpower for the white settlers. There was, however, never quite enough black labor to fulfill the voracious need of white farmers—in part because many Zulu men resisted doing agricultural work, which they saw as women's labor—and the colony in 1860 resorted to importing Indian laborers whose descendants still form a substantial segment of the KwaZulu-Natal population, although they are not present in large numbers in the Ingwavuma area.

Little changed in Ingwavuma after Natal became part of the new Union of South Africa in 1910. The area remained largely black, although a handful of white trading families controlled the bulk of commerce in the area, building for themselves colonial enclaves where they played tennis and drank afternoon tea in the dense African air. A handful of government officials, English and Afrikaans, ran a prison and a court. Later, in the 1950s, the missionaries arrived. Protestants came to build a hospital, Mosvold, which is now run by the South African government, and the Catholics to build schools.

In 1959, Ingwavuma became part of KwaZulu, one of the black "homelands" that South Africa claimed were self-governing states, although that fiction wasn't believed anywhere else. The map of the old KwaZulu shows a series of unconnected areas whose main criteria for inclusion in the homeland was that they were poor, primarily occupied by blacks, and consisted of land for which whites had no use. Like Native Americans in the nineteenth century, South African blacks were given the excess, unwanted bits of a fertile and plentiful land and told that there they could preserve their culture and continue to develop in their own separate ways. In the eyes of the South African government, of course, the African way of development didn't require education, electrification, or other modern accoutrements.

The establishment of the homelands, or "Bantustans," conveniently allowed the South African government to strip blacks of South African citizenship, making them in essence foreign workers in "white" areas. In theory, every black African belonged to one of these homelands, no matter how many generations of his family had lived in the city. Any black African who ran afoul of the strict pass laws that governed which blacks could live in white areas could be deported back to his designated "ancestral home," even if he had no family or connections there. That the homelands were not large enough to support the populations that theoretically were supposed to live there was conveniently ignored. By the government's own calculations, there was enough land to support only half the country's blacks even at the time of the establishment of the homelands in 1951.[3]

Shortly after the 1994 election, the new South African government embarked on an ambitious development program to erase the legacy of centuries of colonial and apartheid rule and to improve life for the nation's poorest people. The country's idealistic constitution guarantees citizens not only political rights, such as freedom and equality, but also social rights, such as access to basic health care, education, and housing, as well as clean water and sanitation. The task of providing these, however, would prove enormous, especially in former homeland areas like Ingwavuma.

Mandela and the ANC inherited an economy teetering on the verge of collapse after decades of sanctions, as well as a bloated and inefficient civil service that had existed in large part to provide jobs for loyal Afrikaners. The new government's grand social projects immediately hit economic and capacity constraints, and they struggled to balance the competing needs of stabilizing the economy, diversifying the civil service, and providing social services.

BY 2004, when I first started visiting Ingwavuma, some progress was being made, although the changes fell far short of the thunderous revolution most people had expected to accompany the fall of apartheid. After decades of "Bantu education," which dictated that Africans be taught in their mother tongue and only in those subjects the apartheid government deemed suitable for second-class citizens, there were few locals with the skills to implement the government's ambitious plans. Few educated urban blacks wanted to move to rural areas where the quality of living was poorer, especially since their skills were in high demand in the cities, where life was easier and the pay higher. Places like Ingwavuma also had to play decades of catch-up in terms of basic infrastructure. They had few roads and largely lacked electricity, running water, or telephone connections. There weren't enough schools for all the children or clinics for all the sick. Social services were nearly nonexistent, and in the absence of the infrastructure of a modern state, traditional leaders continued to play a powerful role.

Still the evidence of change was often quite visible. The paved road to Ingwavuma, completed in 2001, was modest and already beginning to crack, but it had substantially reduced the area's isolation. More schools had been built and the hospital had expanded, with more than double the number of doctors posted there compared to a decade earlier. The new system of government-provided social grants, disbursed by government employees in a recently built, double-story, yellow brick building, had made a tangible impact on cash poverty for many families like the Mathenjwas, for whom this money was their sole source of income.

Yet this progress paled against the overwhelming need in the region, which seemed to be growing daily. Despite a decade of massive public works projects, most people still lacked access to basic services. Nearly a hundred thousand people lived in the vast, rural area served by the local hospital, Mosvold. Of those, only an estimated 3.6 percent had electricity. Fewer than 5 percent had piped water.[4] Even areas that were served by water, like the one where the Orphan Care center stood, often experienced water shortages that lasted for months at a time. There were more schools, but also more children, and overcrowding remained a problem. Crime was also increasing as young people became more mobile, moving back and forth between the cities and the rural areas.

Most seriously, there were still almost no jobs, and those that did exist paid poorly. The vast majority of employed people worked for the government, and many of those had been recruited from elsewhere. The prosecutors, judges, social workers, nurses, teachers, and doctors who kept the area running often came from areas where there were better educational opportunities. They usually stayed for only a few years, until they could find a better job in a more suitable area. Even nurses, policemen, and teachers, who formed the backbone of the small local middle class, earned only a few hundred dollars a month and many lived, like Zethu's family, in houses without electricity and running water. Mosvold Hospital was the area's single most important employer; by 2004, Orphan Care had become the second largest.

And then there was the growing burden of AIDS, which seemed to undermine every bit of progress that was being made. Mosvold Hospital was expanding, but so was its workload. As at Maluti hospital in Lesotho, the number of admissions and deaths were soaring. Social grants provided a lifeline for the poorest families, but the system failed to keep pace with the growing number of needy families, many of whom, like the Mathenjwas, found themselves suddenly destitute.

It often seemed that the only booming industry in Ingwavuma was the funeral business. Over the period I spent there, during 2004 and 2005, the area's first proper funeral parlor began to rise slowly in a valley next to the Boxer, below the bright yellow building that housed the Women's Center, where Zethu worked. Several smaller entrepreneurs had already set up shop, including one at the door of the hospital, and the Boxer, which sold coffins from a metal shipping crate in the back, did a booming business.

"People are poor, but they don't want to bury their relatives without dignity," I was told by a plump man named Solomon Mathenjwa, who sold coffins and snacks at Mosvold's entrance. In one room, he sold packages of chips to hospital visitors. Next door, piles of coffins were stacked up against the yellowed wall. A pauper's coffin, made of roughly hewn tack board, cost 150 rand, just over $20. The most expensive, a lacquered brown box with a lined interior, retailed for 1,200 rand. Few families, even the most destitute, buried their loved ones in the cheapest option.

The custom of burying people in coffins, though, seemed to have made only a recent appearance in the area. Zethu once pointed out to me the house of the first local man who had been buried in one. The burial had occurred within her memory.

"I was the first African here to sell coffins," Solomon said. "Last week, there were thirty-one people at the hospital who died. I sold five coffins. I never sell less than five a week."

"There's more competition now—two more people are planning to open—but I'm not worried. More people are dying."

By then, across the country, an estimated 950 people were dying of AIDS each day. In KwaZulu-Natal, which had the highest infection rate in South Africa and one of the highest infection rates in the world, an estimated 600,000 people had already died.[5] So many people were dying, a funeral director in Durban told me in 2001, that the cemeteries were full. "There's no place left to bury the dead," he said. According to one study by a doctor at Mosvold, 45 percent of deaths at the hospital in 2003 were AIDS-related. Particularly worrying was the gender disparity. Although women and men seemed to be dying in nearly equal numbers, women were dying nearly a decade younger, many in their thirties, probably because they were being infected at a younger age. Comparing the age of patients dying from HIV-related causes to those dying from other causes, it appeared that AIDS was cutting short the lives of many local women by twenty-five years. Men were losing fifteen years.[6]

AIDS wasn't taking the very old or the very young, as most diseases tend to, but those in the prime of their lives. Left behind were orphans and grandparents, struggling to survive in an upside-down world. This meant good business for the coffin-seller Solomon but, as would become painfully clear to me in the coming months, disaster for the area.

THERE WAS NO PAUPER'S coffin for Nozipho. She had been buried in a coffin her family could ill afford, bought with money saved from the foster-care grant she received for her younger siblings. I often thought of the shiny wooden box underneath the stones of her burial mound and what else the money could have bought. Dying in Africa today is an expensive proposition. There is the coffin to buy and the funeral day feast to provide for dozens, sometimes hundreds of guests. Relatives from far away must be housed and fed, from the time they arrive after first hearing of the death to the day after the burial. Then, several months later, there is another feast to cleanse the homestead and set free the spirit of the recently deceased. Often families emerge from the fog of grief to find themselves deeply in debt, from the combined burden of sickness and death.

By the time Nozipho's family gathered for her cleansing ceremony, a few days after I first met them, they were too poor to fully honor tradition. The family was Christian but, like many in the area, retained many of their traditional beliefs and customs as well.

There was an unusual chill in the air on the day of the ceremony. A cold wind whipped across the hills, and although it was the beginning of the dry winter season, the gray sky threatened rain. At 8:30, when the first guests began arriving, there was still no sign that a ceremony would be held that day. No fire had been lit in the cooking hut, either at the Mathenjwa home or their grandmother's.

In more prosperous days, the family would have slaughtered a cow for the occasion. The animal's intestines would have been placed by the entrance to the homestead, or *kraal*, for visitors to wash their hands in, and its meat stewed in large, black cast-iron pots. But the Mathenjwa family had no cattle of their own, nor did they have the several hundred dollars it would have cost to buy a cow. Instead, the children placed a bowl of water sprinkled with ash from the fire near the gate. When Gogo woke and gathered the family, they cooked a simple meal of rice and watery beef stew, boiled with no spices, and slaughtered a few chickens from Gogo's flock. Visitors would later comment on the sparse meal and lack of salad.

The relatives had gathered in the children's yard long before the food was ready. They were restless because there were only a handful of chairs for the more than seventy guests who milled around near the small graveyard where Lungile and Nozipho were buried. The family had borrowed extra cups and plates from neighbors, but even then there were not enough for everyone. Guests took turns drinking a sweet tea with milk and generous spoonfuls of sugar. As the morning ripened, the group sat in a circle and passed around a white plastic jug of traditional beer, brewed from sorghum.

No one mentioned the disease that had taken Nozipho, although the old women whispered, in general terms, among themselves about the epidemic. Gogo's sister-in-law, who lived down in the flatlands, lamented how many funerals there were these days. In her place it was worse than anywhere else. "No," Gogo countered. "It is worse here."

Only Mkhulu shed tears that day. Nozipho was a good girl, he said. Very kind. He recalled how Nozipho had come to him in her last days. She had fought with Gogo and wanted him to intercede with the old woman. "I remember the things my granddaughter did on her last day," he said sadly. "She never wanted to see Gogo. She was always fighting with her."

The day of the ceremony there was also a fight. While his sisters were preparing the meal, Mfundo was playing with some of the other boys in the neighborhood. He came back crying, his head bruised and bleeding, saying he had been hit by some of the other boys. He claimed they had accused him of breaking a toy car made of wire, which he swore he did not do.

Gogo and Mkhulu did not believe Mfundo's story and were worried about his erratic behavior. "He is not listening at all. He is badly behaved," Gogo complained. "He wants to hit everybody and does not respect his elders."

The boy had, they said, stabbed Sbuka in the hand and had tried to stab his aunt when she was pregnant. Mkhulu took away everything that they thought might be dangerous. The two old people were confused by Mfundo's bad behavior, but did not connect it to the deaths of his parents or sister. Sadness they could understand, but Mfundo's anger mystified them.

Finally, around 10:30, Sbuka and her siblings brought the food down from Gogo's house to their own. When the guests had completed the simple meal, Gogo told Lungile's children to bring

Nozipho's things from the house. There wasn't much. They gathered around the small pile of garments. There were some black shoes, some panties and bras, a few shirts and a mattress. Gogo sprinkled the pile with water and then invited each to take what they wanted.

Sbuka chose a black skirt of shiny rayon, printed with large red roses, that she said was Nozipho's favorite. Gogo asked if anyone wanted a shirt Nozipho had often worn, but no one did. Sbuka said nothing. She just turned her eyes away and blinked back tears, so Gogo put the shirt in a box to remember Nozipho by. "When she was wearing that, she used to be full and strong, but when she was sick she looked very thin and it hung loosely on her," Gogo said sadly. She also took Nozipho's favorite shoes, which caused some quiet giggles, since the old woman rarely wore shoes and could not have fit her swollen, cracked feet into anything Nozipho wore.

As the day drew to a close, the family passed around Nozipho's photo album, which she must have bought second-hand because it had the name of a strange man inscribed on the inside cover. There were pictures of her with friends and with her daughter. She looked young and beautiful and carefree.

10

TWO WAVES OF AIDS

THE FIRST IDENTIFIED AIDS cases in South
Africa came in 1982 and followed the Western rather than the
African model, occurring among homosexual men. Infections
among heterosexual Africans didn't appear until several years later,
and as late as 1990, two-thirds of the country's reported cases were
still among white homosexuals. A decade later, the homosexual epidemic would be dwarfed by the heterosexual one.

Flight attendants working for the state-owned South African
Airways, who were part of a very mobile subculture that was connected to the international gay community, were an important vector for first bringing the virus to South Africa, just as the now
infamous Canadian flight steward Gaetan Dugas is believed to have
played a role in spreading HIV in North America and Europe.[1] Of
the 215 South Africans who had died of AIDS by 1990, twenty-six
were flight attendants for the airline.[2]

A second wave of AIDS came later, but with devastating force.
The country was heavily dependent on imported labor, and so-called
African AIDS—in the form of a heterosexually driven epidemic—
eventually worked its way down the continent and into South
Africa, where it quickly became entrenched.

By the mid-1980s, there were already worrying signs that HIV might be spreading rapidly among black South Africans, although it would be several more years before a confirmed case of heterosexually transmitted AIDS was recorded. In a survey of 35,500 mine workers in 1986, 130 tested HIV-positive, most of them from Malawi. The study found that mine workers from that country already had a 4 percent infection rate.[3] In response, the mining industry in 1987 began screening new mine workers for AIDS and rejecting those who tested positive. Malawi refused to allow its citizens to be tested, so no new mine workers from that country were admitted after that date. Existing employees who tested positive, though, were allowed to remain as long as they could still work, and by 1988, nearly 10 percent of Malawian workers were infected.[4]

The epidemic quickly spread from mine workers to residents of black urban areas. Blood surveys in 1990 of sexually transmitted disease clinics in Johannesburg and Durban, the main city in KwaZulu-Natal (then still called Natal Province), found infection rates of 2.9 and 3.6 percent, respectively.[5] While infection rates among patients of such clinics are generally higher than in the overall population, the substantial presence of infections there indicated that the epidemic had reached the general heterosexual community and that it was spreading alarmingly fast.

In the polarized political environment of the 1980s, the arrival of "African AIDS" in South Africa provided ideal propaganda for the apartheid government and racist whites determined to avoid any kind of multiracial rule. That the virus had first affected gay whites was conveniently ignored. At a campaign appearance in March 1987, South Africa's foreign minister, Pik Botha, responded to a question about the government's response to AIDS by blaming the spread of AIDS on "terrorists" attempting to destabilize the country. "AIDS gets into this country in ways you wouldn't even think of," Botha said. "Terrorists cross our borders carrying a more dangerous bomb in their bodies than in their hands. They come from camps where AIDS is rife."[6]

Right-wing political groups also used AIDS to play on white fears. Anonymous pamphlets advised whites to regularly test their black domestic workers and to insulate themselves from Africans to ensure their survival in "an AIDS sea."[7] In parliament, white political parties traded accusations that their opponents were hyping the epidemic for political motives. The opposition Conservative Party accused the ruling National Party of telling voters that AIDS would make blacks a minority within five years, while the health minister accused a Conservative Party member of saying, "If AIDS stops black population growth, it would be like Father Christmas."[8]

Despite its superior infrastructure and health system, apartheid South Africa did little to respond to the growing epidemic. The country was preoccupied by other, more immediate concerns. In 1990, South Africa spent only $2 million on AIDS prevention, half of what neighboring Mozambique—then wartorn and one of the world's poorest nations—spent the same year. The next year, the AIDS budget rose to only $2.1 million, most of it targeted at white urban areas. The government, dominated by conservative Christians and heavily influenced by the Dutch Reformed Church, resisted making condoms more widely available and teaching about sex in schools. State-controlled television also refused to talk about condoms, which were still subject to a 60 percent import tax.[9]

Given the political environment in the country during the late 1980s and early 1990s, it is unlikely that such messages would have been believed by black South Africans in any case. In the context of the poisoned rhetoric from some whites about AIDS, it is also no wonder that many blacks began to see in AIDS a deadly conspiracy by a government that had already proved its brutality and amorality. In other parts of Africa, the early debate around AIDS and race largely took the form of denial. Many Africans dismissed what they saw as a Western attempt to "blame" Africa for AIDS, as, in the words of Ghana's official newspaper, *The Ghanian Times,* "a shameful, vulgar and foolish attempt by white supremacists to push this latest white man's burden onto the doors of the black man."[10]

In South Africa, however, most blacks were only too willing to believe that AIDS existed and to connect its untimely appearance to the raging political struggle. Rumors flew that the disease was an invention of the apartheid government, intended to kill off blacks, or that the government was trying to lower the black birth rate by tricking them into using condoms. Some people suspected that condoms might actually help spread AIDS, rather than prevent it. Young antiapartheid activists claimed the acronym AIDS really meant "Afrikaner Invention to Deprive Us of Sex."[11]

Such fears were not unreasonable, given the experience of black South Africans. After Mandela's election, it would emerge that Wouter Basson, a cardiologist who ran the apartheid regime's chemical weapons program, used government funds to try to develop a special bacterium that would target only black people. The bacteria project was as scientifically unsound as it was morally abhorrent, yet the existence of such programs, to many black South Africans, made the possibility that AIDS was an apartheid conspiracy seem entirely plausible. Sadly, these conspiracy theories would last long after apartheid itself was dead. Around the time of Basson's trial, in 2001, I encountered young men, barely old enough to remember the apartheid days, who claimed stridently that Basson had created HIV.

The ANC, many of whose members had lived in exile in countries like Zambia and Tanzania where the epidemic was further advanced, already had firsthand experience of AIDS. The party had even lost members to the disease. As the movement prepared for the transition to democracy, it seemed that the ANC might make AIDS prevention a priority.

In 1990, Chris Hani, the popular leader of the ANC's armed branch, Umkhonto we Sizwe, warned that AIDS posed a grave threat to South Africa's future. "Those of us in exile are especially in the unfortunate situation of being in the areas where the incidence of this disease is high. We cannot afford to allow the AIDS epidemic to ruin the realization of our dreams." Although the epidemic in South Africa was still small, Hani—who was tragically assassinated three years later—warned that it could not be ignored. "Unattended, however, this will result in untold damage and suffering by the end of the century."[12]

Two years later, the ANC and the government convened the National AIDS Convention of South Africa (NACOSA), charged with jointly developing an AIDS plan. Mandela himself spoke at its launch. Such collaboration between old enemies was, even for its time, revolutionary. Among the ANC representatives involved in drafting the NACOSA plan were Dr. Nkosazana Dlamini-Zuma and Dr. Manto Tshabalala-Msimang, who would later both play inglorious roles in the AIDS battle as health ministers in postapartheid governments.[13]

In those early years, despite the political turmoil still preoccupying the country, there was a brief period when it seemed the epidemic would be taken more seriously in the new South Africa. At the time, the NACOSA plan was considered one of the most progressive in the world. That hope would quickly be betrayed, and AIDS would slip slowly down the new government's list of priorities, victim to more immediate concerns like forging the peace and tackling South Africa's enormous economic inequalities. Mandela himself would later lament the lost opportunity. In 1990, when South Africa conducted its first survey of pregnant women—the data on which most estimates of HIV prevalence are based—only 0.8 percent of women were infected. The disease had arrived, but it remained potentially controllable. By the time Mandela left office, in 1998, almost 23 percent of pregnant women in the country were HIV-positive.[14]

SOUTH AFRICA WASN'T the only place where the growing AIDS plague was quickly overshadowed by other, more immediate concerns. The brief flurry of interest in global AIDS that occurred in the late 1980s had by the early 1990s quickly faded. Journalists, who had flocked to Central Africa to report about the appearance of African AIDS, disappeared again, off to cover other stories: the fall of the Iron Curtain, the first Iraq war, Mandela's release, and South Africa's transition to multiracial democracy. Even for those specifically attuned to affairs on the African continent, there were plenty of other stories, most of them tragic. Brutal wars were raging in the former Portuguese colonies of Angola and Mozambique. There was anarchy and failed intervention in Somalia and genocide in Rwanda. The continent that only a few decades earlier had grasped freedom with such optimism seemed to be sinking into a morass of political instability, corruption, and human suffering. In the larger context of Africa's troubles at the time, AIDS seemed to be only one small piece.

It soon also became apparent that, despite early fears, the epidemic in America and Europe would not follow the African trajectory. There AIDS remained essentially confined to the same marginalized segments of the population, largely gays and intravenous drug users, who were first stricken. In some urban areas in America the epidemic was beginning to move into the general population, but as the victims were largely poor and black, this development received little attention. When the hypothetical white yuppie couple who had been featured on the cover of *U.S. News and World Report* in 1987 with the headline THE DISEASE OF THEM BECOMES THE DISEASE OF US, ceased to be at risk, the political urgency to understand African AIDS suddenly faded. Activists in America were consumed by their own troubles and had little time for the concerns of the nameless and the faceless dying far away on another continent.

The same virus was killing people on both sides of the Atlantic, yet the experiences of Africans and Westerners with AIDS could not have been more different. In America, the epidemic sparked a political radicalization and cultural flowering among gays, but the demands of this new breed of activist were immediate and localized. They wanted more money for AIDS research, quicker authorization of new drugs, and laws protecting the rights of HIV-positive people. With their friends dying, the first and most important front of the war was at home. In Africa, the shroud of silence lasted for many years.

The global AIDS effort also experienced a leadership vacuum after Jonathan Mann fell out with the new head of the World Health Organization, Hiroshi Nakajima, in 1990. The agency's former head, Halfdan Mahler, had given the iconoclastic American enormous freedom to build and run WHO's AIDS program as he saw fit. From a staff consisting of a single half-time secretary when he began in 1986, Mann turned the Global Program on AIDS (GPA) into one of the agency's largest and most visible programs. By 1989, it had a budget of $90 million and a staff of nearly four hundred.[15]

Nakajima, a political appointee and rigid bureaucrat, was uncomfortable with Mann's independence and believed AIDS had received too much attention in comparison to other global health problems, such as malaria, that at the time were still killing more people. Nakajima tried to rein in the GPA, to Mann's fury.

After months of tension between the two men, Mann quit in March 1990 when he failed to receive official permission to attend a conference on AIDS in the Soviet Union and other Eastern-bloc countries. He went public with the reasons, attributing his decision to "issues of principle" and "major disagreements" with Nakajima. For several years after Mann's departure, international efforts to slow the spread of the virus were stalled.

ANN BARNARD, the British doctor who founded Ingwavuma Orphan Care, was slightly plump, with straight blond hair and a shy, awkward manner. She had a fierce little dog, named Impi after the Zulu word for "warrior," who followed her everywhere. When Ann drove, Impi would sit on her lap and put her paws on the steering wheel, as if she was helping direct the car. "See that house," Ann once heard a small child telling a friend, "that's where the woman lives who has the dog that can drive!"

Ann first came to South Africa to work at Mosvold in 1997 at the age of twenty-seven. The child of a British father and a Russian mother who had met while teaching in Ghana, she had grown up in a secular family but became an evangelical Christian as a teenager. Like her parents, she wanted to work in Africa.

She had read an article about the hospital in a magazine for evangelical British doctors and written to the director asking if they had any posts for doctors. At the time, she thought she would stay in South Africa for only a short while before she moved on to the "real Africa," where people were poorer and the need for doctors greater. When she got to Ingwavuma, however, she realized that there was plenty there for a doctor to do. The area may have been part of the continent's most developed nation, but it had far more in common with neighboring areas in Swaziland and Mozambique than with the bright lights of Johannesburg. The primary health problems in Ingwavuma were largely the same ones that were ravaging other parts of the continent: malaria, tuberculosis, diarrhea diseases, and accidents. AIDS, the hospital's administrator assured her before she arrived, was not yet widespread. "I didn't want anything to do with AIDS," she recalled. Soon she would have no choice.

When Ann arrived in Ingwavuma, life there was rustic but comfortable. The doctors all lived on the hospital grounds, where they were given small houses with running water and electricity. The paved road had not yet been built, and cell phone service had yet to reach the area, so incoming and outgoing calls had to be routed through the hospital switchboard. She was pleasantly surprised at the quality of the hospital. "Things were well-run," she said. "They even had an ultrasound machine."

At the time, the hospital had dealt with only a few patients who had progressed to full-blown AIDS. "The major medical problem then was malaria," she said. "There were hospitalizations even in winter. Sometimes it was really hectic. There was a bit of AIDS, but not that much." One summer, in early 2000, a major malaria epidemic broke out after unusually heavy rains. Mosvold hospital was flooded with patients, and the harried doctors put three people in each bed. When the beds were full, they put new arrivals on the floor. In all, they treated more than thirty thousand patients at the hospital and local clinics.

Ingwavuma's small white and expatriate community was centered at the hospital, and many were, like Ann, evangelical Christians. Since there were few jobs in Ingwavuma, their spouses busied themselves with improving the community in other ways. Two doctor's wives, Beni Williams, a black Zimbabwean, and Maryna Heese, a white Afrikaner, applied for government money to build a women's center. Others founded Nansindlela School, which Sbuka would later attend.

Despite her initial lack of interest in AIDS, Ann soon found herself treating an increasing number of cases. Within a few years, it had overtaken malaria as the most important health problem faced by the hospital. Partially this was because improved efforts at fighting malaria, including spraying with DDT, had drastically lowered the incidence of that disease. Largely, though, it was because the thousands who had been infected with HIV in previous years were beginning to fall sick and die.

It was Ann's work in the pediatric ward that first moved her to action. There was a little boy of eight or nine named Siyabonga, which means "thank you," who had been abandoned at the hospital after his mother died there. His father came to visit once or twice but never took him home. The nurses looked after him and gave him what comfort they could, but a hospital was no replacement for a family. Ann was moved by the boy's plight. "He was quite miserable all the time."

As the number of deaths from AIDS increased, an increasing number of children were being abandoned in the hospital. Some, like Siyabonga, were sick and themselves HIV-positive. Others were simply abandoned when their parents died. There was no government structure in Ingwavuma to deal with abandoned children. The problem had never existed before, so the children became the hospital's problem.

Sometimes the infants would be adopted by hospital staff. The Heeses took in two, despite opposition from Maryna's conservative Afrikaans family. A teacher named Bridget Walters adopted two others. Ann wanted to take in some children but thought that they needed two parents. Instead, she decided to found Ingwavuma Orphan Care.

In the beginning, the organization was run out of a small building on the hospital grounds, and Ann ran the project on top of her regular duties as a doctor. It started small. She asked government community workers to inform her of struggling families and would go to the Boxer to buy them food. When a volunteer from England came for a few months in late 1999, Ann put him to work identifying families and helping them to build food gardens. But he left after a short time, frustrated by the slow pace of working in such a vast area without a car. In the coming years, the problem of transportation would prove a major obstacle for the small organization, as well as for government efforts to expand social services to the area.

In 2000, the organization received some donations to buy a pickup truck and hire a staff member. Ann officially registered Ingwavuma Orphan Care as a nonprofit and formed a management committee with local community leaders. They hired a man named Johnson Gwala to identify orphans, organize food parcels, and help find money to pay for the children's school fees. But within two weeks of starting, he crashed the new vehicle. It took six months to repair and always leaked oil afterward.

Still, under Gwala the program grew. Almost a thousand orphans were identified. The program was featured on a local television news program and in the country's largest paper, *The Sunday Times*. Gwala was hailed as a local hero. In a story that inspired a group of schoolchildren in the township of Soweto to collect food and clothes for Ingwavuma orphans, *The Sunday Times* called him the "Angel of the AIDS Orphans." The truth, it turned out, was not quite so rosy.[16]

When Orphan Care started receiving more funding and hired additional staff, the new employees began to notice certain discrepancies. Gwala had bought a personal car, and rumor had it that he had opened a tuck shop, a small stall that sells goods in a remote area. They wanted to know where he was getting the money. Ann had strong suspicions that he was stealing from the organization, but nothing could be proven. Eventually he was caught using the organization's gasoline card to fill his personal car. After a long fight that went to a labor tribunal, the board of Orphan Care fired him.

Later one of the board members discovered that Gwala had applied for a grant from the British Council in the name of Ingwavuma Orphan Care. He received 30,000 rand (more than $4,500) which was put into an account that Ann knew nothing about. She informed the British Council, but nothing was ever done about it. Ann doesn't know what happened to the money.

By the time I first visited Ingwavuma in April 2004, Ingwavuma Orphan Care had blossomed into a large organization that did far more than help orphans. The need was overwhelming, and they soon found themselves running support groups, school prevention campaigns, programs to treat sick people at home, and programs to encourage entrepreneurship.

A few months earlier, the organization had moved out of the hospital and into a cluster of cheery pale pink buildings on the outskirts of Ingwavuma. One building housed the organization's new office, complete with a small meeting room, a storeroom, and a tiny kitchen. Three others were built as housing for staff and volunteers.

Although most of the organization's employees were locals, many lived too far away to commute to the office on a daily basis. Good housing in the immediate area was hard to find. Since there were no hotels in Ingwavuma, or for that matter anywhere near, I stayed there as well when I was in town, paying the organization a small amount of "rent" each time.

A year before I met her, Ann had left the hospital to work full-time for Ingwavuma Orphan Care. The organization had grown, and she had trouble juggling her time between the NGO and her work at the hospital. Her church in England, Cornerstone Evangelical Church in Nottingham, agreed to pay her a salary to run a charity for orphans. When she left the hospital, Ann also lost her right to live on hospital grounds. She moved into an oddly shaped house that had been built by an eccentric Portuguese woman. It had running water—sporadically, as with every other house in the area—but no electricity and no hot water. The fridge and stove ran on natural gas, and the only light came from a few dim bulbs that ran off solar batteries. It was a rustic, and rather lonely, existence.

I often thought Ann epitomized the best of the Western missionary tradition. She was selfless and dedicated, without being self-important and judgmental. In personality, Ann couldn't have been more different from Barbara Kingsolver's angry, hell-and-damnation missionary in *The Poisonwood Bible*. She was, in fact, almost painfully shy and ran the organization quietly from behind the scenes, guiding rather than imposing her will. Orphan Care struggled with the inevitable cultural misunderstandings, and occasional tensions, inherent to an organization run by a well-educated, European woman and staffed largely by rural, African employees. Yet

Ann's nonaggressive style kept tension to a minimum and generally suited the sensibilities of her staff's largely nonconfrontational Zulu culture.

Orphan Care was not an overtly religious organization, although it maintained a quietly Christian flavor. The week was opened with a prayer, led in rotation by different staff members, but there was little other overt talk of God. On issues such as condom use, Ann was also pragmatic. While the organization did not actively promote them, their prevention programs for youth did address condom use. In this, Ann said her views had changed since coming to Africa. The cultural context of sex and condom use was different.

"Some women here don't have a choice about sex," she said. In Ingwavuma too, in the era of AIDS, sex could have deadly consequences.

Keeping Orphan Care's various programs funded and running was a constant battle. The main problem, at least in South Africa, was not a lack of money. There was plenty of money available for AIDS work; in fact, there was more money than organizations to absorb it, and as an established, reputable NGO, Orphan Care was frequently contacted by donors who had money for specific projects that they were struggling to spend.

The problem was that each of these grants came with its own application process, laundry list of rules and regulations, and reporting requirements. Many donors wanted grant recipients to open a unique bank account exclusively for their money; for Ann, this required a drive of nearly two hours to the nearest full-service bank, and at times, she was juggling a dozen different accounts. Grants from the American government often required recipients to get three different quotes before buying new equipment such as computers, while European Union programs often limited organizations to buying locally or European-produced goods. If the best and cheapest computers happened to be from China—or, for that matter, if the only available computers happened to come from there—too bad.

Most AIDS money is also earmarked for specific purposes. This often meant that international donors, who were out of touch with what was happening on the ground, set the agenda. Even the best local organizations sometimes found themselves following the money, starting programs to please donors rather than in response to local needs. Different approaches and causes would go in and out of fashion. Sometimes there would be lots of money for orphans or home-based care programs, then suddenly everyone would want to fund prevention programs with an abstinence theme. The result was overlap and a lack of continuity. In late 2005, for example, the European Union asked for applications for grants. The Women's Center applied for money to help fund a program to make and distribute bed nets that could guard against malaria, but for some reason got money to start a program to treat sick people in their homes. Orphan Care already had a home-based care program, and the two groups began jostling for patients and carers. At the time, though, home-based care was the vogue issue.

Since most funding periods were short, usually only a year, local organizations like Orphan Care struggled to keep reinventing themselves in response to donor demands. Programs would just be finding their feet when the funding would run out. "It takes a year to train someone," Ann said. "Most of the staff have never had jobs before. You have to start from the very beginning."

Ann spent the bulk of her time applying for and managing grants. It was a constant battle to keep the organization running and the staff paid, especially since many donors were notoriously late in distributing payments. More than once I arrived in Ingwavuma to find Ann scrambling to use money that she had suddenly received but had to spend in the next month before the end of some organization's fiscal year. On October 22, 2004, for example, Ann finally received funds for a fourteen-month-long project to build food gardens for vulnerable families. The funds were supposed to be frozen on October 31, when the project officially ended.

Orphan Care was large enough, and its sources of funding diverse enough, that Ann usually managed to make things work. If one grant came late, she could usually dig up money from somewhere else to keep everyone paid until the promised funds came through. But smaller organizations that depended on a single grant often found themselves paralyzed while they waited for money.

Employees whose salaries didn't come through had to stop working and find other ways to support their families. Supplies couldn't be bought or office expenses paid. Then, when the money did finally come through, it couldn't be spent quickly enough or was misused.

It was nearly impossible for small, grassroots organizations to qualify for and manage international donor funds. I doubt even the best of Orphan Care's local staff would have been able to keep the organization afloat. A few of the rules made sense and were intended to protect against fraud by people like Johnson Gwala. But more often the rules had to do with the donors' own inefficiencies, not to mention their desire to be able to show the world exactly how much good work they'd done. In many cases, the donor's own waste and inefficiency was far worse than anything perpetrated by the grassroots organizations. Some spent more money coming to see how their money had been spent than they actually donated. The most egregious case of this that I witnessed in Ingwavuma was the South African office of the pharmaceutical company Eli Lilly, which twice sent executives to visit Orphan Care on trips that must have cost hundreds, if not thousands of dollars. In the end, all they gave the organization were some T-shirts.

ALTHOUGH THERE WERE many indicators of the increasing impact of AIDS on Ingwavuma—the rising number of orphans, more frequent funerals, and full hospital wards—public awareness of the epidemic seemed lower than in Maseru. Everywhere there were T-shirts with AIDS messages, but useful news about the epidemic seemed hard to find.

AIDS-themed T-shirts were quite common in Ingwavuma, though their popularity probably had less to do with their message than with the fact that they were usually free. "Sometimes I worry that people here associate AIDS with free T-shirts," Ann sighed after a big AIDS rally thrown by the local government. Hundreds of people had attended the event, but it seemed that most of them had appeared only at the end when free food and shirts were distributed.

Few people had access to any mass media—news in Ingwavuma

still traveled primarily from person to person, on foot or more recently over cell phones—and people lived spread out across vast distances. There were certainly increasing numbers of sick people, but most retreated behind the walls of their homesteads.

Early one morning I met up with Marcus Shongwe, one of Orphan Care's home-based care workers, as he prepared to do his rounds in Machobeni, the area where the Mathenjwas lived. I wanted to see what was happening behind closed doors.

A short, smiling man with thick glasses, Marcus worked with 150 patients in several different neighborhoods, visiting each at least once a month. About half of those knew they were HIV-positive; he guessed that more probably were but had not yet been tested. In Machobeni, home perhaps to a few hundred families, Marcus knew of about ten families in which someone was actively sick from AIDS. He suspected that this was just a fraction of the total number who were ill—and of course the vast majority of infected people were not yet symptomatic. He had no car and spent much of his time simply walking or bicycling from house to house; in the home-based care program, as with many of Orphan Care's other projects, a lack of good transportation was a major barrier to efficient work.

Our first stop was a house within sight of the Mathenjwas'. We found a fat, middle-aged woman sunning herself in the yard of her house. She was HIV-positive and suffering from kidney problems, but had not taken her medicine for two weeks because her friend, who had gone to the hospital to fetch more pills for her, had lost the small paper booklet that served as her medical record. Hospitals in Africa usually don't keep their own files; instead they rely on patients to carry around their own records. Now the woman needed to get a new booklet and to be reexamined, but she had no transportation and could not walk that far on her own. Marcus promised to do what he could to organize a ride for her.

Next we visited an old woman with severe arthritis. Mina was the only old person we saw all day; the rest were young or middle-aged. It was a curious inversion of the natural order of things. When Marcus first found her, she was in so much pain that she couldn't walk. Sylvia, a Swiss nurse who managed the home-based care project, helped her get arthritis medication and now she could walk around again and even garden. When we arrived, she clapped her hands in welcome and told me that Marcus was her savior.

"The most important thing we do is explain to people how to access services," Marcus told me after we bid the old woman farewell. Many people, especially old people, aren't used to relying on the government for help. Some, like the old woman with arthritis, have never been to a doctor.

"The hardest part, though, is when you find a patient at home who has no transport," he continued. Sometimes Orphan Care could help, but not always. At the time, home-based care had only one vehicle and a single nurse.

Marcus took some pills to a woman who had recently had an operation for a false pregnancy and checked on the status of a young man who had broken his leg. But the rest of our visits that day were to families where someone was sick from AIDS. At one small cluster of houses, Marcus started pointing at each in turn: "The husband there died of AIDS last year. In that one, the man went to the hospital a few weeks ago. And the man from that house, he is in the hospital too."

When he started doing home-based care work three years earlier, Marcus told me it was depressing because he knew all the patients with AIDS would eventually die. Marcus would give patients Bactrim, the same antibiotic that Bongy was prescribed in Lesotho, and provide diapers for people with diarrhea. To the caretakers, he gave gloves and advice about how to protect themselves and which traditional healing techniques could be dangerous for the patient and caregiver.

Cleansing of the anus, as Gogo had done to Lungile and Nozipho, was commonly practiced, as was the rubbing of open sores with salt or stones. Enemas, often composed of dish-washing or laundry detergent, were also widely used; people thought if the soap could clean dishes and clothes, it could also cleanse bad things from the body. Marcus said he knew several old women who had been infected with AIDS while administering these therapies.

At first, some of his patients thought it was strange for a man to be doing this work. Nursing was considered a woman's job. But Marcus didn't mind. He said he was doing God's work.

At one house, we found an old man named John who had been left lying all day in his own urine and feces. He and his wife were both HIV-positive, although his disease had progressed further than hers. We had passed her on the road working on a repair crew fixing potholes, part of a government program to create jobs in poor areas. John had been left alone and was too weak to drag himself to the outhouse.

John had had a stroke and seemed to be suffering from AIDS-related dementia. For him there was probably no return. Still, when we arrived, he made a valiant effort at hospitality. He pulled himself up from his bed and leaned against the wall for support. Was I Marcus's girlfriend, he asked? When Marcus said no, the man grinned. "Then you will make a good wife for my son. He is young and handsome," John told me, spit dribbling down his chin. "And he could use a white wife," he joked.

As we left, I thought of Zachariah and the tenderness with which Tsidi had nursed him. "His wife is a drunkard," Marcus explained. John was always filthy when he arrived; Marcus did what he could to help, but a visit once a month from a near stranger could not replace the care of a loving relative.

I was amazed by Marcus's memory. He knew the names of all 150 of his patients, as well as their stories and family situations. Half his work, it seemed, was simply to come and chat, to bring a little joy to their lives. At each house we visited, I saw faces light up when people recognized him.

Our last patient of the day, a young man I'll call Sibusiso, was too weak to even greet us. Just twenty years old, he had been working as a mechanic in a nearby town until he fell sick. His father had died of AIDS several years earlier, and his mother, who was nursing him, was HIV-positive as well. Sibusiso was being treated for TB and was supposed to receive a visit each week from a nurse who would bring his medication. That week, though, no one had come. "I wish the hospital would let us deliver the TB medicine," Marcus said. "I would not have forgotten to bring it."

On our way home, we stopped at one last house for a more personal reason. A little girl ran to the gate, and Marcus gave her a two-rand coin. She was his daughter, he said, but the girl's mother had left him when he lost his previous job, before he started working for Orphan Care. They could not get married because he didn't have enough money to pay *lobola*.

"The problem is for the black people, that if a man falls in love, the girl's father says you must pay eleven cows," he said. "The problem with young people is that we have no money." Young people were no longer getting married, he said, because they couldn't afford to.

11

THE OLD WAYS ARE DYING

WHEN I SAW GOGO and Mkhulu together,
I often thought of the old nursery rhyme about Jack Sprat, who
could eat no fat, and his wife, who could eat no lean. Gogo was
fleshy and soft, all plump folds, despite her hard life. Her husband,
in contrast, was thin and wiry, without a spare inch of flesh on him.
With his deeply lined face, he looked far older than Gogo, whose
skin was still smooth. The Mathenjwa grandchildren most closely
resembled Gogo and had her luminescent skin and wide, flat nose.
There was little doubt that her blood ran in their veins.

Mkhulu rarely ventured to his grandchildren's house, though it
was just next door, but he always seemed happy to see them when
they visited. He was an old-fashioned patriarch and thought it was
proper that they should come to him. When I came to visit, I usually
stopped first at the old people's homestead to pay my respects and to
exchange with Mkhulu the complex and formulaic Zulu greetings
that must be completed in full before any real business can be discussed. It was considered rude to jump right to the point. Zethu still
acted as an intermediary, since my Zulu did not extend beyond standard inquiries after someone's health. Over time, Mkhulu and I
developed our own routine. The old man always asked if I would
become his second wife. I responded that my parents would want a

very big *lobola*—bride-price—maybe fifty cows. He always laughed.

When I first started visiting, Gogo would limp down to the Mathenjwa homestead with me, usually followed by a small horde of children. It was impossible to count how many people lived with Gogo and Mkhulu. The number was always changing, but there were almost always at least ten children and grandchildren living at the old people's *kraal*. Gogo would sit on the ground, on a mat brought by one of the younger children, but I was always offered one of the white chairs Nozipho had bought. One of Gogo's grand-daughters, a girl of five or six, was mentally disabled and shy of strangers; you could see from the shape of her face that there was something not right, and she was not as quick and sturdy as her cousins. She stayed close to Gogo and often hid in her skirts. The others were always rambunctious and loud, asking me to take their picture or for a ride in my car. Sometimes they rode with me down the road a way, even though they had to walk back, just for the novelty.

I was often struck by the cheerfulness of Gogo and Mkhulu. Like Tsidi in Lesotho, who had joked with me on the way to the hospital with her dying son, Zachariah, both Gogo and Mkhulu seemed to use laughter as a shield against the misfortunes of their lives. They were as apt to try to make me laugh as to complain about their problems. Often these jokes didn't even require a translator; their meaning was made clear through hand gestures and facial expressions. Gogo, for example, would ask me when I was getting pregnant by pointing at me and using her hand to show a big belly. Then she would grin widely and wave her hand at her own large family.

Gogo herself had given birth to eight children, including two sets of twins. Five were still alive, along with a great brood of grandchildren and several great-grandchildren, but none had jobs. They were supposed to support her in her old age; instead, she found herself at the head of a large and increasingly poor family that still depended on her, and her pension, for survival.

She had come to Ingwavuma many years before in search of a job as a young girl after her own parents had died. "My breasts were still firm," she joked, lifting her now sagging ones with both hands.

She met Mkhulu and became his third wife. His first had died after giving birth, and the second had run off with the local magistrate.

Mkhulu paid twelve cows for Gogo's *lobola,* bought from money saved working in the mines. Now, however, the family had no livestock, only a few chickens. Like many families in the area, they had in the intervening decades grown poorer. Mkhulu was now too old to work in the mines, and the land no longer yielded so plentiful a bounty. Drought and disease had killed their cows, the traditional symbol of wealth, many years before, and they had had no money since to replace them. Sometimes, Gogo told me, in the days before she started receiving her pension, they survived on bananas from the small grove on the edge of the homestead.

Lungile had been Gogo's eldest child. At the time of her birth, Gogo was still very young, and she said she felt alone and scared so far away from her own family. But she was told to be brave by the woman who had come to act as midwife. "I was crying when I gave birth to Nozipho's mother, and people said I was going to give birth to a crocodile. When the baby came out, I was scared and looked quickly to see what it was," she told me laughing. The next time she gave birth, to twins, she did it alone in her hut, calling no one to help her. She had learned to bear her trials alone.

Both old people wanted to pass on the responsibility of caring for the family to the next generation, but there was no one to carry the burden. Some of their children had left for the city in search of work. Lungile and her brother had died. The ones still left in Machobeni could find no jobs. Nor, complained Gogo and Mkhulu, did they want to help with the planting.

Mkhulu sometimes still hunted, walking for miles into neighboring Swaziland where some game still roamed. In the old days he would find buck or sometimes some baboons. These days he was lucky to catch a monkey or a cane rat, a large hairy rodent. His sons and grandsons told him the days of hunting were over. In the eyes of the old people, many things were changing, not all for the best.

"It's this disease," Gogo told me one day as we sat in their yard, chickens and children racing around in the dirt. "It is changing everything."

Mkhulu agreed. "I'm old enough to die. They are still young, they still have a life ahead," he said, pointing at his grandchildren. "That's why they're supposed to take care of themselves. I've seen the world. I've had children, though some of them have died."

"We still wonder where this disease came from," Gogo continued. "We hear it came from far away, but now it is killing the whole world." She asked me if I knew where this disease had come from. When I told her that scientists thought it came from another African country far to the north, but that it was killing people all over the world, even in my own country, she shook her head sadly. We were silent for a while.

"Gogo and I don't have parents," Mkhulu said. "The children don't have parents. So we must shoulder this together."

"We'll bury each other," Gogo added, patting her husband on the hand.

COMPARED TO THEIR grandparents, the Mathenjwa grandchildren often seemed somber and withdrawn. Occasionally, though, they would slip into childhood and allow themselves to be silly and carefree. Mfundo would climb a tree and shout down for everyone to look or pull a funny face to make his siblings laugh. Sbuka would throw something at him. But often they simply seemed sad. Sbuka, in particular, was moody and depressed, although I could never tell how much was simply normal teenage hormones and how much was a reaction to the unusual degree of sorrow in their lives. No doubt both played a role.

I often felt that, of all the Mathenjwas, Sbuka was most affected by the deaths of her sister and mother. She clearly felt isolated at home, where she had only her brothers for company. Phumlani was often away, playing soccer or out with friends. Mfundo was still only a child. Sbuka too started avoiding home and often returned from school late or not at all. She would tell Phumlani and Gogo that she was staying with a friend, but Phumlani began to suspect she had a boyfriend.

"These children," Gogo complained to me, "they don't listen to their elders. They just run around and do what they want." More than once she told me she wanted to wash her hands of them. Phumlani, she said, could apply for the grants, and she would no longer be responsible for them.

While they waited for their grants to be processed, the Mathenjwas' economic situation was precarious. Their only food came from Gogo. Mfundo was fed lunch at school, but his two older siblings usually went without until the evening meal. They never had luxuries like sugar or tea or candles.

Usually it was Sbuka's responsibility to cook, but as her presence at home became infrequent, the job often fell to Mfundo. At first, he was embarrassed when I arrived to find him stirring a pot of beans over the red-hot coals of the fire. Cooking was a woman's job, he clearly thought. I told him that in America men and women cooked and that many women liked a man who could make a good meal. After that, he would show off if I was around and it was his turn to cook. He was so eager for adult attention and praise that when given it he seemed to almost glow.

When I came to visit, I always brought some supplies; usually a bag of maize meal, some beans, a few vegetables, and some soap. Once I brought a packet of candles, which Mfundo grabbed excitedly, saying "Tonight I can study!" I always brought candles after that.

Journalistic convention would likely frown on this, and some might argue that by providing the family with food, I was in essence paying them for their story. Yet I believe regardless of whether or not I helped the family, the expectation would have been there. Not because I was a journalist, but because in their minds I was unimaginably wealthy.

On my first trip to Ingwavuma, I was riding down a bumpy dirt road in a tiny pickup owned by Vee Dlamini, another employee of Ingwavuma Orphan Care. "Are you going to help them?" he demanded to know after I had explained that I wanted to find one family to spend time with over the following year. "I do not think we should help journalists who do not help people. You take people's stories and give nothing in return."

He had a point. Many foreign correspondents would think nothing of taking a politician or the CEO of a company out to an expensive dinner, but would balk at giving a bag of cornmeal to a starving family who had shared their story. Too often, we justify leaving our humanity at the door by clinging to the conventions of our trade. I understand the logic, that it is dangerous to create the expectation of payment because then people might tell you what they think you want to hear; that it is not our job to interfere. Yet I think that in the context of Africa these arguments are often weak. The expectation of help is usually there, no matter what we do, and in areas of great suffering that have been well-trodden by journalists there is often a bitterness that the telling of stories has resulted in no tangible improvement in people's lives. As journalists, we often justify our stance by saying that our reporting will help bring attention to issues and ultimately bring about broader solutions. But the wheels of international aid and politics move slowly. When we report on a famine, it may indeed encourage foreign governments to give money to that cause, yet the specific family featured in any story will likely never benefit. Or help will come too late, especially since journalists often seek out the worst stories and the worst cases to illustrate a story.

As for noninterference, that doctrine works well enough in cases that don't involve life or death or immense human suffering. In many cases, there is simply nothing we can do to help: the scope of the suffering is simply too large and its causes are too complex. I often felt this way in Ingwavuma and other AIDS-stricken African communities. Journalistic ethics often help to shield us from our own impotence. Better to assume that there is nothing we can do, rather than torture ourselves about what we cannot change. But sometimes too it blinds us from seeing cases where we could do good.

To my great shame, as a very green correspondent on a trip to a war-torn city in the Democratic Republic of Congo, I once interviewed a young woman at a hospital who had been through absolute hell. She was more than eight months pregnant when a rebel group called the Mayi-Mayi invaded her village. She and her husband fled to the sounds of their neighbors being raped and mas-sacred behind them. Her husband eventually returned to their vil-lage to see what he could salvage of their lives. She walked for two weeks until she reached the relative safety of a city where UN peace-keepers were based. Not long afterward, the woman went into labor and gave birth to a son, who soon fell sick with meningitis. She went to the local hospital, where the doctors said they could cure her son for a cost of eight dollars. They couldn't give her the medicine for free because if they did that, the hospital would soon close; it received no outside funding and survived entirely on the fees paid by patients.

At the hospital, I heard the woman's story and was moved by it. I'm sure I had $8 in my pocket. Yet I was so entrenched in the belief that it was not my place to interfere that it didn't even occur to me until much later that I could easily have paid for the infant's medi-cine. I don't know if the boy lived or died and never will. There were other dying children in that hospital and perhaps it would have been capricious to save that one child and not the others. Yet I often think about him and his mother; it is, perhaps, the thing I regret most about my time in Africa.

Had I not helped the Mathenjwas, I have no doubt they would have eventually resented me. They would have wondered, perhaps rightly, what kind of person could come and hear about their sor-rows and do nothing to help. My relationship with the family too was of a different sort than the normal reporter/subject interaction. I spent more than a year visiting the Mathenjwas, often eating with them, sometimes going to school with them, and once even sleeping on their floor. I could not, in good conscience, hear their empty bel-lies rumbling and then go home to a hearty dinner without offering some aid.

I decided long before I even met the Mathenjwa family that I could not take without giving anything in return, though I also knew that the little help I could offer would most likely be only tem-porary and transient. I would usually bring some food when I first arrived in town and share a meal with them. Sometimes, as a special treat we would eat takeout food at the Boxer, and a few times—at

Christmas for example—I brought them all small presents. I did not want them to depend on me, however, since I was not always there and would one day leave. To their credit, they never demanded more, although they often held me to promises—for example, to develop some pictures I had taken.

More often, I would try to help them access existing resources in the community or to negotiate the complex bureaucracy of the social welfare department. For clothes we went to Ingwavuma Orphan Care, which had a large room of second-hand donations. When winter struck and they didn't have enough blankets, we went to the Catholic church, which was giving some out. It's not that I begrudged paying for such things, but I knew I wasn't going to be around forever and wanted to help them learn where they might otherwise go for help.

IN 2001, ORPHAN CARE began focusing on helping families secure government foster-care grants. The number of orphans in the area was so large, and growing so fast, that the small organization simply didn't have enough resources to help every needy family. By the beginning of 2002, the organization had identified twelve hundred orphans. When I started visiting the area, the organization's three orphan workers—Thando, Vee, and Hlengiwe Dlamini—were adding new families to the organization's database every week, sometimes every day.

Although it was not really designed as a response to the country's growing orphan problem, Ingwavuma Orphan Care, like many other organizations, had seized on the foster-care grant as a practical way to provide long-term financial help to families. The problem was that applying for the grant was a long and drawn-out process that took a minimum of several months and was almost impossible for a poor, uneducated family to do on their own.

Before Orphan Care began helping families apply for the grants, not a single foster-care grant had been processed in the area. In 2001, the first year the organization began working on grants, thirty-three were successfully processed in the Ingwavuma area. The next year, things improved, and 180 additional children began receiving grants. But although each year more families were able to access government money, many others, like the Mathenjwas, waited months or years for their grants to be processed.

To start the process of acquiring a grant, the prospective foster parent had to file an application with the social welfare department. This alone required documentation that many families lacked, including birth certificates for the children and death certificates for the parents, as well as government-issued identity books for the foster parents. Before the end of apartheid, many black families in rural areas saw little reason to officially register their births and deaths. They could not vote and received no pensions or benefits from the government. Only men who left for the mines had a real reason for registering; older women in particular often had no identification documents.

The second step of the process involved a home visit by a social worker, who had to file a case at the local court saying the household was safe and the prospective foster parent fit. The foster parent and children then had to appear before the magistrate—a local judge—who reviewed the evidence and gave the adult legal custody over the children in question. All the paperwork then had to be submitted to a central social welfare office, which was flooded with new applications for grants. The whole process was supposed to take no more than three months; it sometimes took years.

There were many steps along the way where an application could falter. Families that did not have the right documentation had to apply to the Department of Home Affairs. Sometimes this application required the signature of the local *induna,* or headman, who had to vouch for the individual's identity and his or her right to South African documentation. Although it was illegal, some *indunas* charged for this service.

The process of getting documentation alone could take months. Ingwavuma did have a small home-affairs office that could process identification documents, but that office had no power to make decisions. It could only accept applications, which then had to be sent to a larger office in a bigger city. Ann and the staff at Orphan Care tried many innovative ways to speed up the process. At first they wanted to take home-affairs officials to different areas, where they could accept a large number of applications at one time. But the department told them that they only had one stamp, which couldn't leave the office. Then they tried busing people from their areas to the office. This had its problems too. News would spread that a bus was coming to take people to Home Affairs to organize their papers and more people would show up than could be accommodated. And since things very rarely started on time (though government offices always seemed to close at the right hour), there would often be time to process only a few of the people who had come.

The next step was getting a social worker to visit. When Orphan Care started operating, Ingwavuma had a brand-new social welfare office but only one social worker, a small, plump woman named Gugu Dubazana. She had a car and a license but couldn't drive. Orphan Care workers, who received interest-free loans from the organization to buy cars, often had to take the social worker to visit families. Eventually they paid for Gugu to take driving lessons. Later more social workers were hired, but there were never enough cars. The cars were constantly broken, due to bad roads, bad driving, and the tendency of livestock to wander into the path of oncoming traffic.

The social workers had to write a report about the family's condition, which was submitted to the local magistrate. But at first there were no computers, so each report had to be laboriously written by hand. Eventually the department got computers, but no one seemed to know how to use them. Nor were the computers connected by the Internet to other social welfare offices in the province. All communication still took place the old-fashioned way, through paper files that shuttled back and forth between offices.

Once the report was submitted to the magistrate, a court date was set that had to be attended by the magistrate, the children, and the potential foster parent. This alone could be a struggle; since most families had no telephones, the visit could be arranged only if a foster parent came to check on the status of the application at the social welfare office or if the social worker drove out to their homestead to inform them of the date. Some families were so poor and lived so far away that they struggled to get to Ingwavuma for their court date. Here too Orphan Care often had to assist.

The court appearances, which often took place in the magistrate's office since there weren't enough courtrooms, were brief, informal affairs. I sat in on a few with a young social worker named Zipho Gumede. The children and their foster parent, usually a grandmother or an auntie, sat quietly at the back of the room. The magistrate, who couldn't speak Zulu, asked through the social worker if the children wanted to live with the person who had applied to be their foster parent. In the presence of their relative, they always said yes. He asked the same question of the foster parent. In the three cases I watched one afternoon, the woman always replied the same way, with a rhetorical question: "What choice do I have? There is no one else to take care of them."

Theoretically, this system was intended to prevent children from being placed in abusive homes, but in reality it had little protective value. The backlog of desperate families waiting for grants was long, and the priority of the social workers and magistrate was simply to process as many applications as possible. Because they spent so much time processing grants, they had little time left over to address the growing number of cases of abuse and neglect.

For many families, the grants meant the difference between malnutrition and full stomachs. I met one woman, Noomsa Mbamali, who was struggling to feed her brother's six children and one child of her own on a small monthly support grant of about twenty-five dollars. When her brother was alive, the family had survived on his disability grant. When he died, three months after Nozipho, the government cut off that grant. A year and a half after I met them, they had still not received the new grants, and the eldest daughter, age seventeen, had given birth to a daughter of her own. The youngest child, whose mother had died when she was only a few months old, was almost certainly HIV-positive but often ate nothing but corn porridge because Noomsa could not afford formula. Noomsa was genuinely trying to do her best for her nephews and nieces under difficult circumstances.

Often, though, the grants were used to support entire families, and the children who were the intended beneficiaries saw little tangible benefit. When one orphan was taken in by a large family, the grant would almost always be used to pay for household expenses. While the money raised the standard of living for the whole family, the orphan benefited only as part of the whole. Too often, orphans would find themselves at the bottom of the hierarchy and the last to benefit.

In the worst-case scenarios, the money was stolen entirely by greedy relatives. When I first met Ann, a young man named Bongilani Nywao lived with her. One of the first orphans the organization had assisted, he had come to stay with her earlier that year so he could attend a marginally better high school in Ingwavuma. He wanted to learn to speak English better; at his former school, he told me, the other children laughed at him for using English.

When Bongilani's parents died, his uncle registered for foster-care grants for his younger siblings. They came through, but he gave none of the money to Bongilani and his siblings, who continued to live in their parents' house. As the eldest child, Bongilani did his best to keep the children fed and clothed. He watched his neighbors plant gardens and tried to grow his own. He tried to find odd jobs. After he turned twenty-one, he considered trying to get the grants for his siblings transferred into his name. But when his uncle heard of this plan, he threatened to kill Bongilani. "He said he would send a witch doctor to bewitch me," Bongilani told me in a matter-of-fact way.

Today, as an adult, Bongilani shows clear signs of childhood malnutrition. He is short for his age, with a head too big for his body. He had had almost no adult guidance in his teenage years; fortunately, he turned to God instead of crime, unlike many other young men his age. Before he met Ann, he had lived a life of extreme deprivation. When he first came to stay with her, Ann told me, she found him curled up on the concrete floor, sleeping under some curtains. He had never slept in a bed.

SADLY, ABUSE OF ORPHANS by family members was becoming an all too frequent phenomenon in Ingwavuma. It was nearly impossible to determine the exact scope of the problem since most cases never made it to court or into the files of the local social welfare department. But anecdotal evidence suggested that the problem was growing as extended family structures creaked under the stress of rising poverty and the increasing number of orphans.

Abuse and neglect of children was certainly not limited to orphans or families affected by AIDS, but to Ann and the other staff members at Ingwavuma Orphan Care it was clear that orphaned children were uniquely vulnerable. Sometimes, as in the case of Bongilani, the relatives were simply cruel or uncaring. In many more cases, the abuse stemmed from ignorance or poverty.

Some time before I arrived in Ingwavuma, the staff at Orphan Care dealt with the case of one young boy, just a toddler really, whose mother had died of AIDS. The surviving family members were so afraid of catching the virus that they refused to touch him. In a society where young children are often in close physical contact with their mothers for the first years of their life, carried on their backs and sleeping in the same bed, the confused little boy was denied physical affection. No one bathed him, and while he was given food, the family refused to share cups, plates, and utensils with him. Until Hlengiwe Dlamini, one of the orphan workers, intervened and counseled the family, the poor little boy who had just lost his mother was a pariah in his own home.

Orphan Care got involved with another family, whom I will call the Myeni family. After the death of their mother, the five Myeni children were sent to live with their aunt, who kept the children in a squalid hut, separate from the house where her own children lived, failed to feed them properly, and generally neglected to look after them.

When Leigh-Ann Mathys, an Australian–South African of mixed-racial heritage who joined Orphan Care in 2005, found them, the youngest children had bad cases of scabies, a contagious skin disorder caused by tiny mites that burrow into the skin and lay eggs there. The children's arms and legs were covered in the tiny, itchy bites. The aunt had done nothing to treat them, and even when Leigh-Ann gave her medicine for the children, she failed to administer it properly. Leigh-Ann eventually had to take the children to the Orphan Center for the weekend so she could oversee their treatment and the cleansing of their clothes and bedding. The eldest girl, who was only fifteen, was later diagnosed with a sexually transmitted infection.

The strained social welfare bureaucracy in Ingwavuma, which when I arrived had only three social workers to deal with a population of more than a hundred thousand, lacked the manpower and skill to adequately address the problem. The social workers spent the vast majority of their time processing new social welfare grants. They did almost no follow-up with families to ensure that the grant was being used for the benefit of the orphans or that the children were being cared for properly.

In part, this failure was due to manpower constraints—although the social workers could certainly have used their time far more efficiently—but it also stemmed from an uncertainty about how to handle such cases. Even when a suspected case of child abuse was brought to their attention, the social workers were often unsure how to proceed. Often traditional ideas of family responsibility clashed with modern ideas of child rights. Even the very concept of what constituted abuse was in the process of being defined.

"Zulu culture says that children should be disciplined, but no marks should be left. They can be hit with a hand or small stick," Gugu Dubazana, the social worker, told me, "so sometimes it is hard for us to tell where the line for abuse starts."

The idea that child abuse, physical or sexual, should concern the state was a relatively new concept in the area. Formerly such problems had been handled within families or, in extreme cases, by *indunas* or chiefs. The ANC-led government, however, was slowly replacing the power of traditional leaders with a modern, state-run infrastructure. In theory, the social welfare system they were building emphasized the rights of the child over the traditional authority of the family. In practice, however, in places like Ingwavuma, local custom had not yet caught up with the new legal paradigm. Although the law allowed the state to remove children from dangerous or abusive environments, in Ingwavuma there were few places to put abused children if they were taken from their homes. Nor, it seemed, were the local social workers entirely convinced that it was the role of the state to interfere.

"The problem is, the father has paid *lobola,* so the uncle is right that the children belong to him," Noctula Gumede, who managed Ingwavuma's three social workers, explained to me about one case that had been dragging on for many months. Bridget Walters, a teacher who had been involved with the family, had been pushing the department to remove a group of siblings from their uncle's care. One of their brothers, who was disabled, had died of a seizure that Bridget believed was brought on by persistent beatings from the uncle.

Without Bridget's constant pressure, the case would likely have stalled entirely. The social workers were afraid of the uncle, who had once come drunk to the welfare office and made a scene. There was also the problem of where the children would be put if they were removed. A maternal aunt agreed to take them if she received social welfare grants for them, but the uncle objected, saying the children had to stay with the paternal line.

Noctula was sympathetic to his claim. According to customary law, if a man has paid *lobola,* his children belong by right to the father's family. Part of the idea of *lobola* is that the family is paying for the right to count a woman's children as belonging to their name and lineage. In Zulu culture, children call their paternal uncles "father" and their cousins on their paternal side "brother" and "sister."

In theory, this system also ensured that if the children were orphaned, the father's family had responsibility for taking care of them. In practice, however, many orphans were being cared for by whoever would take them, in part because an increasing number were being born outside of official wedlock and in part because the paternal family could not always afford to take on additional children.

The biggest burden, for many families, were HIV-positive children. Twice a month, Ingwavuma Orphan Care hosted support groups for the caretakers of HIV-positive children. At the end of 2004 there were 130 children enrolled at two different sites, and on the days the group met at the Orphan Center, the small office became a chaotic jumble of spilled juice and bread crumbs.

Almost all the caretakers were women—mothers, aunties, or grandmothers—who trudged to the center in long skirts, their hair wrapped in muted scarves, as was traditional for married women. The children themselves, who came along for a snack of polony (a bright pink, toxic-looking lunch meat that they all seemed to love) and cheese, had the unnatural quietness of kids who had spent too much of their lives sick and in pain. Some were covered in sores or had oversized heads perched on bodies that were too thin. Few knew or understood that they were HIV-positive, although Hlengiwe Dlamini, who ran the program, encouraged the caretakers to try to explain to the children. "We encourage them to disclose to everyone, but there are problems because of stigma," she told me after one support group. "Yesterday, for example, one child came home from school crying, saying that the other kids made fun of him because he was HIV-positive."

Hlengiwe, who had studied psychology, began the group in 2002 in response to the case of the little boy whose family refused to touch him after his mother died. "He was four years old and he wasn't being washed or held. He was dirty and had flies all over him," Hlengiwe told me. "The reason the child was neglected was because they were afraid they would catch AIDS from him, so I decided that it was important that we explain to the caretakers that they couldn't become HIV-positive from holding him or feeding him."

For the caretakers, who included both mothers who were themselves HIV-positive and relatives who had taken in orphaned children, the support group was a safe place where they could express their frustrations and ask questions of other women in similar situations. "It's hard for them," Hlengiwe said. "They feel depressed because they know this child could die any day. Some of them say they become angry at these children, like if they have diarrhea, and then they feel bad afterward, but they are overwhelmed."

Ann gave each of the children a basic checkup and treated any obvious opportunistic infections with drugs provided by the hospital. She also gave each child a vitamin syrup, Bactrim, and Sutherlandia, a traditional herb with immune-boosting properties that many local doctors had seen good results with on HIV-positive patients and that was in the process of being tested more fully.

One by one, the children filed into the office being used as an examination room with wide eyes and grave faces. None of them said a word. In June 2004, Ann took blood samples from sixty of the children to see how many needed antiretroviral drugs. Twenty-five children needed the drugs immediately, but it was unclear when the drugs would become available for children in the area.

12

FILES AND PHOTOS

Sᴇᴇ ᴛʜɪs ᴘʟᴀᴄᴇ?" Gogo said to me one day, pointing to a dusty corner of the Mathenjwas' yard. "When the grant comes, I will build them a hut to keep chickens so they can have eggs and meat." But the months passed and still no money appeared.

In August, five months after Gogo applied to have the grants for Sbuka and Mfundo transferred from Nozipho's name to hers, they had still not arrived. When, and if, the grants were finally approved, she would receive back payments for each month dating to her application, a colossal sum in her mind. But the months dragged on, and she was becoming desperate. Food was always scarce, and she had not yet paid the Mathenjwas' school fees. The school year would end in a few months, and if the fees were not paid by then, the children would not receive their grades and would be forced to repeat the year.

Early one morning, Gogo and I went to the social welfare office, a yellow brick edifice in the center of Ingwavuma, to try and find out what the problem was. We arrived at six and waited outside with the other women until the offices opened at eight. More than two hours later, we were finally ushered inside.

Usually the office building seemed curiously empty, as if its occupants had not yet fully moved in. Business took place there only in the mornings, and inquiries about specific issues were attended to on specific days of the week, sometimes only once a month. That day the social welfare office was checking the status of grants that had been applied for but not yet processed.

When we finally reached the front of the line, the clock on the wall said it was nearly ten. Gogo sat stiffly in front of a desk while an employee, not a social worker but one of the secretaries, licked her finger to flip through the thick manila file of grant applications. But she could find no record of Gogo's application. Gogo's normal smile disappeared.

"What do I do now?" she asked the woman. The clerk shrugged and said someone would have to write to the central office in Ulundi, where the grants are processed, to try to find out what has happened. I was skeptical that this languid woman, dressed in a too-small polyester suit of black and red, would do anything once we left the room. She looked to me like the kind of official some Africans call a "jobs-worth" for their habit of doing exactly their job and no more. Her job was to check the status of files that were already there, not to go chasing after missing ones. She told Gogo to come back next month and simply shrugged at my questions about who would follow up with the file.

Later that day, I went in search of Gugu Dubazana, the white-haired social worker who was in charge of Machobeni, the area where Gogo lives. It was she who had filed the application in the first place, with substantial help (and continual prodding) from Thando. That morning, however, she was not there.

When I finally tracked her down, she remembered the family and was surprised that they had not yet received their grants. She promised to look into the matter and said she would make sure the file was found. A couple of months later, when I next returned to Ingwavuma, the application had still not been processed, and Gugu had no recollection of her earlier promise to ensure that it was found.

THE ANC'S AUSPICIOUS beginning in regard to AIDS soon proved false. Soon after the party took the reins of power in 1994, a number of tragic missteps would sour the new government's attitude toward the issue. In 1995, health minister Nkosazana Dlamini-Zuma decided to commission a traveling musical play that would teach South Africans about AIDS and how to protect themselves from it. To write the play, the department hired renowned South African playwright and composer Mbongeni Ngema, who dubbed the project *Sarafina II* after his successful musical about apartheid, which later became a movie starring Whoopi Goldberg.

When the play was launched, it was quickly panned by AIDS experts, who questioned the usefulness of its message as a prevention tool. Then, a 1996 government inquiry conducted at the request of an opposition party found that the play had cost a small fortune, more than 14 million rand—$3.8 million—and had been commissioned in violation of state regulations.[1] The health department's entire 1995–1996 budget for HIV/AIDS prevention, counseling, and care was only 13 million rand.[2] The press cried corruption, and civic groups lamented the project as a colossal waste of money and said it was representative of the mess the government had made of its AIDS programs.

By the end of the year, in part because of the *Sarafina II* scandal, a major rift had begun to develop between the government and civil society over the AIDS issue. For the first several years after South Africa's 1994 election, the ANC had enjoyed a honeymoon of sorts during which criticism of the new government was largely muted. *Sarafina II* shattered that tacit truce and caught the new government, used to a sympathetic press, off guard. In the following years, a new generation of activists would emerge in South Africa, many of whom had their roots in the antiapartheid movement. Only this time their target was the very government they had helped to bring to power, but which they now accused of callously looking the other way while millions died.

Before *Sarafina II* had faded from memory, Dlamini-Zuma was embroiled in another damaging scandal, this time over Virodene, a locally invented medicine that its makers claimed could "cure" AIDS. The Medicine Control Council (MCC)—South Africa's equivalent of the U.S. Food and Drug Administration—refused permission for human trials of the drug, saying it was dangerous and ineffective. But Dlamini-Zuma and deputy president Thabo Mbeki, who would become the country's second postapartheid leader in 1999, took up the drug as a personal crusade.

In early 1997, when Mbeki invited Virodene researchers to speak before a special meeting of his cabinet, they presented a handful of patients who claimed miraculous cures. Impressed, the ministers were happy to believe the researchers' argument that the real reason they had been stopped from conducting their research was because the international pharmaceutical industry stood to lose billions of dollars when their product came to market. To the iconoclastic Mbeki this argument rang true.[3]

At the time, great strides in AIDS treatment had been made in the West. In the late 1980s, the drug AZT had been embraced with enthusiasm by AIDS patients and their doctors, who found that it suppressed replication of the virus. However, eventually the virus became resistant to the drug and patients began to fall sick again. The same problem occurred with other antiretroviral drugs. By 1996, however, researchers discovered that a cocktail of three antiretroviral drugs could virtually eliminate the presence of the virus in a patient's blood.[4]

The cocktail, which became known as highly active antiretroviral therapy, or HAART, quickly became standard treatment in Western countries, sharply reducing AIDS-related deaths. These new miracle drugs, though, cost about $20,000 a year and were too expensive for the vast majority of Africans with AIDS. The drug regimes were also enormously complicated, requiring close medical supervision and dozens of pills a day. In addition, they merely suppressed the virus without actually killing it, condemning patients to a lifetime of complicated and expensive treatment.[5]

Common consensus in the medical community and among international donors was that triple-cocktail therapy was too expensive and too complicated for a continent that struggled just to treat simpler diseases like diarrhea, malaria, and tuberculosis and to provide universal vaccination to children. Given the poor medical infrastructure in most of the countries hardest-hit by AIDS and the high price of treatment, they argued, the scarce money available to fight the epidemic was best used for prevention.[6]

Virodene's makers claimed their cure was cheap and effective; moreover, its success would prove to the world that Africa could find solutions to its own problems and that it no longer need rely on Western money and technical expertise. Mbeki, who had long dreamed of an African renaissance, thought Virodene might be just the thing to jump-start a rehabilitation of the continent's image.

With Mbeki's support, Dlamini-Zuma tried to push Virodene's approval through, over the objections of the MCC. Eventually, an investigation into Virodene ordered by the cabinet found that the main ingredient in the drug was an industrial solvent known to cause liver damage. "Virodene is nonsense," Professor Malegapuru Makgoba, the well-respected president of the Medical Research Council, finally declared.[7]

Significantly, Mbeki at this point did not deny that AIDS posed a major threat to South Africa, as he would later do. "The great sand storms generated by all these vexatious proceedings have served to obscure the fact that what confronts us all is the pressing crisis of an escalating pandemic of HIV/AIDS," he wrote, in his typically pedantic way, of the Virodene scandal.[8] Yet his flirtation with the drug, in defiance of established medical and scientific opinion, was evidence of Mbeki's deeper distrust of the intellectual mainstream. In successive years, he would grow increasingly hostile to what he saw as the AIDS establishment. Eventually he would call into question the fundamental premises of the disease: that HIV causes AIDS and that the virus is spread primarily through sex.

Through all of this, President Mandela would stay largely silent; during his five-year presidency he rarely spoke about AIDS at all. Much later, he would rue his failure to effectively confront the issue, calling the epidemic a tragedy worse even than apartheid, the evil he had spent his lifetime fighting against.

THE MATHENJWA CHILDREN had only a few mementoes of their parents. When I asked to see the family pictures, Mfundo brought out a colorful poster of Jesus inscribed with the Lord's Prayer that had been printed on cardboard and covered in clear plastic, which was now ripped and fading. "Give us this day our daily bread," the poster read in script intended to imitate a child's scribbles. The children had placed their own pictures under the plastic, along the edges. There was the small black-and-white photograph of their mother, torn from her state identity book, and a few of Nozipho and her daughter. It was hard, from that small picture, to draw any conclusions about Lungile.

There was also an old picture of a young man in jeans and large sunglasses with rounded lenses standing in front of a brown background with large flowers. The photograph looked like it was from the 1970s but must have been much more recent. "Who's that?" I asked.

"Baba," Mfundo replied. Father. A few minutes earlier he had been bouncing around. Now he was suddenly quiet. I looked more closely. Someone had cut out words from magazines and placed them over the photograph. *Baba,* they read, *you were a man of men. Rest in peace.*

Mfundo doesn't remember much about his father, who died when he was very young, though probably not of AIDS. That picture is the only memento he has. Gogo and Mkhulu said their son-in-law had died because he was "short of blood." Sometimes, they said, he had to go to the hospital to get more.

"He was a good man, kind," Gogo assured me. "Once when he came here and slept in the house, he took the mat to Nozipho's mother to show her he had slept here and not with another woman."

"No, Phumlani's father was not killed by HIV. The disease came with his mother. She fell in love with another man and had a child by him. Mfundo was still breast-feeding then," Gogo recalled.

It was a bad thing, she thought, the way that young people ran around these days. Phumlani and Mfundo's father paid *lobola* for Lungile, five cows in total. She should have stayed and raised her children in her husband's family, as custom dictated, but not long after he died she ran away with another man. The old ways, lamented Gogo, were dying.

"It used to be that when you slaughtered a goat, you would share with everyone. But that is no longer true."

Mfundo's violent behavior, which Gogo and Mkhulu had been so worried about around the time of Nozipho's cleansing ceremony, stopped a few months later. He no longer got into fights with the other children in the neighborhood or threatened his siblings. Mfundo was a bright boy, with a flair for mechanics. Once he built a radio using salvaged parts and an old plastic water drum. I asked him how he had learned to make radios; he told me that he had watched an old man take them apart and put them back together again. I was impressed and told him so. He smiled for the rest of the day.

It was sometimes easy to forget how young Mfundo still was. He was only twelve when we met, although in the months that followed he suddenly hit a growth spurt and was soon taller than me. Like his brother Phumlani, he would be a tall man. For the time being, though, he was still just a little boy who missed his mother.

For the Mathenjwas, education was a ticket out of the poverty in which they lived. All five of Lungile's children were still in school when I met the family, even Phumlani and Khanya, who, in their twenties, were still struggling to graduate from high school.

School is not free in South Africa, although in theory no child can be turned away for inability to pay. Most schools receive money for teacher salaries from the government, but little else. Many principals are even expected to raise money to construct the buildings for their schools. School fees cover the salaries of additional teachers, helping to lower class sizes and pay for building materials and construction. In Ingwavuma, most schools charged only a few dollars a year. But for families like the Mathenjwas, even this was an impossible sum. Including the five Mathenjwa children, there were at least ten school-age children in Gogo's family. And in addition to the fees, there was the cost of uniforms, which was at least 200 rand, about $25, per child.

Most schools allowed children who had not paid their school

fees to continue attending classes, but if the fees hadn't been paid by the end of the year, the children did not receive their results and had to repeat. Failing is very common; it was the reason Phumlani and Khanya were so far behind for their age level. At twenty-two, Khanya was still in the ninth grade, and at twenty-one, Phumlani was in grade eleven.

Orphan Care had grants to provide some orphans with uniforms and to pay their school fees, but the number of children in need exceeded the amount of the funding. The program was also a logistical nightmare. There were hundreds of schools in the area that Orphan Care served, each with a slightly different uniform. The orphans at each had to be identified, counted, and measured. The uniforms then had to be ordered and, after they arrived, delivered to each school. Often the uniforms failed to appear until halfway through the year.

The Mathenjwas' faith in schooling was admirable, but I feared the education system would fail them. There were schools everywhere in Ingwavuma, all bursting at the seams with children, but few provided their pupils with anything approaching an adequate education. In order to graduate, students had to pass the same standardized test taken by rich white kids in Johannesburg. Pass rates at most Ingwavuma schools were, understandably, notoriously low.

The students' poor English was one of the major problems. The apartheid government had insisted that African students be taught in their native language and that, as a second language, all students learn Afrikaans. When apartheid fell, black parents began demanding that their children be taught in English, which they thought would prepare them better for the job market. As a result, almost all the schools in the area used English as the primary language of instruction.

The problem was that many students didn't understand English well enough to comprehend the subjects they were studying. I sat in one day at classes at Ingwavuma High, the school Bongilani, the orphan who lived with Ann, attended. During most classes, the students sat silently and struggled to copy down everything the teacher wrote on the blackboard. But it was clear most students were simply writing down letters and numbers, with little understanding of what they meant. Often the teacher would explain something and then ask a question pertaining directly to what she had just discussed. In agriculture class, for example, the teacher explained the purpose of fertilizer, writing on the board a long list of its uses. Then, immediately afterward, she asked her students why it was important to use fertilizer. No one raised their hand. Only in Zulu-language class were the students more animated. It was the only class where most of them could actually understand the lesson.

Sbuka's school was the one exception. She had won a scholarship to Nansindlela—the name means "this is the way"—a sort of charter school that had been founded by a missionary, a doctor's wife, and a teacher. The fees there were astronomically high for Ingwavuma, around twenty-five dollars a month, and most of the paying students were the children of the local middle class: teachers, nurses, policemen, and civil servants. Unlike most schools in the area, which were little more than boxy concrete buildings with dirt yards, Nansindlela had well-manicured grounds, complete with a playground, a library, and classrooms decorated with maps and posters.

Sbuka, I realized when I went to school with her one day, was old for her class. She was sixteen, but was only in the eighth grade. Most of the other girls in her class still looked like children. In contrast, Sbuka had the body of a woman. She was a head taller than her classmates, and while they still had the slender, boyish bodies of young girls, Sbuka had already developed a woman's curves.

At home, Sbuka was loud and bossy, spending much of her time telling her brother Mfundo what to do. But she was shy around the other students, embarrassed by her mismatched uniform and towering height. During breaks, she often sat by herself or with girls from an older grade. Sometimes she was unable to participate fully in lessons because she had no money for supplies. Sbuka's science teacher had asked each child to bring in a flashlight, a piece of cardboard, or a pair of scissors for a demonstration about light. But Sbuka had none of these things at home nor any money to buy them. Fortunately, most of the other students had forgotten that day, so she did not stand out so much. In English class a few hours later, Sbuka had to borrow a pen from a classmate for a test on pronouns. And at lunchtime, most of the students ate food brought from home or snacks bought from the vendor just outside the school grounds. Had I not been there, Sbuka would have eaten nothing.

At Nansindlela, unlike other schools, the children were encouraged to think, and classes were sometimes even fun. The method of teaching at Nansindlela was far more interactive than at Ingwavuma High School. In arts and culture class, the students presented plays they had written in small groups. Sbuka played a policewoman investigating a murder, and struggled to keep from laughing as she said her lines.

Through her scholarship at Nansindlela, Sbuka had greater opportunity than her siblings, yet I wondered whether she would be able to survive another four years of schooling. She was surrounded by temptations and disincentives: the lure of men and boys and their promises of support and comfort, the embarrassment of poverty, the demanding self-discipline required to get up each day and walk four miles to school, rain or shine.

Most days Sbuka walked to school and back on an empty stomach, and she struggled to find money for basic supplies like pens and paper or soap to wash her uniform at night. I feared that one day she would simply give up.

13

A NEW MORALITY

News of the AIDS epidemic reached Ingwavuma surprisingly early considering its relative isolation from the rest of the world. In 1983, an Irish brother who had been stationed at the Catholic mission there since the mid-1950s returned to South Africa after several years in Dublin, where he had gone to train with the Jesuits for the priesthood. Among the news brought back by Father Camillus was talk of a new disease striking gay men in Europe and America. At the time, of course, he had no idea that AIDS would one day become the most serious threat to the area's survival. It was just idle talk of the outside world that he brought home to his isolated colleagues.

Father Camillus, known to his parishioners as "Father Kagsha," was still living in the area when I first began to visit. A few months earlier, he had fallen off the roof of the Ingwavuma mission house while making repairs and had been sent to recuperate in Mtubatuba, a town near the coast about two hours away. I found him in a large white house down a muddy lane that he shared with several other elderly priests, all former missionaries. He was a tiny, wizened man with a musical Irish brogue who had survived a half century of living among the Zulu. He also had an old man's nostalgia for a world that was no more, a world he now believes he helped to destroy.

Father Camillus first began seeing cases of the new disease in Ingwavuma eight or nine years after his return from Ireland. In the early 1990s, his former students, many of whom had gone off to work in the mines, began returning home to die.

"The lads I taught then, they're all dead now," he said sadly. "It was the mines. So many went to the mines and they had sexual business there. They came home and they just faded away to nothing."

Father Camillus remembers one boy in particular, a former student who had returned home from the mines at the age of twenty. He went to visit the young man's family and found him lying in bed with his mother sitting next to him, spooning sips of water into his mouth. His former student should have been a strong young man ready to begin his own family, but he had been reduced by disease to a state of infancy. The sight shocked Father Camillus deeply. He asked the mother if her son had AIDS, and she said no, it was tuberculosis. But Father Camillus believes otherwise. He had seen many cases of TB, but none quite like that one. To his sorrow, in the coming years, many more cases would follow.

"AIDS," he shook his head. "There's no end to it now."

I suppose I expected Father Camillus to be one of those stern, dogmatic priests that my mother remembered from her childhood attending Catholic schools in Southern California. I imagined him, clad in a long black cassock, standing in front of a room full of frightened school boys, rapping lessons into their heads with repetition and a cane.

In the early years of the mission, he told me, my image wasn't far from the truth. The old-school Irish priests sent to Ingwavuma saw it as their duty to bring Christianity and civilization to the "pagan" Zulu. They set out to eliminate promiscuity and godless rituals. "The schools were very rigid. Any boys caught with girls were dismissed," he said. Students were hit for misbehaving or not learning their lessons, and were taught to abandon the beliefs of their fathers as the path to salvation.

The Irish father, whose outlook on the world and whose own work in Africa was deeply influenced by his training with the Jesuits, had a tendency to romanticize Ingwavuma's past. He interpreted its story as that of an untouched, "pure" society corrupted by contact with the West. "The Africans lived a peaceful, quiet rural life. And they were very respectful," he told me. "There was no stealing, no raping and all that. Western infiltration has destroyed this society."

Father Camillus believes this corruption occurred very recently, within his memory. He says when he arrived in Ingwavuma, the vast majority of people still depended almost entirely on subsistence farming. Most wore traditional clothing and owned few modern material possessions. The one Western commodity he recalled being highly prized were great big heavy army coats; those who owned them would wear them winter and summer. Theft was uncommon and children outside of marriage rare, though polygamy was still widely practiced.

Things began changing, Father Camillus said, in the second half of the 1970s, after nearby Mozambique won its independence from Portugal. When the Marxist Frelimo party, which was sympathetic to the ANC, came to power on South Africa's northern border, the area around Ingwavuma became a front line in the global war against communism. The South African government built up its defenses there, constructing the first proper roads into the remote region in order to deploy troops along the border. A region that had once taken days to reach suddenly became accessible in hours.

Around this time, Father Camillus said, crime began to increase and the mission began to see its first unwed mothers. "The pregnancies started about thirty years ago and got really bad about twenty years ago," he said. He blamed the change on the road, which brought soldiers and a cash economy.

From other historical accounts, however, there seems to be little doubt that the contact with the outside world—the corruption of traditional culture, as Father Camillus saw it—began decades before, with the impositions of hut taxes, the arrival of migrant labor, and annexation by the British, who brought with them Western law. Yet in Ingwavuma, as in Lesotho, recent decades have also been a period of rapid and unsettling change; the world that Gogo's generation was born into has long since vanished.

By the time I first visited Ingwavuma, in 2004, traditional round huts had given way to squat, ugly buildings of concrete or stone like the ones the Mathenjwas lived in. Even those families too poor to buy modern building materials had abandoned the traditional round shape that was common when Father Camillus had arrived. The only building I saw of that kind was one a local primary school had constructed to teach its students how their ancestors had lived.

By the beginning of the twenty-first century most people in the area considered themselves Christian, although the adoption of Christianity did not require an abandonment of all traditional beliefs. Many people believed in Jesus and the spirits of their ancestors, the power of priests and bewitchment. Gogo was a Methodist and on Sundays wore a red dress with a white collar that had become the uniform dress of her faith, but she still insisted that the homestead be cleansed according to tradition so that Nozipho's spirit could be set free.

There were some traditions, though, especially those related to what the priests saw as immoral sex, that the church had worked hard to stamp out. Father Camillus recalls that when he arrived, young men and girls were allowed to gather together, without adult supervision, in certain homesteads marked by a colored flag. Sexual activity took place but was limited to nonpenetrative acts. "There was a certain sexual acceptance, but the rule was you don't make babies." The practice was banned by local chiefs, he believes, more than twenty years ago at the instigation of Catholic and Protestant missionaries.

I had never heard of this particular tradition before, and it is possible that in this specific form, it was unique to the Ingwavuma area. Yet the tradition of nonpenetrative sex, which often involved a young woman bringing a man to ejaculation with her thighs, has a long history in Zulu culture. Called *ukuHlobonga* or *ukusoma* in Zulu, it was considered an acceptable form of sexual experimentation without the risk of impregnating the female partner, whose virginity was highly prized by the Zulu. A. T. Bryant, a missionary who was one of the first white men to live among the Zulu, wrote with surprise that during his many years among them, he can recall only a single case of rape and not one of illegitimacy, despite the fact that they were all "heathens."[1]

Sadly, thigh sex has been largely abandoned, and I met few young Zulu who even knew of the old tradition. Many young women also told me that their boyfriends defined sex as the penetrative act, rather than more broadly as anything that brought about orgasm. Oral sex or mutual masturbation might be engaged in as an entrée, they told me, but the act itself was not complete without penetration. Girls were expected to be passive, and if they attempted to initiate oral sex, for example, they risked being considered loose. "Your boyfriend will ask where you learned such things and think you are sleeping around with other boys," one girl told me. "So even if we know how to do these things, we must wait until he shows us how." Young women in Ingwavuma also said that many men saw sex as a proof of love and that young women were under enormous pressure to sleep with their boyfriends in order to prove their devotion. If a girl tried to insist that her partner use a condom, she was often accused of being unfaithful, and girls who became too wet during sex were considered loose.

While *ukusoma* was primarily about male pleasure, with women as the providers rather than recipients of gratification, the tradition might have served as the basis for a safer modern sexuality in the era of AIDS. Inherent in the tradition is a recognition that there are alternative ways of expressing sexuality other than penetrative sex, an idea that seems to have largely disappeared among young people in the area. *Ukusoma*, mutual masturbation, and oral sex are all forms of sexual behavior that, though not entirely safe, certainly carry less risk of infection, not to mention of pregnancy. Yet from my admittedly anecdotal surveys of young people in the area—who usually found my questions highly embarrassing—they seem not to be widely practiced. Sex in Ingwavuma seemed to be an all or nothing affair.

While the AIDS epidemic in Africa is sometimes blamed by Western observers on a certain liberalism in regards to sex—too much sex with too many partners—it seemed to me that sexual conservatism was the more powerful driving force. If the experience of my young informants was representative, many young Africans had become hemmed into a very narrow definition of sexuality. When I was a teenager in Colorado, even those girls who took pride in the fact that they were virgins had engaged in their share of sexual experimentation. They had simply drawn the line at "sex," which was defined as penetration. Young people in Ingwavuma seemed to have less social freedom in this sense than their parents' or grandparents' generations had had.

Conservativism toward sexual behavior may also play a role in attitudes about number of partners. In the monogamously oriented West, we are encouraged to seek sexual novelty through experimentation within our primary relationship. Whole industries, from Oprah to *Cosmopolitan* magazine, have arisen to teach Americans how to keep their sex lives interesting. In Ingwavuma, however, it seemed far more socially acceptable for men to add flavor to their sex lives by seeking out different partners than trying different methods of sex.

The widespread promotion of condoms seems to have largely failed as an AIDS-prevention technique, and abstinence before marriage is an untenable proposition for most people in a culture where the very institution of marriage seems to be near extinction, due in large part to economic factors that have made it nearly impossible for young men to save enough for *lobola*. Given this situation, I often wondered whether what Africa needed was a massive sex therapy campaign aimed at making "safer" forms of sex more widely accepted. In Africa, as in America, the idea would be controversial, but it might be made more locally acceptable if it could be connected with traditions like *ukusoma*.

A handful of groups in Africa have already begun promoting masturbation as an alternative form of sexuality. I went to a UNICEF-sponsored AIDS workshop in Swaziland where the participants, all members of Christian youth groups, were encouraged to debate the merits of masturbation. The men took a more conservative stance than the women, saying self-gratification was sinful, though their reasons for arguing this varied. Some of the young men believed that any sexual thought outside marriage was sinful, others that sex was intended by God for procreation and that any sex for other aims, such as merely for pleasure, was wrong. The women tended to be more practical. They thought the promotion of masturbation might help take some of the pressure off women to have sex.

I was impressed by the frankness of the debate and the earnestness with which the young people involved considered the question. Over the course of the evening a number of people changed their minds, and by the end of the workshop, masturbation had won greater support. Such openness about sexuality, however, is rare in modern Africa.

FATHER CAMILLUS blames the churches, including his own, for introducing the idea of sin to the Zulu. "We men from Ireland, as far as we were concerned, sex was taboo," he said. It was the missionaries who taught the Zulu to hide away what had once been discussed openly. "Now they don't discuss it," he contends. "But in the old days they did."

Another old missionary, Don Morrill, who worked as a doctor at Mosvold hospital from 1950 to 1975, told me that miners coming home from the cities would often return with sexually transmitted diseases, although not AIDS, since it did not yet exist. I asked if the men were embarrassed or ashamed when they sought treatment. On the contrary, he said. They often saw it as evidence of their prowess.

The difference between AIDS and other sexually transmitted diseases, however, is that even in the 1950s most such diseases were easily curable. AIDS, in contrast, is nearly always eventually fatal. In my time in Ingwavuma, I began to wonder if the central component of the silence wasn't sex, but death. Cultures vary widely in their attitudes toward sex, but we all fear death, even if our rituals of mourning are very different.

We have always placed sexuality at the center of our interpretation of AIDS and believed that the fear and silence surrounding the disease in Africa is a result of the disease's association with sex. In America—where the epidemic first emerged among gay men and where sexually transmitted diseases are often considered highly embarrassing—much of the stigma around AIDS may indeed have been due to its association with sex, and most Western observers assumed the same was true of Africa as well.

Perhaps, though, we overestimate the degree to which Africans have adopted Western, Christian attitudes toward sexuality. Silence has often been used as a form of protest by colonized and oppressed people. Outwardly, a dominated people adopt the attitudes of their oppressors but preserve elements of their own culture and belief by shrouding them in secrecy. In sexual affairs most people in Ingwavuma have adopted the Western pattern of one husband for one wife, but as in Lesotho, a secret, informal system of multiple partnerships has developed. While the Christian institution of monogamous marriage is promoted, there are few social sanctions around extramarital relationships. More than half of children in Ingwavuma are born to unwed, and usually non-cohabitating, mothers. Yet single mothers face little social stigma there. Why, then, do we assume that people with AIDS will be discriminated against because their disease was contracted through sex?

I asked one of Father Camillus's colleagues, Father Mthembu, who was born in the area, educated in the mission school, and later joined the priesthood, if he thought sex was at the root of people's unwillingness to confront the AIDS epidemic.

"There is a taboo around AIDS because of its association with death," he told me as we drank tea in the mission house one afternoon. "We always see death as something evil that can't come from God. Death is not seen as natural, and immediately when one has to deal with AIDS, you have to deal with death."

Sex contributed to the fear, Father Mthembu continued, but death was the more powerful component. Extramarital sex, and the children it produced, were accepted because they resulted in life. Sex that resulted in death was a different thing entirely; it was a perversion of the natural order.

Many local people, even his own parishioners, Father Mthembu also said, still believed that AIDS was caused by witchcraft. Sex, he explained, might be the mechanism of transfer, but it was not the root cause.

The fundamental premise of our Western, post-Enlightenment worldview is that the world is rational, that it can be understood and to a large degree controlled. If someone falls sick, we look for a biological cause and seek a cure. We even try to prevent against potential harm by wearing seatbelts to protect ourselves in a car crash or by losing weight to prevent a heart attack. Our failure to act on good advice—to stop smoking, for example, or to wear a condom in a casual sexual encounter—is more often a failure of will than of faith. It is not that we don't believe that stopping smoking will reduce our chance of getting lung cancer; rather we judge that the short-term cost is not worth the long-term potential gain. Misfortune, in our understanding, is usually the result of our own failure to effectively control the world around us.

This worldview is a product of the scientific revolution; as we began to understand more about the world, we looked for rational rather than spiritual answers to misfortune. But it also has its roots in the Christian concept of sin. The idea that humanity can be saved, through confession or good works or faith, is the ultimate testament to man's ability to control his destiny. Perhaps we underestimate, however, how new such a perspective is even in our own society.

According to Father Mthembu, who has lived with one foot in his traditional culture and the other in the Church, many rural Africans look for more immediate causes of their misfortune, usually another person. People think, "Someone must be guilty," he said.

Sociologist Adam Ashforth argues that while there is no single, uniform system of belief in South Africa—much less across Africa—there is nonetheless what he calls a "witchcraft paradigm" to which most people turn when asking why they have become the victim of misfortune. "The basic hypothesis of witchcraft, the chain of reasoning that distinguishes talk of witchcraft from other hypotheses about invisible powers (such as divine retribution, or punishment by ancestors for infringing taboos, or sin) is that the origin of misfortune is social. It is another person, ordinarily conceived, who is hypothesized to have caused the harm."[2]

If evil is caused by other people, then it is much harder to protect against. This belief system has potentially profound implications for AIDS prevention, which has largely been based on the assumption that people believe they have the power to protect themselves against the virus.

THAT DECEMBER was hot and dry; once again the rains were late. Phumlani had halfheartedly cleared a plot of land and planted it with corn, but the small stalks were already brown and dead, and looked unlikely to yield much food. Nine months had passed since Thando, from Orphan Care, had started the processes of having the grants transferred to Gogo's name and still she had received nothing. Gogo had been told to stop coming every month to the social welfare office. Someone would come to tell her when the grants arrived.

One day, Zethu and I found Sbuka at home with her cousin Celiwe, who was braiding cheap extensions into her hair as they sat outside under an avocado tree. Five young people now lived in the little house. Celiwe had moved in, and Khanya, the children's oldest sister, whom I had not yet met because she had been living in the flatlands in a place called Ndumo, had come home after a fight with her boyfriend, a teacher. He had pulled a knife on her and threatened to kill her.

Sbuka, her siblings told me, had been staying away a lot lately. Sometimes she would not come home for days. She told her siblings that she was staying with a friend whose mother worked as a nurse in the hospital, but Khanya believed that she was out with different boys. Gogo said Khanya was just trying to stir up trouble because she and Sbuka had recently fought. The older girl had slapped her younger sister one night in a fight over supper. But there were also rumors in the neighborhood that Sbuka was sleeping around. One local girl told Zethu that she hoped Sbuka got pregnant so she would stop stealing all the other girls' boyfriends.

I didn't know whom to believe. Neither Zethu nor I had seen Sbuka with a boy, and she always denied to us that she had a boyfriend. She seemed less lonely at home now, but she was still withdrawn and depressed. On the other hand, we often passed Celiwe on the main road through Ingwavuma talking to different men. It is possible that the rumors about Sbuka were simply the product of jealousy. She had a scholarship to attend Nansindlela, the best school in the area, and a quiet pride that I could see might rankle other girls. She sometimes laughed, but not often, and there was often a wryness even to her smiles. In my heart, I doubted that Sbuka was running around with lots of different boys.

Still, if she had turned to boys, or men, to ease the loneliness of her days, she would not have been the first. Orphaned teenage girls have higher rates of pregnancy and HIV-infection than other girls.[3] Some look for men who can provide for their material needs, while others hope they will simply fill the emotional vacuum in their lives.

"Some of the girls, they look to a rich man because they think, okay, this man will take care of me. But it's really just abuse," Thando told me once, after we had visited a family where a recently orphaned seventeen-year-old girl had suddenly revealed that she was six months pregnant. The girl's boyfriend was a decade older and had been a drinking partner of her father.

Gogo limped down to speak to us. She had been to the hospital that day for her knee, which was swollen and painful with gout. She was angry. "Sbuka wants to go live in Johannesburg with her teacher's mother," she told us.

The teacher had promised to pay her school fees, feed her, and buy her clothes in return for helping around the house. Sbuka had also told Gogo that her scholarship at Nansindlela was ending, which I later found out was a lie. Gogo didn't want to let her go.

"If Sbuka leaves, the police might come and arrest me for applying for a grant on her behalf," Gogo said. She was also angry that the teacher had not come and spoken directly to her and Mkhulu, as would have been proper.

Sbuka said nothing as Gogo told us this story. She turned her back to us and started crying softly.

"Why hasn't your teacher come to speak to us?" Gogo demanded. "I cannot give my child to someone I do not even know."

Still Sbuka said nothing. As Zethu and I got up to leave, she followed us to the car.

"Gogo will not even talk to me about it," she sniffled. "I want to go, but my teacher is leaving in the morning, early, and Gogo will not talk about it." I asked her why she wanted to go.

"I am unhappy because I never have money to participate in class activities," she confided. "We were supposed to give gifts to each other at the end of the year, but I had nothing to give. All the other students have better uniforms and clothes, and sometimes they make fun of me."

Her teacher, Sbuka said, picked her because she was shy and quiet in class, and could tell she was unhappy. "If I go to stay with her mother, she will pay for my school fees and clothes and buy me food so I won't feel different anymore."

I could see why Sbuka wanted to go, but also why Gogo was concerned. Sbuka saw the offer as a way out of the grinding poverty of her life and, perhaps, a chance for a new family. Although at Nansindlela she was receiving a better education than her siblings, her poverty was also on greater display there.

But it also seemed strange to me that Sbuka's teacher would make such an offer and expect it to be accepted without ever speaking to her guardians. I wondered too why she wanted to bring a girl all the way from Ingwavuma when there were probably many girls who needed homes nearer where she lived. If something did go wrong—if the woman was abusive or simply neglectful of her—Sbuka would be far away from anyone she knew. She had been to Johannesburg once, on a school trip, but knew little about the city or its ways.

I didn't want to take sides on the issue but agreed to drive Gogo to the teacher's house if she wanted to go. When we found Gogo, she was sitting in her yard under a tree, wrapped in a pink towel. She said she could not leave without permission from Mkhulu, who was sleeping. Sbuka wanted me and Zethu to speak to her teacher anyway—probably because she hoped we would help to convince Gogo—so the three of us hopped in my car and drove the short distance to the teacher's house. I made it clear that it was not my place to interfere but wanted to hear what the teacher had to say.

The teacher said she had offered a new home to Sbuka, but that it was in a township outside Odenkraal, a small town in the Free State, hours from Johannesburg and not far from the border with Lesotho. It was a Sesotho-speaking area, Adeline's language, although the teacher thought there might be a Zulu-language school in the town.

"The last of my mother's children will be leaving soon, so she wants a girl to come help her at the house and to help take care of the grandchild who is staying with her," she said. "I thought of Sbuka because I knew she was an orphan and she is always so well-behaved in school."

I explained that Sbuka's grandparents were unwilling to let her go without meeting her. She shrugged and said it was too late. She was leaving the following morning. Perhaps she would come and speak with them when she returned for the new school year, if her mother had not yet found someone.

The next day, Gogo and Mkhulu told me they would not let Sbuka go, even if the teacher came to them. If she took Sbuka without their permission, they would go to the police to say it had been done without their consent.

"When their mother died, these children were given to me to care for, but if she does whatever she wants then I am no longer responsible," Gogo said. "Why did this woman not come to speak to me? I do not believe such a woman would take good care of my child."

From that point on, Sbuka stopped speaking to her grandmother. It was the beginning of a rift that would grow deeper in the coming months until the Mathenjwas were barely speaking with their grandparents and Gogo had stopped giving them any food.

14

THE SCOURGE OF POVERTY

S BUKA NEVER WENT to Johannesburg, or even the Free State. Instead, we went to the beach. Mfundo, Phumlani, and Sbuka had all passed their exams and would progress to the next grade level, so as a treat I agreed to take them to the ocean.

I picked them up early one Saturday morning and we drove about sixty miles to Sodwana Bay, a popular beach inside a government park. Armed with a cooler full of bread, Coke, cheese, and polony, we found a free spot and spread out our towels and blankets in the soft sand.

The other beachgoers had segregated themselves. On one side of the beach, a small number of whites kept to themselves near a row of 4x4s they had backed onto the sand near the water. Closer to where we sat, a spirited crowd of blacks from the nearby town partied to the competing sounds of various thumping stereos. We were, without a doubt, the only mixed-race group on the beach and elicited curious and sometimes hostile looks.

Only Phumlani had a swimsuit; the rest of the family made do with whatever they had. Khanya wore a bra, while Sbuka donned a yellow T-shirt and a pair of running shorts. But the lack of appropriate gear did nothing to stop their fun. They splashed in the warm Indian Ocean for hours, happier than I had ever seen them.

Phumlani disappeared somewhere down the beach, perhaps worried that it was not cool to be hanging out with his family. But the others seemed happy to splash together.

"It's so big," Mfundo cried, looking at the ocean. "It goes on forever and ever."

"The people who stay here are lucky," Sbuka said wistfully. "They can come here anytime." Although she lived only an hour and a half away, Sbuka had been to the ocean only once before. The family lived in an area dotted with internationally famous wildlife parks, some known for their rhinoceros conservation, but they had never had the chance to visit. Sbuka had once seen an elephant, but at the zoo in Johannesburg on a class trip.

As I sat under the fierce summer sun, I was struck by how isolated the Mathenjwas were even from the mainstream of South African culture, not to mention global culture. The other young blacks on the beach that day, most of whom came from a nearby town, all seemed far more worldly. In their taste in music and clothing, they were part of a new urban, black culture that I was familiar with in Johannesburg. Even Adeline in Lesotho had been far more connected to this new, modern African identity. She knew the latest hit songs and followed the dramas of South African soap operas.

In the context of the new South Africa, poor, rural young people like the Mathenjwas were increasingly being left behind. There were two worlds in South Africa, as there had been under apartheid, but the divisions in the country were no longer just black and white. The divide between urban and rural had become equally significant.

With their poor English and substandard education, most of the young people in places like Ingwavuma would have a hard time ever finding a place in the country's increasingly competitive job market. The lives their grandparents had lived were slowly disappearing, never to return again. Subsistence farming was an increasingly untenable form of survival and the unskilled jobs that had once been abundant were vanishing as South Africa's economy moved away from labor-intensive industries such as mining and agriculture. I doubted whether the girls could even find work as domestic workers, the kind of job their mothers would likely have taken had they moved to the cities. Sbuka's desire to go to Johannesburg, I thought, reflected her understanding that if she stayed in Ingwavuma, she would be trapped there.

As orphans, the Mathenjwas were particularly disadvantaged. When their parents died, they lost the guidance of the generation most able to help them make the transition into this new world. Their grandparents were even less worldly than they were and could offer little help.

There was clearly important knowledge that was being lost in this generational gap, although how much of it was simply a result of changing times and how much was directly related to the loss of their parents was hard to tell. Sbuka's mother had taught her things like how to cook and keep the house clean. Their floor was always swept and their few belongings neatly stored. There was never any of the chaos one might expect, for example, in a similarly composed household of children and teenagers living on their own in the United States.

But no one had, for example, ever taught them how to keep a garden. Their diet, which largely consisted of pap and beans, was frighteningly bereft of any green vegetables. There were a few fruit trees in the garden, but by and large their diet was heavy on starch and low on just about everything else. Once, while I was away, Zethu had brought them a few seedlings from which they could grow a garden. When she returned a few weeks later, Sbuka told her that the seedlings had died. Zethu asked where and how she had planted them; Sbuka, it turned out, had done everything wrong. She had planted them in an unprotected space where the neighbor's chickens could reach them and where the sun hit them too directly.

On my next visit we brought more seedlings, and this time Zethu showed them how to build a proper garden. When I had first met them, the remnants of a small garden still existed in front of the house. But over the months, it had become increasingly overgrown and the family had begun using it as a trash heap.

Under Zethu's guidance, we spent all morning clearing the plot and creating a barrier of thorny branches. The garden was full of ripped clothes, old bottles and cans, and planks of wood. There was even the door of a refrigerator. Zethu taught them how to dig long trenches and plant the seedlings at the top so the water would seep into the roots without drowning the plants.

We had brought dozens of small plants, purchased from a project run by the women's center where Zethu volunteered: cabbage, spinach, onions, tomatoes, and beetroot. She and I had dropped the plants off the night before, but by the time we arrived the next morning some of them were missing. The tomato plants were almost entirely gone.

"The rats," Sbuka explained, pointing at the house. "They're so hungry they even eat Mfundo's pants."

We left the beach early, not long after lunch. Sbuka and her siblings wanted to make a detour on the way home to pick up their youngest sister, Makhisi, who was supposed to spend the summer school holidays, and Christmas, with them. But they didn't have enough money to fetch her by taxi and hoped that I would agree to pick her up. I wondered where we would put her—the four of them were already squeezed into the backseat of my car, with Zethu and me in the front—but readily agreed.

I had not yet met Makhisi, who had been staying with the family of her father and had not seen her siblings since Nozipho's funeral in March. Then eleven, she was a slight girl with a smooth, round face and a deliciously wicked grin. When we found her at her uncle's house, she was wearing a torn sundress that was too big for her and slipped off her shoulders, making her look a bit like a little girl playing dress-up in her mother's clothes. When we left, she took with her only a small backpack.

Makhisi reminded me of her grandmother. She had the same grin and the same sense of humor. I hoped she would bring a ray of humor into the often somber Mathenjwa house.

ONE OF MANDELA's few public statements on AIDS during his presidency took place in Mtubatuba, the town Father Camillus moved to after his fall. It was 1998 and Mandela was preparing to step down as president, becoming one of only a handful of African leaders to have done so voluntarily. After decades of struggle, he planned to take up the life of an elder statesman who could finally rest on his laurels.

By then, Mtubatuba was widely recognized as having one of the highest recorded AIDS-infection rates in the world. That year, it had become temporarily famous for its unmatched HIV-infection rate: 29 percent of pregnant women there tested HIV-positive.[1] Standing with Dr. Peter Piot, the Belgian researcher who had worked at Project SIDA in Kinshasa and who had, a few years earlier, been appointed to head the United Nations' new AIDS organization, UNAIDS, Mandela called on South Africans to break the silence on the epidemic.

"Although AIDS has been a part of our lives for fifteen years or more, we have kept silent about its true presence in our midst," he said. "We have too often spoken of it as if it was someone else's problem. . . . Because this disease is so new, and because it spreads mainly through sex, prevention requires of us that we speak [of] it in a way [for which] our traditions, our cultures and our religions provide little guidance."[2]

As Mandela was awakening to the scale of the epidemic, frustrated activists were beginning to band together to demand that the government take more action. Nine days after Mandela appeared in Mtubatuba, a new organization, the Treatment Action Campaign (TAC), announced its formation and called on the government to take steps to provide free AZT to pregnant women in order to prevent them from passing the virus on to their children, and to take steps toward developing a "comprehensive and affordable treatment plan for all people living with HIV/AIDS."[3]

The TAC's call for treatment for people with AIDS challenged conventional wisdom that triple-cocktail therapy was too expensive and too complicated for Africa. Previously AIDS had been seen largely as a development problem, but the members of the TAC and their allies saw it as a human rights issue. They argued that the primary barrier to treatment for HIV/AIDS in the developing world was the price of the drugs, which were expensive not because they were difficult to make but because they were protected by international patents intended to enrich pharmaceutical companies. In the TAC's stark formulation, millions of Africans were dying so that rich drug companies could get richer.

The TAC's argument was, in many ways, a natural outgrowth of South Africa's revolutionary new approach to the very idea of rights. The country's 1996 constitution is widely regarded as the world's most progressive and includes not only political rights, like freedom of speech and religion, but also a whole range of new social rights like the right to housing, education, clean water, sanitation, and health care.

What was not detailed in the constitution, and what would later become the point of contention between the government and groups like the TAC, is how much health care the state owed its citizens. Did the right to health care include the right to any treatment, no matter what the cost? And more specifically, did it include the right to antiretroviral drugs?

The TAC first campaigned for the provision of antiretroviral drugs for pregnant women and rape victims. Unlike HAART, which had to be taken for a lifetime, short-courses of AZT for pregnant women or for rape victims at risk of being infected by their attackers could prevent the virus from taking hold in the body. They could, in essence, prevent AIDS infection.

The main focus of the group's activism in its early days was pharmaceutical companies, which the TAC saw as greedy and amoral. "In 1998 there was no reason to suspect that pseudo-scientific opinions about HIV would be embraced by some ANC leaders and intrude adversely upon government policy," Mark Heywood, another TAC leader, later wrote.[4]

A few months before the TAC's official launch, the health department had decided not to offer AZT to pregnant women, citing the drug's high cost as the major barrier. But the health minister, Nkosazana Dlamini-Zuma, gave her blessing to efforts to try to reduce the price of the drugs: "If you want to fight for affordable treatment then I will be with you all the way," she said.[5]

At the time, the South African government was waging its own fight against international drug companies. The TAC should have been a natural, and effective, ally in this struggle; instead the relationship between the activist group and the government quickly deteriorated into outright hostility. In 1997, the South African parliament had passed an amendment to the Medicines and Related Substances Control Act that allowed the government to bring down the price of certain essential medicines through parallel importation—buying the drugs from another country where they are cheaper—or compulsory licensing, which would allow South African companies to make generic versions of drugs before their international patent ran out. While the law had not been passed specifically with the intention of securing cheaper antiretroviral drugs, the TAC quickly realized that it could give South Africa a key weapon in the fight to bring affordable treatment to the masses.

Although World Trade Organization agreements allow countries to take such steps in cases of health emergencies, South Africa was under enormous international pressure not to put such a waiver into practice. The United States, home to many of the world's largest drug companies and much of the globe's pharmaceutical research, was particularly virulent in its criticism.

In 1998, thirty-nine drug companies and the South African Pharmaceutical Manufacturers Association slapped the South African government with a lawsuit, alleging that the law violated its international intellectual property rights. The U.S. government— then under the leadership of President Bill Clinton, who would later become one of the world's most important advocates for affordable AIDS treatment—supported the drug companies and threatened South Africa with trade sanctions if the law was not repealed.[6]

For the drug companies involved, the lawsuit turned out to be a public relations nightmare, in large part because of the activism of the TAC and other AIDS activist organizations. The suit, which was eventually resolved out of court in 2001, made the TAC famous and painted the international pharmaceutical companies as representatives of a coldhearted industry that callously placed profits above lives.

When the pharmaceutical companies withdrew their suit, Mbeki's new health minister, Manto Tshabalala-Msimang, claimed the government had won a victory for human rights in the face of opposition from a heartless corporate entity. "The resolution of this court case only confirms our view that international markets, which play an increasingly important role in all our lives, have no inbuilt conscience. But governments and ordinary people acting collectively have a precious responsibility to make the huge companies that dominate the markets accountable for how they respond to the most critical issues of our times."[7]

The patent trial marked the beginning of a new phase in the epidemic. The price of antiretroviral drugs across the continent suddenly plummeted as the makers of antiretroviral drugs scrambled to rebuild their international reputations. The pharmaceutical companies that held patents for these drugs agreed to allow poor countries to purchase them from generic makers in India or to license local companies to produce them. Many also started offering them to African governments and nongovernmental organizations working on the continent for free or at cut-rate prices. Treatment that had once cost tens of thousands of dollars a year could suddenly be acquired for a few hundred dollars a year, and the idea of treating millions of infected people in the world's poorest countries suddenly seemed within reach. In 2002, the World Health Organization pledged that three million people would begin receiving the life-prolonging treatment by 2005.

The alliance between government and civil society over the drugs suit, however, masked a deeper and growing hostility between the two sides. The transition of power from Mandela to Mbeki in mid-1999 marked the beginning of a new period in South Africa's AIDS fight, in which failure of leadership would become outright denial.

While the South African government fought pharmaceutical companies in the courts, Mbeki continued to flirt with dissident theories regarding HIV and AIDS, apparently using the Internet to dig up information. He began to question whether AZT was toxic, saying there was a "large body" of literature alleging that the drug was harmful to human health.[8] In early 2000, he set up the Presidential Advisory Council on AIDS and invited dissident American scientists David Rasnick and Peter Duesberg, who questioned the link between HIV and AIDS and claimed that antiretroviral drugs were toxic, to take part.[9]

Advocates of AZT and other antiretrovirals had never claimed that the drugs had no side effects, but they pointed out that all drugs do. Furthermore, they argued that the potential benefits—reducing the chance that the deadly virus would be passed from mother to child, protecting a rape victim from becoming infected, or extending the life of an HIV-positive person otherwise certain to die—far outweighed any potential side effects.

Mbeki has never explicitly denied that HIV causes AIDS. He has, however, frequently questioned whether the link between the virus and the syndrome has been proven. In one of the more exquisitely embarrassing moments of South Africa's postapartheid history, Mbeki even used his opening speech at the Durban AIDS Conference in 2000—where thousands of the world's most prominent AIDS activists and researchers had gathered in the South African coastal city—to question whether AIDS or poverty was killing his people. The world's biggest killer and the greatest cause of ill health and suffering across the globe, he said, is "extreme poverty." He also said that the country's health problems could not be blamed on a "single virus."[10]

Increasingly, it seemed that Mbeki was living in a bubble. He accused the CIA of taking part in a plot to promote the idea that HIV causes AIDS and began to speak about the syndrome—on the rare occasions he referred to it at all—as if it were some strange, racist conspiracy to paint Africa as a cesspool of disease and promiscuity.[11] "Convinced that we are but natural-born, promiscuous carriers of germs, unique in the world, they proclaim that our continent is doomed to an inevitable mortal end because of our unconquerable devotion to the sin of lust," he said in October 2001, during a speech at a traditionally black South African university, Fort Hare.[12] And although South Africa had more HIV-positive people than any other country in the world, he also claimed to be untouched by the epidemic, telling the *Washington Post* in 2003: "Personally, I don't know anybody who has died of AIDS. I really, honestly don't." [13]

In Ingwavuma, there is no doubt that poverty is a potent force. It is evident in the tattered uniforms of the children walking to school in the early dawn light and the weary faces of old women waiting patiently in the midday sun for their monthly pensions.

In a sense, Mbeki's AIDS panel was right. Poverty *was* intricately connected to Ingwavuma's AIDS epidemic, though it is not itself the sole cause of the rising tide of death. No one I spoke to there, from old Gogo and Father Camillus to the doctors at Mosvold and the local *indunas,* had any doubt that something new and terrifying had arrived in Ingwavuma; what was happening there was more than a new variation on an old theme.

The arrival of HIV had helped to upset an already precarious existence, and the area was now trapped in a downward spiral of poverty and AIDS. While there was no direct correlation in Ingwavuma between individual wealth and HIV infection rates—middle-class nurses and teachers were as likely to succumb as members of the poorest families—the endemic poverty of the region, and the sense of hopelessness that poverty created, certainly contributed to the spread of the epidemic, especially among young people.

At some local high schools, nearly half the girls got pregnant before graduating; their teachers speculated that some were intentionally getting pregnant in order to claim the monthly twenty-five dollar child-support grant given to any mother of a child under fourteen. Whether this was true, or simply a myth born out of a deep-seated cynicism about what was happening in their community, it nonetheless reflected the local reality that poverty was so deeply entrenched that twenty-five dollars a month seemed to many like a great deal of money. It wasn't so hard to believe, in a place where few children had hopes of going to college or getting a good job, that being paid to have a baby might seem like a good deal.

Most of the young people in the area who dragged themselves

out of bed before dawn each day to walk miles to school in hope of a better life eventually gave up long before they graduated. The eldest Mathenjwa sister, Khanya, for example, stopped going to school in late 2005 after her boyfriend attacked her for a second time, this time beating her so badly that she was hospitalized. Once again she fled home for safety, abandoning her studies and her son.

Khanya talked vaguely about going back to school, but I doubted she ever would. She was by this time twenty-three and had a five-year-old son. When she was separated from her boyfriend, she said she might go to Durban to try to find a job as a maid. But before long she was back with him, despite the abuse. He gave her money each month, and since Gogo had by this time stopped giving them anything—and the grants had still not come through—Khanya and her siblings relied on the money from him to survive. The only other income in the house was Khanya's child-care grant, although her son actually stayed with his paternal grandparents. She was trapped by poverty in an abusive relationship and one in which, I suspected, she was also at high risk of becoming infected by AIDS. Unlike Adeline in Lesotho, she lacked the social support and economic resources to leave her boyfriend.[14]

Thando, Vee, and the other Orphan Care workers watched as AIDS also led to the rapid economic decline, and sometimes disintegration, of families. The Mathenjwas were a classic example of this, if not by any means the most extreme. Five years ago, they were a two-parent family with a stepfather who brought in cash doing odd jobs and a mother who kept a garden and grew corn. First, the death of their stepfather stripped them of their cash income. Then their mother grew too sick to maintain the agricultural work that kept some food in their bellies. They had never been rich, but the death of their parents suddenly made them destitute.

I often wondered if there was anything I could do that would provide more lasting help to the Mathenjwas, aside from trying to push through their foster-care grant, which would at least provide them some income. Even with that, I was having little luck. I felt defeated by the systemic poverty in which they were entrenched. I could not give them better educations or teach them English or find them jobs. Had any of them expressed a specific desire to start a business or seek technical training, I would have funded it. But none of them seemed to have any idea how to escape their predicament.

There were a few local children who somehow managed to get out of Ingwavuma and find good jobs or go to college, but most of them were, like Zethu, the children of comparatively middle-class parents. There were a handful of exceptions. Nathi, who was another one of the first orphans assisted by Ann, had finished high school while taking care of his younger siblings and was now working as the receptionist at Orphan Care. He had undergone special training to learn how to use computers and was, during the period I spent in Ingwavuma, studying Web design.

I met another young man from the area, Thando Mpontshane, who had miraculously won admission to the country's top medical school, although he had not gone to school at all until he was twelve. He had passed the national high school graduation exam (even though his father had died the week before he took the test) and had applied to the University of Witwatersrand in Johannesburg with the help of his teachers, who chipped in their own money to send him two hundred miles away to Durban for the admission exam. No one, though, had explained to him the need to apply for a scholarship, and a few weeks before the term started he found himself with a letter of admission but no money to pay the school fees or even to get to Johannesburg.

Once again Orphan Care intervened, and the organization's new operations manager, Leigh-Ann Mathys, took it on herself to raise the money to ensure he got there. Thando was the hardest worker I had ever met, and I gladly lent a hand, keeping an eye on him in Johannesburg and, with my family, chipping in to help pay for his residential fees. For Thando, who had spent his entire life in rural South Africa and Swaziland, Johannesburg was a mystifying—and sometimes terrifying—place. Once I took him to watch a soccer match on television at a bar outside Soweto. As we drove home through the city after dark, he looked with awe at the city skyscrapers. "There are so many lights. In Ingwavuma, everyone would be asleep by now!" It was 8 p.m.

Neither Nathi nor Thando could have succeeded without the help of more worldly people who helped them to access opportunities and navigate the world outside Ingwavuma. They were both clearly highly intelligent. But there was something else that contributed to their success, some special spark of desire that came from inside. I often pestered Thando about why he thought he had succeeded.

He always just shrugged. "I just wanted to be a doctor," he would say.

YOUNG PEOPLE like Thando and Nathi, however, were the rare exception in Ingwavuma and were unusual even in the context of their own families. Thando's brother became a petty criminal; while Nathi's teenage sister got pregnant before finishing school. Indeed, most observers in Ingwavuma agreed that the deepening poverty and expanding AIDS epidemic were taking a terrible toll on the social fabric of the area. Crime had increased dramatically, including many offenses that had been previously almost unknown, such as sexual assaults against children.

"The morality here has gone down," Father Mthembu had told me sadly. "AIDS has rendered people subhuman. And because of poverty, people will do anything to keep themselves alive."

Each time I arrived in Ingwavuma, I would be inundated with new stories of recent events that reflected the breakdown in social morality.

Once I returned to hear there had been a flurry of attacks on local whites, many of them associated with the hospital. One of the female doctors had been attacked while jogging and had narrowly escaped being raped. A male doctor was mugged at the ATM, which is located inside the Boxer supermarket, while withdrawing money. A local white man who did odd jobs and construction work was severely beaten. And the house of Sylvia, the Swiss nurse who had run Orphan Care's home-based care program, and her husband, who was a doctor at the hospital, was robbed.

Few of the victims thought the primary motive of the criminals was predominately racial: the number of attacks against whites simply reflected the economic reality that most of the small local white community was comparatively wealthy. Prosperous blacks also suffered greatly from attacks. The year before, Thando Mbhamali, the employee at Orphan Care who was working with the Mathenjwas, had been hijacked and his car stolen. Most of the victims of violence, in Ingwavuma as across South Africa, were black.

One of the local prosecutors, a young Zulu man from Durban, told me he was shocked at the kind of crimes he was seeing in Ingwavuma. He expected to spend most of his time there handling stock theft and the occasional assault. Instead, he found that most of his cases were rapes, often against children. In the two years he had worked in the office, he had prosecuted 223 rape cases, and that was only a small fraction of the number he suspected were occurring in the area. At the time, near the end of 2005, he was working on a case involving a five-year-old girl who had been raped. "The people here think that if you sleep with a virgin, you can be cured of AIDS," he said. He could think of no other reason that so many young children were being victimized.

There were also a surprising number of murders. "Usually here they use a *panga,*" he said, using the local word for machete. He showed me a few files of cases he was currently working on, warning: "It's pretty gruesome."

One particularly horrible recent case had involved a family associated with Orphan Care. An elderly grandmother who had been taking care of five AIDS orphans was brutally murdered in her bed, along with her young grandson. Her throat had been cut and she had been disemboweled.

Ann knew the family well; she had written her master's thesis in part about their father's struggles to continue to feed his family as he was dying of AIDS. After his death, Orphan Care helped the woman take care of her grandchildren. When she was killed, the surviving orphans came to stay for a while at the orphan center and were taken care of by staff. Their family was too afraid to take them since the motive for the killing was suspected to be witchcraft.

"It was so brutal you'd think there'd have to be something other than normal jealousy," Ann said sadly. "Apparently she was so badly mutilated that they couldn't recognize the body."

The prosecutor said he was dealing with four or five murder cases believed to be witchcraft-related, including the case of the grandmother and grandson. Most, though not all, of the victims were old women who were accused of practicing witchcraft. Ann suspected the killing might have been related to an Orphan Care project she was involved with. The old woman was going to receive a large chunk of money to build a community garden; someone, Ann speculated, must have been jealous and accused the woman of using witchcraft to increase her luck. Now there would likely be no garden.

Accusations of witchcraft and the killing of witches, while they have their roots in traditional beliefs, tend to become more common in times of social tension. When the community as a whole struggles, people look for someone to blame, and old women make easy targets. There were several attacks against old women during my time in Ingwavuma, where everyone whispered that the motive was witchcraft. In at least two of these cases, the prime suspect was a relative of a neighbor who had recently died of AIDS.

One of the more terrible recent murders, however, had nothing to do with witchcraft and everything to do with poverty. A young orphan girl who was a friend of Bongilani, the boy who lived with Ann, became pregnant. Not long before she was due to give birth, she was caught stealing from the Boxer. The court released her from prison so she could give birth, but rather than going to the hospital when she went into labor, she had the baby in an outhouse and then dumped the baby down the toilet and into the pit of sewage below. By early 2006, the girl had still not been found.

LIKE FATHER CAMILLUS, many locals believed the increasing crime, rising number of teen pregnancies, and spread of AIDS were all rooted in the breakdown of traditional culture. In rural, conservative Ingwavuma, where fewer people saw the benefits of modernity than had felt its costs, many had begun to believe that the solutions to contemporary problems could be found only in a return to their own history and culture. History, though, was often remembered selectively. In the context of AIDS, the most powerful example of this conservative desire was the "revival" of virginity testing, which has been embraced by many Zulu, including some at Orphan Care, as an effective way of combating AIDS among young people. If girls faced social sanction for sexual activity, the idea went, then perhaps more would choose to remain virgins, thus stemming the spread of AIDS.

Despite claims by its supporters that this practice has deep roots, and although virginity was certainly highly prized; historically, there is little evidence that routine testing traditionally occurred in Zulu communities. In its modern incarnation, the practice dates perhaps to the mid-1990s; largely a response to the growing AIDS epidemic in KwaZulu-Natal, it takes the form of public spectacle. Teenage girls are brought by their mothers or grandmothers to public ceremonies where their virginity is "tested" by a female practitioner who has established herself for this purpose.

The test can range from a physical examination of the vagina to a glance into the girl's eyes, which are believed by many practitioners to betray whether the girl has known a man. The state of the hymen is only one of several physical signs looked for by virginity testers; other, usually more important ones, are the color of the labia, the size of the vaginal opening, and the amount of lubrication.[15] The strongest supporters of virginity testing are often older, rural women like Gogo who have been left caring for the illegitimate children and orphans of their own children. They are supported by a number of powerful Zulu men like Chief Mangosuthu Buthelezi, leader of the Inkatha Freedom Party, and Mbeki's first deputy president, Jacob Zuma, who see the revival of virginity testing as part of a broader movement to preserve, and when necessary revive, indigenous Zulu culture.

The idea of a coming African renaissance, which would include African solutions to African problems, has powerful currency in a postapartheid landscape in which the new government and black intellectuals are trying to find a third way between the Western model and the failed African leadership of the immediate postcolonial period. Some, though not all, South Africans saw virginity testing in that context, despite its questionable authenticity: whereas condoms were an imported, and largely unsuccessful, response to the AIDS problem, virginity testing was homegrown and therefore, its supporters believed, more likely to succeed.

"We do it because it has good outcomes, but some say it violates human rights," S'thembiso Mpontshane, who ran Orphan Care's youth outreach programs and supported virginity testing, told me. "We do not think this is true. Rural Africans believe that you grow up not for yourself, but for your community."

Far from seeing the widespread adoption of Western-style human rights as the solution to contemporary problems, many Zulu blamed the Western emphasis on individuality for the breakdown of social morality. Young Zulu people today, he believed, have been told by radio and television that they can do whatever they want and no longer have respect for their responsibilities to their families and communities. S'thembiso also saw a direct correlation between the rise of women's rights and his community's problems.

"You have a lot of women jockeying for power, but in my opinion, that will never happen. Women will never be equal to men," he said. "In South Africa, men have always been leaders, and if you play around with that system, men will become dangerous to society. Men, they lost self-confidence through the transformation process that has empowered women. Most of the men who would be powerful are in jail, not in the community."

Virginity testing censures young women for sexual activity yet ignores the role of men and boys. S'thembiso saw no contradiction in placing the responsibility for controlling AIDS on women without giving them greater social power to control their sexuality. In the old days—in Zulu culture as in Sotho—there were social sanctions against men for impregnating young women before marriage; the man's family would have to pay a penalty, usually one cow, to the woman's family. But while many Zulu men were keen to revive traditions that helped preserve male power, few advocated bringing back those that ensured men used that power responsibly. In Ingwavuma, as in many areas, the past was remembered only selectively.

To be fair, S'thembiso did believe that there should be more AIDS-related programs that focused on men, though he seemed to want them to encourage a return to a more traditional masculinity. He wanted to start a local group called *Amandla Amatota,* which means "Men's Power," but had been unable to find someone to fund the program. "We need to make men talk about it. Women are talking about it, but they don't have the power. Most of the projects target women."

15

ANOTHER DEATH

In January 2005, the Scorpions, South Africa's version of the FBI, seized all the files in Ingwavuma's social welfare office as part of a nationwide crackdown on corruption in the social welfare system. The investigation was supposed to last for three months, but it took more than six before the files were returned. During that time, work at the social welfare office came to a virtual standstill. Gogo's application, which still had not been processed, got caught up in the turmoil and sat frozen while the investigation continued.

South Africa's minister of social welfare estimated that corruption in the grant system was costing the country hundreds of millions of dollars a year. Mostly it was petty corruption, but on a massive scale. Across the country, there were thousands of perfectly healthy people who had received doctors' notes saying they were sick so they could receive monthly disability pensions or old people who had died but whose families continued to collect their old-age pensions. Many of these families were desperately poor and saw what they were doing simply as a means of survival. But there were also, the government estimated, thousands of civil servants who were collecting grants, such as twenty-five dollar monthly child-care stipends, despite having incomes that should have disqualified them from receiving public assistance.

Ingwavuma hadn't been specifically targeted in the fraud probe. All the social welfare offices in the area were being investigated. The investigators didn't seem to suspect any organized corruption there, although one man was arrested during the initial raid for allegedly stealing money from the office. When the Scorpions arrived, he spontaneously confessed. In Ingwavuma, however, as across the country, the problem was vast.

The government offered amnesty to people who came forward within a certain period of time and admitted they were receiving illegal grants. The new head of the social welfare office, who had arrived a few months earlier as part of a management shake-up, told me that eight hundred people had asked for amnesty in the Ingwavuma area alone.

Among them were several employees of Orphan Care, who had continued to receive child-support grants even though they had jobs. Ann was embarrassed, but the employees hadn't seen what they were doing as wrong. No one in Ingwavuma canceled a grant once they had begun receiving it, whether they had a job or not. Before the investigation, no one was even sure how to go about deregistering.

In the distribution of social grants, South Africa confronted the classic bureaucratic tension in the developing world between efficiency and preventing corruption. If the process was too simple, and local offices were given too much control over decision-making, there would be a great deal of space for corruption and error. If, on the other hand, the application process was too complicated and centralized, efficiency would suffer and the people who needed help most would have difficulty accessing it.

The system as it stood when I arrived in Ingwavuma was both centralized and, as the Scorpions investigation demonstrated, corrupt. Applications for grants had to be sent to a town called Ulundi for processing. The office there was so overloaded with applications that they had no time to investigate whether the grants were legitimate, and there was an ever-growing backlog of applications that was made worse by the investigation. The poor communication between offices also ensured that legitimate applications that had some small problem disappeared into a bureaucratic black hole. There seemed to be little hope that Gogo's grants would ever be processed.

When I tracked down Gugu Dubazana in April 2005 to harass her again about the Mathenjwas' application, she looked through her files and then asked if Gogo was receiving an old-age pension. "That's the problem," she said. "You can't receive both."

I was confused. I had met other old women who were certainly receiving both pensions and foster-care grants. When I asked Ann about the situation, she said she had never heard about such a rule. Nor had anyone else in the social welfare office. It seemed more likely that the application was simply lost, disappeared into the bureaucratic black hole that was South Africa's social welfare system. The Mathenjwas family had given up hope. In any case, given the state of relations between Gogo and the children, I wondered how much they would benefit if the grants did eventually come through.

Sbuka and Gogo hadn't spoken since January, since the conclusion of the fight over whether Sbuka could go to Odenkraal to stay with the family of her teacher. The teacher had returned to Ingwavuma just before the school year and had come to Gogo and Mkhulu, wanting to take Sbuka away. Gogo wouldn't let Sbuka go unless the teacher signed a statement at the police station saying she was taking full responsibility for the teenager. The statement was signed, but Sbuka never went. "Gogo didn't want me to go," she told me and left it at that. She stopped speaking to her grandmother entirely.

On August 21, 2001, just four months after the pharmaceutical companies retreated in the case against South Africa, the Treatment Action Campaign filed suit against the government demanding that the health department immediately make the antiretroviral drug Nevirapine available to all pregnant women. Despite plentiful evidence of the drug's effectiveness at reducing the transmission of the virus from mother to baby, doctors at state hospitals were not allowed to prescribe the drug. The TAC argued that the government had a moral and constitutional duty to make the drug freely available to all women who wanted it. In court, the government said providing Nevirapine was too expensive, even though the drug's maker had offered to provide it free to pregnant women. But the government said the real cost of the program was in infrastructure and human resources.[1] The issue of cost, though, was a red herring. It seemed clear that the real reason was Mbeki's strange views on AIDS and his belief that antiretroviral drugs were toxic.

In December, the court ruled that the government had a constitutional duty to roll out a national program to prevent mother-to-child transmission and set a deadline for March of the following year. The government at first refused to accept the court's ruling but, after a series of appeals, finally agreed in July 2002 to begin making Nevirapine available to pregnant women across the country. Several provinces not controlled by the ANC, including KwaZulu-Natal, had already begun making the drug available.[2]

For the TAC, though, the fight had just begun. The court victory meant that thousands of children would be spared an early and painful death, but an estimated five million South Africans were already HIV-positive, and the TAC extended its call for antiretroviral drugs to one for universal treatment for people with AIDS. The price of drugs, they pointed out, had fallen dramatically since the Pretoria court case and international donors were lining up to fund treatment programs. In other countries, efforts to make AIDS treatment available were under way, but in South Africa the government continued to express doubts about the effectiveness and toxicity of antiretroviral regimes.

In cooperation with other civil society groups, the organization stepped up its public protest campaign. The activists marched on parliament, protested outside pharmaceutical companies, and haunted every step of the health minister, Manto Tshabalala-Msimang, whom they accused of being a mass murderer.[3] Inspired by apartheid-era community activism, the organization mobilized a vast, nationwide network of HIV-positive people and their supporters who participated in public protests and helped educate people about the need for treatment. They illegally imported cheap generic versions of AIDS drugs from countries, such as Brazil, that produced them in defiance of international patent law.

The most visible face of the movement was Zackie Achmat, a charismatic, HIV-positive former male prostitute and anti-apartheid activist from Cape Town, who pledged not to take antiretroviral drugs until the government made them available to everyone who needed them.[4]

Throughout this time of protest, which was embarrassing to the government, the now-retired Mandela had remained publicly silent, preferring to try to influence policy from behind the scenes. As time passed, though, the Nobel laureate began giving subtle public signs that he supported the TAC's call for universal AIDS treatment. In July 2002, an aging and increasingly frail Mandela appeared at the bedside of Achmat, giving his tacit support to the TAC's fight against the government. "What I've come here to do," he said, "is to find out under what conditions he [Achmat] will then be able to take treatment." Mandela promised to meet with Mbeki to argue Achmat's case for treatment. "I have a case to take to the president to acquaint him with his position."[5]

Under fire domestically and internationally, the South African government finally grudgingly pledged in March 2003 to roll out universal treatment for people with AIDS, but the first drugs did not start reaching patients until more than a year later, a few weeks before South Africa's April 2004 election.[6] Stung by the bad press he had received, Mbeki said he would leave the AIDS issue to experts and, since then, has rarely publicly mentioned the epidemic.

Once the national government gave the green light for treatment, hospitals across the country began slowly preparing to offer the drugs. The speed at which they became available to ordinary citizens, however, seemed to depend largely on the management of the individual hospital.

At Mosvold in Ingwavuma, it would take more than a year for the first patients to be enrolled. On September 16, 2004, a few months after I first visited the area, the first eighteen patients began treatment. There were, however, thousands more in immediate need. Due to lack of staff, and because they were developing the program as they went along with little help from outside, the hospital was adding only five new patients a month. But each week, dozens of others were dying.

Still, despite the minute numbers actually receiving antiretrovirals, news of the new treatment had given many hope. Ever so slowly, the silence around the disease began to crumble.

"If I think they have AIDS, I tell them to get tested. Most go now because of the ARVs," Marcus, the home-based caregiver told me. "I told them how ARVs work, and now most of them are less afraid about HIV."

ONE EVENING, Zethu and I picked up some supplies for dinner—chicken, rice, a few vegetables, and some spices—and headed to the Mathenjwa house, with a plan to sleep there that night. I wanted to see how they spent their evenings after the sun had gone down.

The whole family seemed happier now that Makhisi was there. When we had picked her up from her uncle's house a few months earlier, she had planned to visit for only a few weeks, until the new school year began. But she had missed her siblings and decided to stay, even though life was harder there. Makhisi was now going to the same school as Mfundo, but her teachers yelled at her every day because she had the wrong school uniform. But with her at home, there was more laughter, and Sbuka spent more time there.

Makhisi looked at our offerings wide-eyed—it was rare that they ate meat of any kind—and said with a giggle that she wanted to cook. But it quickly became clear that she had no idea how, so Zethu took charge.

The kitchen that had stood next to the house when I first met the family had disappeared. They had burned most of the wood in the fire and now cooked in a narrow, triangular space between the house wall and the pieces of sheet metal that had previously served as the kitchen roof. That night it was blustery and cold, and we struggled to build a fire with only the rattling metal for shelter.

The family owned only two pots and two knives, both so dull that I struggled to cut an onion with them. While we sat in the dirt near the makeshift kitchen chopping potatoes and onions for the stew, an old man who lived nearby arrived at the gate of the homestead and began shouting for Sbuka.

"Where is my money?" he demanded. "Are you trying to steal my money?" Sbuka giggled nervously and kept hidden. The man was mad, she said, pointing to her head. A few days earlier, he had handed her some scraps of paper that he told her to take to her teachers. For some reason, he thought that they would give her money for them. The papers were meaningless, just pieces of trash, but now he came every day to demand his money.

It was dark by the time dinner was finished, and a soft rain had begun to fall. Zethu and I ate at the white table with Sbuka, Makhisi, and Mfundo. Phumlani took his dinner into the bedroom he shared with Mfundo; he always kept his distance when I came to visit. Sbuka said he just liked to keep to himself. Mfundo ate ravenously, as a growing boy should, though he complained that he didn't like chicken and said he wished we had brought beef.

With no electricity and no entertainment except each other, the day usually ended with the setting of the sun. As we prepared for bed, Sbuka offered me some water in a shallow plastic bucket to wash my face.

Zethu and I slept on the floor in the girls' room, while Sbuka and Makhisi shared a sagging bed. They had another mattress, which had been given to them by the Department of Social Welfare, but even if they began the night in separate beds, by morning Makhisi ended up next to Sbuka. "If I sleep on the floor, by the end of the night she is there. If I sleep on the bed, she comes and sleeps with me there!"

The two girls thought my sleeping bag was the funniest thing they had ever seen. Why didn't I just sleep under blankets, they wanted to know? Even Zethu thought it strange. The miner's flashlight I had brought, with a strap that went around my head, elicited even greater laughter.

In the silence, the rats—or perhaps they were mice—came out. We could hear them running around in the walls and across the floor. Once, in the middle of the night, Zethu smashed me in the face with her hand. I had moved and she thought I was a rat. The next morning, she said one had jumped onto her face during the night.

Sbuka woke well before dawn, before the alarm on my cell phone went off. It was not yet five in the morning. The sun had not yet risen, and it was wet and foggy outside, but somehow her internal clock had told her when to get up. She had to walk four miles to school each morning, and although I had promised to drive her that day, she kept to her normal routine.

As I struggled into wakefulness, Sbuka was already up and moving around the house in the predawn light. I realized in shock that the bucket I had used to wash my face in the previous night doubled as a chamber pot. The girls were afraid to go to the outhouse at night, so they used the bucket. And since they had only one bucket, they used it for both purposes. Sbuka warmed the leftover food from the night before on the ashes of the fire and, after emptying the bucket of the previous night's waste, washed her face in cold water. After a quick breakfast of warmed chicken, eaten hurriedly standing up, we walked outside into the rain and off to school.

Sbuka and her siblings each had only one uniform, so every night before Sbuka went to bed she washed her shirt and in the morning smoothed out the wrinkles with an iron warmed in the ashes of the previous night's fire. More than once, I had found Mfundo or Makhisi at home during the day because their school uniform was dirty or had not dried during the night. I marveled that they went to school at all. I couldn't imagine American children diligently washing their uniforms each night and waking on their own to walk miles to school.

A FEW MONTHS LATER, Mkhulu—the children's grandfather—fell ill. As a young man, he had mined coal and then later gold, and his lungs were ruined from years underground. He suffered from asthma so severe that it qualified him for a government disability grant. But that September, he began losing the struggle for air. His whole body swelled, and Gogo had to help him walk and even go to the toilet.

One night he became so ill that Gogo called the hospital, which sent an ambulance to fetch him. She went to visit him the next morning and he seemed better. A few hours after she returned home, though, he died.

The family buried Mkhulu nearby, and relatives from all around came to his funeral. Sbuka and some of her cousins sang a song that Mkhulu loved, and Khanya wrote a poem for him, asking why he had left them behind without anyone to take care of them.

I was shocked by the suddenness of his death. Although I knew he received a disability grant, he had never seemed particularly sick. The last time I had seen him, he had showed me the fruits of his most recent hunting trip: two large furry rodents that were unlike anything I had ever seen but that I guessed were cane rats.

Mkhulu's death prompted Gogo and her grandchildren to call a temporary truce, but within a few months they were again fighting. "We stopped for a while," Khanya shrugged. "But without Mkhulu, we started fighting again. Now we don't talk or even see each other."

Khanya, it seemed, was back home for good. She was still together with her boyfriend, but had decided to come live with her siblings and planned to apply for foster-care grants for them as soon as she could get Makhisi's birth certificate from the family of the girl's father. For the time being, though, she didn't have enough money for a bus trip to Manyiseni, where the certificate was being held.

On my last trip to Ingwavuma, not long after Mkhulu's death, I found myself abandoning my journalistic role entirely. I bought them all new school uniforms—they had grown out of their shoes and their uniforms were in tatters—and gave Zethu money to pay their school fees.

I also felt a probably futile compulsion to beg them to protect themselves against AIDS. In the many months I had spent with them, we had rarely spoken overtly about the virus. Gogo talked about the epidemic often, though she rarely used the word *AIDS*, but the children were even more circumspect. They didn't mind talking about their late sister and mother but never talked about what had killed them. They knew why I was there—Thando from

Orphan Care, Zethu, and I had all explained it as best we could numerous times—but they just didn't want to talk about AIDS, I suspected in part because they had not yet truly come to terms with the reasons for Lungile and Nozipho's deaths. I had generally respected this, as I felt my role was to observe, not to counsel.

But I was becoming increasingly worried about the children and whether they knew enough to protect themselves. Certainly, especially for the girls, knowledge alone is often not enough, but it is an essential starting point. And over the months, it had become clear to me that they actually knew very little about the virus and how to protect themselves. In addition, because they were unwilling to really accept the effect the virus had already had on their family, they still did not connect themselves to the epidemic.

They were in a buoyant mood as we arrived back at their homestead after a shopping trip. They were more excited over the new uniforms than I'd ever seen them; it was the first time they'd had new ones. On the way back, Mfundo begged me to let him steer the car, as I had occasionally let him do before on the long, flat road from Ingwavuma to their house. "One day I will own a car too!" he promised. Sbuka said she would miss me and asked if I could take her to America one day.

I hated to break the mood. It was rare to see them so carefree. But Zethu agreed with me that we could not leave without tackling the issue head-on. "You know what it is that took your mother and sister," Zethu told them as we sat inside the house a little while later. "It was AIDS." They grew suddenly silent and looked shocked at the serious turn of the conversation. Finally they nodded. "We're worried about you," I added. "We want to make sure that you stay healthy and live a long time. Do you know what you can do to protect yourselves from AIDS?" They squirmed. The whole situation seemed ridiculous, not to mention useless, and I began to regret having started the discussion.

Zethu tried to come to the rescue. "Don't listen to the boys if they tell you you must have sex with them. If you do have sex, you must use condoms," she said, adding, "You can get them at the hospital for free." We asked them if they had any questions about AIDS and how it spreads, but they were silent. Our little lecture seemed so impotent. Zethu and I both knew that, especially for Khanya and Sbuka, the ability to protect themselves likely lay outside their power. I doubted Khanya could ever convince her boyfriend to use a condom, and fear of catching AIDS was not likely to make her leave an abusive man to whom she had returned again and again. If Sbuka had something bigger to dream for, she might stay away from boys and focus on her studies. But even she knew that the odds were stacked against her. To pretend it was a simple choice, ignoring their poverty, loneliness, and orphanhood, seemed almost insulting. Yet what else could we do?

"Please," I finally said, "just be careful."

PART III
HOPE

OTSE, BOTSWANA

16

HOMECOMING

I'T'S MAY 2004. A young woman named Seeletso Isaacs is sitting in the front of my car with her son, Thabang, on her lap. We're driving slowly along rutted dirt roads with the speakers blasting Lauryn Hill. I keep turning the volume down and Seeletso keeps leaning forward to turn it up again. She loves the album and sings along, off key, to many of the tunes.

Seeletso is giving me a tour of her village, Otse, located in the vast, arid Southern African nation of Botswana. By African standards, the village is a prosperous one. Most of the houses are made of concrete and many have cars parked in their yards. The schools in Botswana are free, and there is a small clinic, staffed by a nurse and always stocked with drugs, just for the thirty-five hundred people in the village.

Otse is long and narrow, sandwiched between Botswana's main highway and Vulture Mountain, where there is a small reserve for endangered birds. Most of this part of the country is flat and dry, but Otse sits in a valley, bordered on all sides by mountains that look like sleeping giants. One, Mount Otse, is Botswana's highest point at a mere 4,885 feet.[1]

The village straddles a set of railroad tracks. Seeletso tells me that cows often get hit on the tracks and occasionally people too, usually drunk ones who are not watching what they are doing. The richer families generally live closer to the highway, but Seeletso and her family live on the poorer side of Otse, on the last road before Vulture Mountain. Most of the houses near where they live are humble structures of only a few rooms, constructed of bare concrete blocks and set in dusty yards. Unlike Ingwavuma, though, which is spread out over a vast distance, Otse feels like a proper town. Each house is set in its own small plot that is usually bordered by fencing of some sort.

When she was young, Seeletso says, the village was far larger and more dispersed, but people have been moving closer in to town to take advantage of new services, like running water and electricity. Every house has its own tap, though few have connected it to any kind of indoor plumbing, and most people still use outhouses with pit latrines. Seeletso's house doesn't have electricity. Her family is too poor to afford it, but the woman who lives across the street has a television and sometimes Seeletso goes there to watch. She is currently obsessed with a bad American soap opera about a witch, called *Passions*, that is played twice daily.

Otse has a few small shops, a handful of modest government buildings, and a small hotel, called Baratani Lodge, that is always empty. Along the highway there are several bars and nightclubs that are frequented not only by residents of Otse, but also by students at the nearby police and teachers' colleges. Seeletso points to her favorite, A Thousand Days, and promises to take me there some night. At this time of day, the building is shuttered and looks, to my eyes, slightly seedy.

From Seeletso's house, we turn left and start driving to the outskirts of the village. Seeletso points to the house of her grandmother, who is toothless and more than eighty years old. Nearby, she shows me the shell of a house where she used to live before her family moved closer to town.

Lauryn Hill is still thumping, uncomfortably loud for my taste, but Thabang seems to enjoy it. Although his fifth birthday is only a few days away, he is still tiny, the size of an eighteen-month-old baby. His head seems too large for his body and lolls strangely to one side. He is severely disabled and can't talk, sit up by himself, or walk, but it is hard to tell whether his brain is damaged too. He can understand what Seeletso says to him, though she usually talks to him in baby talk, and he responds to her with grunts or jerky motions of his hand. As we drive, he is jerking to the beat. "*Bina,* Thabang, *Bina,*" Seeletso encourages him. "Dance, Thabang, dance."

Not far outside the village, the landscape quickly turns to rugged scrubland. Much of Botswana is covered by the vast Kalahari Desert, and even here, along the narrow strip of land on the country's eastern border that is home to most of the nation's small population, it is dry and infertile. Corn, the staple crop farther south, is grown here, but most families also plant sorghum, which is more drought-resistant.

We park near a small cluster of buildings, one of which looks like an unfinished shell. "This is where rich Uncle Isaacs lives," Seeletso confides. "This man is a rich man. He has hundreds of cows."

There are many Isaacs in Otse, and this one seems to be defined by the fact that he is rich. He doesn't look rich to me, though. The house is run-down, and there are rusting corpses of cars scattered around the yard. There are also several dogs, a caged monkey named Jackie, and birds of every type in the yard: chickens, ducks, turkeys, and, strangely, peacocks. Seeletso points to one of the brightly colored birds. "See those birds? They protect against lightning." I wonder how the people here began to believe that a bird from Asia could have protective powers.

While I am trying to take everything in, Seeletso hands me Thabang, whom she carries everywhere, and disappears with a young woman. She returns a few minutes later with a large plastic bag of corn on the cob, called mealies. I realize that this is the real reason for our visit.

I had met Seeletso the day before, through her cousin Brenda Fonteyn, who with her husband runs an Otse-based center for orphans called Dula Sentle, which means "stay well" in Setswana, the local language. Seeletso's mother, Matlodi, and Brenda's mother are sisters and part of the large Isaacs clan, which seems to comprise half of Otse village.

The day before, Brenda had taken me to see Seeletso at her house, and we sat chatting for a while in the small room she shares with Thabang and three siblings. In that first visit, Seeletso was shy and withdrawn and answered my questions in Setswana, which Brenda translated. The younger woman was painfully thin, with wild, unkempt hair and a sundress that was too big and kept falling off her shoulder, exposing her breast. On her face, above her left eye, there was a painful dark patch that oozed yellow pus.

Today, however, Seeletso has taken charge, and I quickly realize that I have misjudged her entirely. She is loud and assertive, with a cackling laugh that verges on the vulgar. Her English is confident, if ungrammatical, and as we drive around the village she directs me in imperatives, ordering me to turn here and go there. The purpose of the trip, I suspect, is as much to show me off as to show me around.

After we leave the house of rich Uncle Isaacs, Seeletso tells me to pull into a small lane that runs off to the right, and we enter a graveyard. This, Seeletso tells me, is the Isaacs family burial place. She points to the biggest grave, which like the others seems to be on top of the ground rather than under it. "That one belongs to my grandfather," she said. She points to two others. One belongs to her Uncle Michael, her mother's brother, who died the previous year. The other, she says, belongs to a cousin who had died a month before of AIDS.

She is quiet for a while. Unspoken between us is how close she came to being buried there as well.

EARLY ONE TUESDAY morning more than a year earlier, two friends helped Seeletso into an old tan bus in Botswana's capital city, Gaborone. The bus was bound for Otse, Seeletso's village, which the twenty-two-year-old had not seen for almost four years. That day, her friends were taking her home to die.

As the bus rattled down the two-lane highway leading out of Gaborone, the three friends said little. They all guessed, but would not say, what sickness had stricken Seeletso. In recent months, the young woman's two friends, Cynthia and Naledi, had watched as she had slowly wasted away, shrinking from a weight of 130 pounds to just over 80. Only one disease they knew caused such symptoms in someone so young.

After forty-five minutes of near silence, the three young women disembarked by the side of the road near Otse. Seeletso's friends half helped, half carried her across the village, stopping frequently so that she could rest. "I was so sick," Seeletso recalled, shaking her head. "I was walking, but slowly. Some of them said I was dead already because I was so sick."

Seeletso's home was a modest, two-room building of concrete bricks. The family had been planning for many years to build more rooms, but there was never enough money. Seeletso was surprised, though, that so little had changed since she had left four years earlier.

When the three young women arrived, Seeletso's mother burst into tears. "I didn't know where Seeletso was. I had not heard from her in many years. People in the neighborhood said she was in Gaborone and that the area where she was living was a dump, a bad place," Matlodi recalled later. "When she came back, I thought, is this my child?"

As shocked as she was by Seeletso's appearance, Matlodi had little time to spare for her daughter. Matlodi's brother Michael had died only a few days earlier, and the family was consumed with preparations for the funeral. A delegation had gone to collect his body from the northern city of Francistown, where he had worked as a policeman. Other family and friends were gathering at the house of Seeletso's grandmother, on the other side of the village, where the funeral feast would be held. All the visitors had to be fed and housed, and there was much drinking of beer, singing of songs, and telling of stories. Matlodi's place was there, with her mother, sisters, and brothers.

Seeletso too grieved for her uncle, with whom she had lived for several years when she was a child. She had seen and heard nothing of him for a long time. In the years since she had run away from Otse, Seeletso had had almost no contact with her family. She had never been back to visit, for fear that they would try to make her stay. Nor had she seen her son, Thabang, since he was six months old.

Seeletso had known even then that there was something not right with him. When he reached the age that other babies had begun to make sounds and grab things, Thabang still lay helpless. He couldn't sit up or control his hands properly. His tongue curled strangely in his mouth and he failed to grow. By the time he reached the age of two months, it was clear there was something seriously wrong.

When Thabang was six months old, Seeletso said she was going to visit friends and never came home. With two friends, she stole off to Gaborone, where she hoped to make a living doing odd jobs or cleaning the houses of wealthier families. She ended up hanging out in seedy bars, begging drinks from the men who frequented them. She lived with her friend Cynthia in a squalid room in a run-down neighborhood, at the back of a house belonging to a traditional healer. It was a precarious existence, but she was free. "I didn't work, I just drank and partied all the time," she said.

She says she left home because her mother was a drunkard and would shout at her when she drank, but her cousin Brenda suspects she also left because she was overwhelmed by Thabang, who would never grow up and become independent like other children.

In recent months, though, Seeletso's health had begun to fail. By the time she returned to Otse, she had grown skeletal and her skin had acquired a chalky pallor. Her hair was wild and unkempt because she had no energy to maintain it, and she looked half-starved. The twenty-two-year-old woman who had returned to Otse was a pale shadow of the buoyant teenager who had left only a few years before.

In most African countries, Seeletso would have soon been buried next to her uncle. The virus had already grown strong by the time she came home from Gaborone, and it was only a matter of time before it would have overwhelmed her body's defenses completely, leaving her powerless against an onslaught of invisible microbes. She might have lived for a few more months, or maybe even a few more years, but eventually she would have succumbed to the virus.

Seeletso didn't come from a wealthy family, though even the poorest families in Botswana were better off than most families in neighboring countries. Her mother received a small disability pension from the government and earned a little cash teaching English and brewing traditional beer. Her stepfather worked as a night watchman and repaired shoes during the day. The family also had a small plot of land outside the village where Matlodi planted corn and sorghum, and they kept a few chickens and ducks in the yard.

Though they never went hungry, there was no extra money to pay for visits to a private doctor or to buy expensive drugs. Had the government of Botswana not launched an ambitious and extraordinary experiment, becoming the first country in Africa to offer free antiretroviral treatment to its citizens with AIDS, Seeletso and her son Thabang would both have died.

AN ARID, SPARSELY populated country of just 1.7 million, Botswana is known internationally primarily for its vast diamond wealth and fabulous game reserves. Like Lesotho, the country became independent only in 1966, as the British Empire freed the last of its African territories. The two countries, whose languages and cultures are closely related, were both woefully unprepared for existence as modern states. At the time of independence, though, Botswana seemed even more unlikely to succeed than its smaller, more fertile neighbor. It was bigger, drier, and equally undeveloped.

But where postcolonial politics in Lesotho quickly degenerated into internecine conflict, Botswana made a peaceful transition from protectorate to independent state under the guidance of a British-educated chief's son named Seretse Khama. Under his steady hand, the small nation gradually prospered and began to make the slow transition from traditional, rural society to modern state. When vast reserves of diamonds were discovered beneath its desert landscape, the government controlled that wealth in the name of the people, using it to build roads, schools, and health clinics.

During the years after independence, Botswana grew from one of the poorest countries in the world to become a middle-income country. It is also one of the rare African nations whose postcolonial history is unmarked by either dictatorship or violent transitions of power. Although one party has controlled the government through the country's entire history, the presidency has changed hands without incident three times. Elections have been generally peaceful, and opposition parties control a substantial part of parliament, though the current government sometimes shows a worrying disregard for free speech from people who disagree with its policies.[2]

When Festus Mogae—a short, solemn man with pepper gray hair—became Botswana's third president in 1998, he inherited a country whose economy and social development were the envy of the continent. Even powerful, prosperous South Africa performed more poorly on most indicators measuring poverty and development. But Botswana was also a society teetering on the brink of disaster. For more than a decade, AIDS had been silently weaving its way into villages and neighborhoods across the country.

At first the number of deaths had risen only slowly, starting from a single AIDS-related case in 1985. Then by 1994, a quarter of all pregnant women were HIV-positive. By 2000, the vast desert nation would have the highest recorded HIV-infection rate in the world: a staggering 38 percent of pregnant women carried the virus in their blood.[3]

Mogae, an Oxford-educated economist who had worked at the International Monetary Fund, quickly realized the threat that the epidemic posed to the development of his small nation. Already, Botswana's achievements in raising life expectancy and reducing maternal deaths were slipping.

Under the new president's guidance, Botswana quickly rolled out ambitious AIDS education programs, new testing centers, food packages and free schooling for orphans, and short-course antiretroviral programs to help prevent mothers from passing the virus on to their babies during birth. By 2000, the country had one of the most progressive AIDS programs in the world.

Perhaps more important, Mogae broke the international silence that had surrounded the epidemic in Africa. He encouraged his people to be tested, to take measures to protect themselves, and to treat those already infected with dignity and respect. To the international community, he acknowledged the scope of the crisis and called for assistance. At risk, Mogae warned, was his nation's very survival.

"I stand before you to claim the dubious distinction of being leader of a country most seriously affected by HIV/AIDS in the whole world," he told world leaders at the United Nations Millennium Summit in New York in 2000. "The fight against HIV/AIDS is therefore for us the challenge of the millennium. In the last 25 years we achieved economic growth rates comparable to those of the Asian tigers, attained human development indices that were the envy of many, practiced multiparty democracy, accountable and transparent governance, maintained an open society and ran an open economy.

"Now we daily witness elderly mothers mourning the untimely deaths of their beloved children, babies born today only to be buried the next day and a growing population of orphans yearning for parental love and care. These are the traumatizing realities of HIV/AIDS with which we live and have to contend."[4]

In following years, Mogae would repeatedly use words like "extinction" and "annihilation" to describe the fate that lay ahead for his nation. Even with the increased attention given to the issue, the infection rate continued to rise. By 2001, in a few urban areas such as the diamond mining center of Selebi-Phikwe, nearly 50 percent of pregnant women were HIV-positive. Mogae and others in his government soon came to the realization that it was no longer enough to simply stop new infections.[5]

In 2000, Mogae and his finance minister did some "back of the envelope calculations," said Dr. Banu Khan, a slight physician and public health expert of Indian origin who at the time ran Botswana's AIDS program in the department of health. They concluded that the economic consequences of doing nothing to treat people with AIDS was far greater even than the enormous cost of providing treatment. It was an argument that the TAC had been making in South Africa, but to little avail.

"Both looked at what was happening to economic development

and the investment that the country had made in improving development," said Khan, who later served as the first head of the country's National AIDS Coordinating Agency, from the office of her private practice after she had retired from public life. "They decided that if they provided ARVs, they could delay illness or death and also delay orphanhood. Just those savings would justify the costs." There was also the ethical issue of whether the state had an obligation to women with AIDS whose children had been spared through the program to prevent transmission from mother to child. Was it right to save the babies and do nothing for the mothers, if the means existed to help them?

"There wasn't a debate about whether this was the right thing to do. We realized this was something we had to do."

In March 2001, Mogae announced that the government of Botswana hoped to begin offering antiretroviral treatment to people with AIDS by the end of the year, becoming the first country in Africa to do so. The president, though, offered few details. How much the program would cost, who would be the first to benefit, and where the drugs would be sourced from—whether from the international brand-name drug companies that held the patents or from generic suppliers in India—remained unanswered.

The program was made possible in part by generous donations the previous year from the Bill and Melinda Gates Foundation and from Merck, the international pharmaceutical company. But, Mogae made clear, the bulk of the cost would be borne by the government, which faced a moral imperative to provide the lifesaving treatment to its citizens. The president also warned that treatment was no replacement for prevention. If AIDS infection rates did not begin to fall, he said, Botswana faced "blank extinction." "The implications," he said, "are too horrendous to contemplate." [6]

International reaction to the announcement was mixed. Many public health experts still questioned whether such a program was possible in Africa. Although the price of drugs had fallen dramatically and the medical regimes were far simpler to administer than they had been even a few years before, many experts worried that Botswana would fail to adequately monitor and track patients, resulting in high levels of resistance and ultimately drugs with reduced efficacy. They also worried whether, once begun, the program would falter in a few years as international and local enthusiasm dwindled for such an expensive endeavor. ARV treatment, they warned, was for life.

The tide of opinion, however, was beginning to change. The work of advocacy groups like the Treatment Action Campaign in South Africa had begun to change mind-sets, and an increasing number of AIDS experts and international political leaders were beginning to believe that it was no longer a question of whether ARVs should be provided in Africa, but when and how. Botswana would show it could be done. "We see before us the most dramatic experiment on the continent. If it succeeds, it will give heart to absolutely every country worldwide," said Stephen Lewis, the United Nations envoy on HIV/AIDS in Africa.[7]

Changing international public opinion, however, did little to influence the South African government, which became more intransigent on the issue as time passed.

"We have no plans to introduce the wholesale administration of these drugs in the public sector," Manto Tshabalala-Msimang told the South African parliament in June, two months after Botswana announced that it would begin providing treatment by the end of the year. "ARVs are not a cure for AIDS."[8]

WHEN SEELETSO came home from Gaborone, weak and sick, it was her cousin Brenda who guessed what was wrong. Brenda and her husband, Gill, who was born in Belgium but had become a naturalized citizen of Botswana, were among the first people in the village to take seriously the threat AIDS posed to their community.

In late 1998, one of Brenda and Gill's friends, Keitumetse, fell sick. In those days, AIDS was still not talked about in Otse, and they knew no one who had died of the disease. For Gill, watching Keitumetse die was a shocking experience. "It was for me the first living example of how HIV/AIDS works—how crude it is, how quickly it takes life." With her last words, Keitumetse begged them to look after her children.

Keitumetse's death was an eye-opener for Gill and Brenda. Newly sensitized to the problem, they began to see more and more evidence that the epidemic was growing. "We knew that there was AIDS, that it was there, and that it was killing people. But we didn't think it was here," Brenda said. Within a few years, however, there was no ignoring what was happening. "In those days, every weekend there were three, four, five funerals. Old people were still trying to take care of daughters and sons without gloves because they weren't provided. Quite a lot of old people became infected."

In 2001, remembering Keitumetse's last words, Gill and Brenda started inviting orphans from the village to come to their house on weekends. They erected a small tent where they played games with the children and gave them hot meals, made with food donated by shops in the nearby city of Lobatse. A few months later, in April 2002, they received a plot of land from the local chief and began building a center for the orphans. By 2004, when I arrived, it was a thriving center with six small buildings, gardens, and a playground.

In many places, as in Ingwavuma, organizations working with orphans spend the bulk of their energy and effort working to secure the children's material well-being, ensuring that they have enough food and clothing, as well as a roof over their heads. In relatively wealthy Botswana, the government sees to these most basic needs. Schooling is free, and the government gives generous food baskets to orphaned children. People in Botswana may be poor, but few are desperate.

Dula Sentle was left to focus on the emotional and social aspects of AIDS. There the children get the love and support they often lack at home. Gill saw it as significant, for example, that by late 2005, not a single one of the older girls had become pregnant.

Brenda—who was also known as Mago Shaba, which means "mother of Shaba," after her eldest son—also tried to help her own family come to terms with the epidemic. When Thabang was only a few years old, she began to fear that he might be positive. The little boy, who had been cared for by family members while Seeletso was in Gaborone, had always been sickly. He suffered from diarrhea and never seemed to grow. Thabang's poor health, combined with his disability, made him a huge burden on the family. When Seeletso ran away to Gaborone, her mother, Matlodi, refused to take care of Thabang. There was no one else in the house who could. Dineo, Seeletso's younger sister, was the only other girl, but she was too young and had to go to school during the day.

Thabang lived for most of that period with Seeletso's aunt, Gertrude, a serious, church-going woman who seemed to be the opposite of her sister Matlodi, who was often drunk. Seeletso's grandmother cared for Thabang during the day, and once, when he had to go to the hospital, she had to stay there with him even though she was old and frail herself. Matlodi often complained to me about how much trouble Seeletso had caused her by leaving Thabang behind. "This girl, she makes me suffer so much," she would complain, even though she had not been the one to take care of the boy.

At first, the family thought Thabang's sickness was related to his disabilities. Eventually, though, Brenda took Thabang to get tested for HIV. He was positive. When Seeletso came back to Otse, Brenda confronted her and encouraged her to get an HIV test too. It was better to know, Brenda told her, and not just to be afraid. The older woman had heard about the government's new program to offer free antiretroviral drugs, and she assured Seeletso that she could get help if she did test positive.

At first, Seeletso resisted. She didn't want to admit that she might have such a terrifying disease. In Botswana, AIDS was often called *phamoleate,* which means "it can kill you anytime."

She was also worried that if she did test positive, other people would find out. Few people in Otse in those days talked openly about the disease, and there was no one in the village who admitted to being infected. Even when people died and everyone knew the cause, no one said it aloud. Some families refused even to allow orphaned children they were taking care of to go to Dula Sentle because they thought people would think the children's parents had died of AIDS. Gill and Brenda tried to explain that Dula Sentle was for any orphans, no matter what disease had claimed their parents, but it was hard to change people's minds.

As she grew weaker, Seeletso became afraid that she might die. Finally, in late 2003, she agreed to go and get tested. She was HIV-positive.

17

A SECOND CHANCE

OTSE HAS A SMALL support program for people with AIDS called Home Based Care, located in a brand-new brick building next to the government-run clinic. The building, which was built with money from the village council and international donors, has a room with a television and pamphlets about AIDS, a few bedrooms, and an office, but there is rarely anyone there except the nurses. Outside, however, there is a garden and a small mobile building with a kitchen where food is prepared. Sick people, or relatives taking care of the sick, can come to collect meals there.

For the handful of HIV-positive people in Otse who were not afraid to be seen there, the Home Based Care center had become a de facto support group. Sometimes Seeletso went there for lunch or simply to chat with other HIV-positive people. They also gave her diapers for Thabang, although they rarely had ones for children, and she often simply made do with large ones designed for adults. She rolled these down at the top, but they still covered half his body.

After Seeletso tested HIV-positive, the nurses there also helped her and Thabang register for the government's antiretroviral program, called the Masa program; *masa* means "new dawn" in

Setswana. They took her to Princess Marina Hospital in Gaborone, which was then the nearest place where the drugs were being distributed by the government. A nurse drew Seeletso's blood to check her CD4 count, and she was told to return two weeks later. Her pink and blue health cards, which she keeps in a tattered manila envelope along with Thabang's, say the result was 200, just low enough to qualify for treatment. Seeletso says her CD4 count was actually 202, but that they wrote down 200 so she could begin immediately.

Even though she was very sick when she first came home to Otse, it took Seeletso a year to begin taking antiretroviral drugs. At first she had delayed getting tested. Then, after she tested positive, she delayed registering for the Masa program because it required that she have an adherence buddy—someone in her house who would help make sure she kept taking her drugs—and she hadn't told anyone in her family that she was HIV-positive. Finally, she told her mother, Matlodi, which she later regretted. When Matlodi got drunk, she would sometimes shout at her daughter and say she was a slut because she had AIDS.

Seeletso took four pills a day, two in the morning and two in the evening. She had to take them at 7 a.m. and 7 p.m. sharp, but the strap on her watch was broken, so she was always asking people the time. One pill contained a combination of two drugs, so altogether she took three different medications. Not very many years ago, the same treatment would have involved dozens of pills a day taken at prescribed intervals. But the treatment regimes for AIDS had become simpler over time.

Thabang drank his medicine, which came in a liquid form specially made for children. The nurses gave Seeletso a small plastic syringe that sucked the brightly colored liquid from a glass bottle. Thabang took the medicine straight from the syringe. He liked the taste and never complained.

When Seeletso first began taking the drugs, she became temporarily sicker than she was before. For two weeks, she lay in her bed, unable to move. A painful sore erupted over her right eye. The doctors told her that it was herpes zoster, which is caused by the same virus as chicken pox. Thabang too was sick when he started taking the drugs, a few months before Seeletso. He just lay there whimpering, and sores broke out all over his face.

Called immune restoration syndrome, this is a common initial response to antiretroviral drugs.[1] Both Thabang and Seeletso were so sick that their bodies had virtually stopped fighting off infections. When they started taking the drugs, their immune systems gained strength again but had to rid the body of all the foreign agents that had lodged there. A battle was being waged in their bodies between their immune systems and the microbes.

WHEN BOTSWANA began developing plans to provide treatment for people with AIDS, it had little guidance on how to do so. No other African country had tried anything similar; at the time there were probably only a few thousand wealthy patients on the whole continent who were receiving antiretroviral therapy. All of them were buying their drugs through private doctors or participating in research trials.

Outside of rich Western nations, only Brazil had a state-funded AIDS treatment program, and that program relied on cheap generic versions of the drugs, which African countries were under international pressure not to use. Brazil's program had been successful: between 1996 and 2002, HIV-related deaths dropped by between 40 and 70 percent, saving an estimated 90,000 lives and helping to avert 58,000 new infections. By the time Botswana began its program, 125,000 Brazilians had been treated with antiretroviral drugs by the government. But this was still a tiny percentage of Brazil's total population. Brazil and Botswana could hardly be more different. In Botswana, an estimated 40 percent of adults were infected, although many did not yet require treatment. Nowhere in the world had such a large percentage of a population ever been treated for a single disease.[2]

To a degree, the fate of Africa's 25 million HIV-positive people lay in Botswana's hands. If their program went disastrously wrong, it would seriously dent confidence in the possibility of such a large public health project. If rich Botswana failed, critics would argue, how could poorer, less-developed African nations like Mozambique, Lesotho, or Uganda possibly hope to roll out effective treatment programs?

In designing a universal ARV program, Botswana faced a number of hurdles. Procuring the drugs at reasonable prices would prove to be one of the easier aspects of the program. More difficult would be creating systems to distribute and track drugs, as well as to monitor patients. Like most African health systems, Botswana relied on patients to keep their own health records and to bring these with them when they accessed medical care. Given the fears about the virus developing resistance to antiretroviral drugs, the government and its donors felt that an integrated system needed to be developed that could track patients and their drug usage across the country. This required computer systems to be built and people to be trained to use them.

Botswana also faced a serious shortage of trained health-care personnel. The country had no medical school of its own, although plans had long been in progress to design one. In the short term, Botswana needed to recruit more doctors, nurses, pharmacists, and lab technicians in a market where such skills were in high demand. Like other African countries, Botswana struggled to compete against richer Western countries, who lured trained medical staff from the continent with promises of higher pay and better working conditions.[3]

There was no roadmap for rolling out an AIDS treatment program on this scale. No one knew, for example, exactly how many of the country's estimated three hundred thousand HIV-infected citizens would require treatment or how time-intensive it would be to treat each patient. One important measure of the program's success would not be simply how many patients were enrolled, but how well those patients adhered to treatment. Even in rich countries, many patients struggled to stick to their drug regimes day after day, month after month. Many experts worried that poor African patients, large numbers of whom were illiterate or lacked formal education, would be even less likely to keep taking their drugs appropriately. Botswana had to design effective ways of helping patients stick to their treatment, which started with educating them about the importance of taking their drugs regularly.

"Part of the Botswana lesson began long before they began to distribute ARVs," reflected Dr. Ernest Darkoh, director of operations for Botswana's antiretroviral program. "They learned about the importance of putting in good systems in order to build a program that would last and that would provide a uniform quality of care across the country."

For advice, the government turned to the international consulting firm McKinsey & Company. One member of the team sent out by the company was Darkoh, an American born to African parents. He had an impressive set of qualifications, including a Harvard medical degree and an MBA, and would end up staying for several years to help launch and run the program he had played a role in designing.

McKinsey estimated that just over 30 percent of the country's people with AIDS, or about 110,000 people, required immediate treatment. Clearly, however, the program could not immediately serve so many. Instead, administrators set a more conservative goal of treating 19,000 patients at four sites by the end of the first year. The general criterion was a CD4 count below 200 or an AIDS-defining illness. Even within these parameters, however, certain groups would have highest priority, including pregnant women and their partners, TB patients, children who had been hospitalized, and inpatient adults.[4]

According to the plan, patients would report first to a hospital site for enrollment, but would later be supported by a network of clinics with smaller staffs that could provide drug refills and deal with minor complications. As a bare minimum, each hospital site would require three doctors, a pediatrician, three nurses, three counselors, a dietician, a clerk, two pharmacists, and two pharmacy assistants. Supporting clinics would have smaller staffs and would refer more complicated cases to the hospital.

Lives were at stake, and despite the normally slow pace of bureaucracy in Botswana, the program came close to meeting the deadline set by Mogae in March 2001. The first patient began receiving ARV treatment in January 2002.

Just over two years later, Seeletso would arrive at Princess Marina with a nurse from Otse's Home Based Care program. By then, thousands of people in Botswana had been granted precious extra time.

ONE MORNING a few days after our tour of Otse, I found Seeletso sweeping her room with a traditional broom made of straw. It was a ritual Seeletso carried out every morning. Thabang sat outside in his Winnie-the-Pooh stroller, straining to turn his head to see what his mother was doing inside. When he saw me, he began waving his hands up and down in excitement, hoping that I would come play. He hated being left alone in his stroller.

I often forgot how old Thabang was, since he was so small. Only his head was normal-sized, but it was perched on the body of a baby. One of Thabang's nicknames was "Matchsticks" because his legs were so skinny. It was also hard to know exactly what was going on in his mind since he couldn't speak. He could answer yes or no questions: he would shake his head to say no and grunt to say yes. But since he looked like a baby, the family usually treated him like one, asking him simple questions and playing games with him that you might play with a one-year-old. "*O batla dijo?*" Seeletso would ask. "Do you want food?" Or she'd ask him where his nose was and he'd point to it and laugh. Little things made Thabang happy: food, attention, playing in the dirt. When he was sad or angry, though, he would look up angrily with big, doe-like eyes framed by long, feminine lashes.

That morning was laundry day, and Seeletso had gathered together a huge pile of dirty clothes to be washed. She had been taking her drugs for only a month, and she was still skinny and frail. But there was work to be done and no one else to do it. Most of the housework seemed to fall to Seeletso. Her two youngest siblings, Pona and Dineo—who everyone called MaPhiri—were at school all day, and her older brothers disappeared early and came back late. They didn't have jobs and spent most days drinking or smoking *dagga*, marijuana.

Matlodi rarely helped either. Often she spent the day drinking, although Seeletso said she had gone that morning to chase baboons away from the family's fields. I wondered who had done the cooking and cleaning before Seeletso returned from Gaborone and who had done it when she was too sick to be of much help.

I offered to help Seeletso with the laundry. She looked at me skeptically and asked if I knew how to do laundry by hand. I confessed that I did not and told her she would have to teach me how. She seemed to like this idea—over the next year I would discover that in general she liked being in charge—and began to instruct me on what to do.

We set up three big tubs in a row and filled them with water. In the first, Seeletso put some washing powder and dumped in a small pile of clothes. She scrubbed each piece vigorously and then handed it to me, soapy and wet. My job was to rinse, once in each bucket, and then wring the clothes out and hang them on the line to dry. Before long, the water in all three buckets was brown and soapy and my back ached. It was hard work, and I wasn't used to leaning over washing buckets. My arms too were tired and sore. Only a month earlier, Seeletso was practically dying, yet by then she had more energy than me. Clearly, my life was too soft.

Seeletso's health seemed to have improved in even the few days I had known her. The day she had showed me around Otse, she had tired easily after walking only a short distance. Now she was lugging heavy washing buckets filled with water. Her spirits had improved too. When we met, her hair was tangled and wild, but she had brushed and braided it together with thick, maroon strands of yarn. The effect was Medusa-like and not particularly attractive, but Brenda saw it as a sign of progress since it was the first time in many months that Seeletso had taken the time to do anything with her hair. The ugly bruise over her right eye, which a few days before had been covered in a dried yellow crust, was less noticeable too, and she had taken more care with her clothes. She had put on a yellow skirt, a shiny, black rayon shirt, and fake diamond earrings.

Since she started taking the drugs, Seeletso said, she had stopped smoking and drinking, although she still kept a small plastic container filled with menthol snuff in her pocket. As we washed the laundry, she occasionally rubbed her hands dry and put a small amount of snuff on the back of her hand, between her thumb and forefinger. "This is what old men do," she said laughing, as she sniffed it. When she did this, Thabang would imitate her and bring his own hand to his nose, pretending to sniff.

Thabang started crying and Seeletso asked him if he was hungry. He grunted, "Mmghhh," and smiled with his big eyes. We stopped washing, and Seeletso showed me how to make sorghum porridge, called *bogobe*. She took a scoop of white sorghum and put it in a plastic container and then added water, which she allowed to slowly soak through. When the fire was hot and the water she had placed on top began to boil, Seeletso slowly added the sorghum paste to the water and stirred. Then she let the pot sit. After twenty minutes, it was thick and gooey, with a yeasty smell. She put some in a bowl for Thabang and stirred in some peanut butter.

Almost all the food in the house came from the government, which gave both Thabang and Seeletso large food baskets each month. They received flour, sorghum, fruit, milk, peanut butter, tinned meat, vegetables, and some soap. The food was nearly enough to feed the whole family for the entire month.

I finished feeding Thabang while Seeletso returned to the washing. Thabang was a lot of work, like a baby. He couldn't do anything for himself and cried if he was left alone and no one paid attention to him. After school, when Seeletso's brothers and sisters and the other neighborhood children were around, it was easier for her. The other kids were good with Thabang. They would carry him around on their backs and play little games with him. If they had a little money to buy sweets or chips from the shop down the street, they always shared with him, sometimes even biting off small amounts of chewy candies for him to suck on. The whole family knew that he was HIV-positive and that he was taking antiretroviral drugs, but no one seemed worried about catching the virus from him.

After he began taking ARV drugs, Thabang was always hungry. He woke up in the morning crying for food. The boy's stomach was like a clock, and Seeletso said she never needed to set an alarm to make sure that she woke up by seven in order to take her medicine and give Thabang his. "I always wake up before seven because this boy wakes up before seven," she says, tickling his stomach affectionately. "He wakes up at half six. When he wakes up, he pulls my hair." If she didn't respond, he would start to cry.

The hunger was a side effect of the drugs, and both Thabang and Seeletso were gaining weight fast. Before, they could hardly hold down any food and were plagued by diarrhea. But the diarrhea had disappeared, and their bodies seemed ravenous for nutrients. Every time I came to visit, Thabang was eating, and Seeletso spent half her day cooking food for him and feeding it to him. He couldn't hold a spoon, so she fed him like a baby, although he could hold small pieces of bread or orange and eat these himself. He couldn't control his hands or tongue well, though, so he always made a huge mess, and by the end of the day he was covered in juice and crumbs.

Thabang also still wore diapers. Seeletso wasn't very good about changing him regularly, in part because she wanted to conserve diapers. Thabang was so used to it that he didn't complain about sitting in his own urine and feces.

I was often frustrated by Thabang's state of cleanliness, especially since Seeletso often handed him to me to hold. More than once, his diaper leaked and he peed all over me. The first time this happened, I experienced a twinge of fear that I could get infected from him. It was unlikely, I knew: urine, like saliva, contains only very low levels of the virus and antiretroviral treatment reduces the virus to almost undetectable levels. But even though I wasn't going to catch AIDS from Thabang, being peed on is unpleasant, and I sometimes refused to carry or hold him unless she cleaned him up first.

Staying clean at Seeletso's house, though, was not easy. The yard served as the living room and kitchen for Seeletso and her family. It was also a playground for the children and the main place of socialization for adults. When I returned to my hotel, or to Dula Sentle, after a day with Seeletso, I was always filthy, my clothes and hair covered in dirt. But I had the luxury of a hot shower.

I understand why Seeletso didn't wash Thabang more often, although it offended my sense of cleanliness. It was not a matter of simply running a tub. She had to build a fire, heat water, and then carry the warm water into the house. The whole process usually took more than an hour. When she did bathe Thabang, though, he loved it. He was so small that his whole body fitted into the small metal washing tub that the family used. He would splash and laugh happily, and then cry when Seeletso tried to take him out. Usually he was dirty again after only a short time. If she had known the story, Seeletso would probably have identified with Sisyphus, condemned in Hades to endlessly roll a heavy stone up a mountain.

Seeletso told me that she thought Thabang was disabled because she had had an accident when she was five months pregnant. One night she was out with friends who started to drive away without her. Seeletso chased the car and tried to grab hold, but missed and fell on her stomach. Afterward, she went to the clinic, where they treated her for a cut, but they didn't check the baby.

Brenda later told me a slightly different version of the story. Seeletso did fall off the car, she said, but it was because she was very drunk. She had tried to chase the car, but it zoomed away and she fell. Ultimately, though, Brenda believes it was the alcohol that made Thabang the way he is. "It was the alcohol, one hundred percent," she said.

Sometimes, Brenda said, she wondered whether it was a good thing that Thabang was getting better. "Sometimes I think it would be better if he would just go. He is suffering, and he is making Seeletso suffer too. She is the only one who is taking care of him, all by herself. There is no one to help her; not even her mother helps her." But Thabang seemed to have a great will to live. He had been sick his whole life, in and out of the hospital, with high fevers and mysterious diseases. "That boy refuses to die," she shook her head. "I swear, he will outlive us all."

Many months later, when I went with Seeletso to see an orthopedic doctor at a nearby hospital, the doctor told us Thabang had cerebral palsy, a neurological disorder caused by damage to the part of the brain that controls muscle movement. Usually the damage occurs before or during birth, so perhaps the fall did indeed cause his disabilities.

With Thabang, though, it is impossible to determine how much of his condition is due to the cerebral palsy and how much to AIDS, which has stunted his growth and made him weak. Seeletso also drank heavily during her pregnancy, and Thabang's face bears some of the distinctive characteristics of fetal alcohol syndrome, which can cause mental impairment.

18

FORGOTTEN CHILDREN

Not long afterward, tragedy struck the Isaacs family twice in quick succession. Just a day after I had helped Seeletso do the laundry, Brenda's mother died of a heart attack in Johannesburg, where she was employed as a domestic worker. Less than a month after that, Seeletso's grandmother passed away.

There was a ritual to death and mourning in Botswana. Both times, as the news spread through the family, relatives gathered at the house of Seeletso's grandmother. For days, until the funeral, friends and family would spend their time together, eating and drinking. The night before the burial, which usually occurred at dawn, everyone stayed awake the whole night, cooking and singing. The Isaacs family was comparatively prosperous—Matlodi's branch was the poorest by far—so a cow would be slaughtered and cooked into stew in giant cast-iron pots.

There was grief, certainly, especially on the day the news was heard and the morning of the burial itself. But funerals had become so common that they had also become central to village social life. Around the cooking pot, as we huddled near the fire in the bitter cold, there was more gossip than sorrow. "Funerals are our only entertainment these days," Brenda once told me sadly as we drove one evening to Ramotswa, a nearby town, for the funeral of an acquaintance. She could stay for only a short while, though, since she was expected at another funeral in Otse.

When her grandmother died, Seeletso called me in Johannesburg, and I drove to Otse to pay my respects at the funeral. By the time I arrived, the night before her burial, the whole family had gathered at the old woman's house to prepare the funeral feast, but I found Seeletso at home alone with Thabang. She was sitting on the single step leading to her room, with her knees to her chest and her head in her hands. She had gained weight and her face had filled out. The bruise over her eye had almost disappeared. At first I thought she was simply waiting for me, so she would not have to walk across the village.

As I approached, Seeletso burst into tears. "My body is weak," she sobbed. I had never seen her like this before. Thabang was sitting in his stroller, watching us curiously. Seeletso had dressed him and herself for the funeral but, exhausted, had not been able to muster the strength to walk to her grandmother's house, which was almost a mile away. I was worried, but didn't know if it was serious. When I offered to drive Seeletso to the clinic, she refused. She wanted to go to her grandmother's house, where her family was preparing for the funeral, to see if there was any food there. She had eaten nothing all day because she was too weak to cook.

Seeletso could barely walk, much less carry Thabang. She kept tripping, and at first I thought it was the high heels on her shoes that were causing the problem. We went to the funeral, but there was no food there yet, so I cooked her some pasta and took her home to bed, before returning to the funeral myself. Seeletso was usually loud and boisterous, but that day she barely said a word. She had no energy to banter with her cousins or play with Thabang. Even Thabang seemed to understand that something was wrong and was unusually quiet.

No one in Seeletso's family seemed to notice that she was sick. Everyone was busy with the funeral preparations. Seeletso was too weak to build a fire and cook for herself, and I wondered if I had not been there if anyone would have made sure she and Thabang had something to eat and drink. Perhaps she would have simply lain at home, helpless for days, while her family put her grandmother to rest.

That evening as we prepared food for the feast, Matlodi told me Seeletso had disappeared for several days the previous week and not taken her medicine. She had left Thabang at home, saying she was going to visit friends for a few hours. Three days later she returned and said she had been in Gaborone. "Hmmph," Matlodi responded when I told her that Seeletso was at home too sick to come to the funeral that evening. "I hope she is scared so she won't run away again and leave us with that boy." Matlodi seemed more concerned about being left with Thabang than about Seeletso's health.

The next day I picked Seeletso up and drove her to the funeral, but she was too weak to even leave the car. She watched the burial of her grandmother through the window. I brought her a plate of food, which she picked at halfheartedly, and then took her to the clinic, where they took her temperature and gave her some aspirin.

I had to return home to Johannesburg that afternoon—I had come only for the weekend for the funeral—but was worried about leaving Seeletso alone. So, after the funeral, I left her in the care of Mmauwi, a wild, freckled little girl who lived next door and who attended Dula Sentle. "Will you stay with Seeletso and Thabang until Matlodi comes home?" I asked Mmauwi. She nodded gravely. We pulled a mattress into the sun for Seeletso and Thabang to lie down on, and I made my farewells.

A few days later, I called Brenda to see if Seeletso was feeling better. Mmauwi had stayed with Seeletso as I had asked until, worried, she had gone to find an adult.

Seeletso was taken to the hospital, where she was diagnosed with anemia, caused when the number of red cells in the blood falls to an abnormally low level. Seeletso was given a blood infusion and prescribed a new mixture of antiretrovirals. The doctors suspected that her anemia had been caused by one of the drugs in her three-drug cocktail.[1]

Several days later, she was home again and feeling better. I, however, felt extremely guilty for leaving her. I had no idea that she was so ill. But I secretly hoped Seeletso was sufficiently scared by the episode that she would not stop taking her drugs again. I also pledged to give Mmauwi a special treat when I returned, to reward her for keeping her promise.

UNLIKE SEELETSO, Thabang had no relapses in those first months. In fact, he seemed to be thriving. His diarrhea stopped and he started to gain weight. He grew stronger and became more alert, as well as more demanding. When I had met him in May, he was as helpless as a baby. Within a few months, he became more lively and interacted more with those around him. By the end of the year, he was sitting up by himself and could walk across a room with Seeletso holding his hands for balance. He didn't like playing that game for long, though, as his muscles were weak from a life-time of disuse, and after a short time he would demand to be carried again.

Seeletso had been told that with intensive physical therapy, Thabang might one day learn to walk by himself, although his doctors doubted whether he would ever talk. Thabang's access to the appropriate care, however, was limited. There was a physical therapist who lived in Otse and who had offered Thabang free therapy, but for some reason Seeletso had stopped taking him there. We had been due to visit the therapist the day Brenda's mother died, but that was the last I ever heard of that. Whenever I brought it up again, Seeletso always dismissed my questions with a wave of her hand.

The hospital in the nearby town of Ramotswa sent a nurse to check up on Thabang once a month and do exercises with him. They had given him a wheelchair, but Seeletso never used it because it was too large and Thabang slipped out through the bottom. They also gave her a wooden contraption that was supposed to help him learn how to sit up, but Seeletso used it as a table and stored her and Thabang's medication there.

Seeletso wanted, desperately, for Thabang to be more independent, but she lacked the self-discipline to ensure that he got the special attention he needed. Even the most dedicated and organized of parents in her situation would likely have struggled, and Seeletso, then just twenty-three, was hardly the most stable of mothers. It was as much as she could handle to keep him clothed and fed and his prescriptions filled.

Brenda said AIDS had matured Seeletso, and in those early months, happy to be alive, she had stopped drinking and smoking. But she was still young and felt chained to Thabang, who would probably require constant care and attention for the rest of his life. When she was with him, she was an attendant and doting mother, and I have no doubt that she had come to love him. "You can never get bored with Thabang because he is always doing something silly," she told me once. But he was also exhausting, and at times she became overwhelmed, Her response then, as when she was a teenager, was simply to run away.

Even without physical therapy, however, Thabang was undergoing a miraculous transformation. The drugs had given him a second chance just in the nick of time.

In mid-May I went with Seeletso to Gaborone, to the special clinic at Princess Marina for children with HIV/AIDS, which was a joint project between Baylor College of Medicine in Texas and the government of Botswana and funded by the international pharmaceutical company Bristol-Myers Squibb. Thabang was scheduled for a checkup.

We arrived early in the morning and joined the other mothers and their children waiting in the center's shiny lobby. The contrast between the facility and its patients was dramatic: the center itself would not have seemed out of place in America or Europe, but the African patients came from a different world. Many were traditional women who wore long skirts and kept their hair covered with scarves. There was a television and a small play area for the children, but most of the kids stuck close to their guardians and watched the television wide-eyed from a distance.

If Botswana's decision to provide treatment to adults with AIDS was revolutionary, its decision to offer antiretroviral treatment to children was even more so. Antiretroviral therapy for children with AIDS is even more complicated and more expensive than for adults. There was also far less data about how it should best be done, and until recently, little new research was being conducted. Since Western countries had never experienced a generalized epidemic of the sort Africa is facing today, there were always far fewer children there born with AIDS. Today, with the discovery that antiretroviral treatment could nearly eliminate the transmission of the virus from mother to child, there are few children in the West still being born with the virus.

In Botswana, however, there were thousands of HIV-positive children. Although in 2000 the government began a program to prevent the transmission of the virus from mothers to children, not all pregnant women were agreeing to be tested. And then there were those, like Thabang, who had been born before such a program became available to them.

Plans for a center to treat children with AIDS actually began independently of Mogae's decision to offer free antiretroviral treatment to adults, but those plans too would have gone nowhere without support from the president himself. The mastermind behind the plan to open a children's AIDS center in Botswana was a tall, striking Kenyan doctor named Gabriel Anabwani, who had first come to Botswana to help the country develop plans for a medical school. When those plans were put on hold, he joined the pediatrics unit at Princess Marina.

Anabwani, called "Prof" by his colleagues, is a specialist in pediatric cardiology, but he soon realized that what Botswana needed was an expert in childhood AIDS. In mid-1998, Anabwani began to see the first spurt of pediatric AIDS cases. The hospital had several cases of children who died of pneumonia. Childhood malnutrition, which had virtually disappeared, suddenly came back. In postmortems, the doctors realized that the underlying cause was AIDS.

Within a short time, he recalled, HIV-related cases were accounting for more than 90 percent of deaths in the pediatric ward and 60 percent of all admissions. "It was keeping other children out of our ward because we could only admit the sickest," he told me.

In late 1998, Anabwani met an American doctor named Mark Kline, who was a specialist in children and HIV at Baylor. Kline had medical students who wanted to learn how to treat children with

AIDS, and Anabwani had patients who needed treatment. They agreed immediately to begin a program to exchange staff and students. When Bristol-Myers Squibb agreed to provide funding, the cooperation expanded into a pilot project to see if children in a developing-world environment could be effectively treated with antiretroviral drugs. This project came so closely on the heels of new advances in treatment that the first drug regime they used combined only two drugs. Later they switched to the now-standard three-drug therapy.

By the end of 2001, the doctors were treating eighty children, but they had no space to expand. They were working out of a temporary building on the hospital grounds. By this time, the plan for adult antiretroviral treatment was in full swing, and Anabwani and Kline began hatching a plan for a special center to treat children with AIDS. After some debate about where the center should be located, the government approved the plan, and Bristol-Myers Squibb, which like other international pharmaceutical companies was under increasing public pressure on the AIDS issue due to the court case in South Africa, agreed to provide the bulk of the funding.

By the time the new building was completed in June 2003, a mixed American and African team of staff, headed by Anabwani, had been recruited to oversee the children's treatment. The Baylor/Bristol-Myers Squibb Children's Clinical Center of Excellence-Botswana was the first dedicated treatment facility for children on the continent; within a few years other clinics modeled on its success were being rolled out in a number of other African countries: Lesotho, Swaziland, Uganda, Tanzania, Malawi, and Burkina Faso would all soon have their own centers for children.

Seeletso and I waited at the children's clinic for a while before realizing that we had come on the wrong day. Thabang's appointment was the next month and Seeletso had misread his medical card. Had I not driven her to Gaborone from Otse, it would have been an expensive mistake. The bus to Gaborone cost 8 pula each way, about $2, a huge sum for Seeletso, who rarely had more than a few thebe—a hundred of which made up a pula—in her pocket. Matlodi usually refused to give her money to go to Gaborone, so Seeletso often ended up begging for change from Brenda or trying to catch a ride with Julia, one of her mother's sisters, who worked in town. She had absolutely no source of cash income of her own, although her food basket ensured that there was always enough to eat.

We were about to leave when one of the doctors asked if Thabang was feeling okay. I mentioned that he had been having a bit of trouble breathing recently, and the nurses whisked us away to an examination room to give him a quick checkup. The nurses all remembered him and treated him fondly. "That one, he was almost dead," one nurse told me, pointing to Thabang as we sat down. "Now, look, he is okay." It was a far cry from the kind of impersonal treatment most African patients receive at government centers. Thabang, of course, was a unique child and not easy to forget.

Later, as Seeletso sat holding Thabang, another nurse came to take his pulse and measure his breathing. As she put the cuff around his still thin but no longer boney arm, she shook it appreciatively, like a matron assessing a particularly nice piece of meat: "He is getting fat! Before he was so weak he could hardly raise his arm." The nurses could find nothing wrong with Thabang, so we bid them farewell and trekked to another part of the hospital to refill Seeletso's medicines.

Botswana's capital, Gaborone, is similar in size to Maseru. But the similarities end there. Where Maseru seems poor and rundown, Gaborone is neat and new. In the years before I began visiting, the city had experienced a building boom, and everywhere there were new office buildings, malls, and car dealerships. Today, the first thing you see as you enter the city is a giant shopping mall, filled with South African chain stores and surrounded by sprawling parking lots. Across the street is a Volvo dealership.

Every three months, often on separate days, Seeletso and Thabang had to go to Gaborone to refill their medications at Princess Marina Hospital, in the center of the city. Thabang went to the Children's Clinical Center of Excellence, while Seeletso went to a series of low, prefabricated buildings at the back of the hospital called the

Infectious Disease Control Center (IDCC), although the only diseases they treated there were AIDS and AIDS-related infections. The adult treatment center was always overcrowded, and often Seeletso had to wait all day to see a doctor or get new pills.

In theory, Dr. Darkoh told me, Seeletso was supposed to start using one of Gaborone's four designated clinics for follow-up and to refill her prescription, but the original model had not been implemented properly, and Princess Marina was overloaded with patients.

By September 2004, Botswana had opened twenty-three sites across the country, including two that were closer to Otse than Princess Marina. But because it had been the first, and because many people preferred the anonymity of a big center even if they had to travel long distances to get there, patients continued to go to Marina. Almost half the patients enrolled in Masa across the country, 10,000 out of a total of 21,000, received their care at Marina.[2]

But despite the long lines, Seeletso liked coming to Princess Marina because it gave her an excuse to come to Gaborone, where many of her old friends still lived. The hospitals in Ramotswa or Lobatse, two towns closer to Otse, would have been easier, but she preferred to keep making the journey to the capital, even if it took all day.

Seeletso's stories about the period when she lived in the capital were often contradictory. Brenda told me she suspected Seeletso had worked as a prostitute and that she was known there as Mma-Bosche, after a white South African woman who had been executed in Gaborone for murder. Brenda doesn't know how she got this nickname, but says maybe it was because she was the mistress of that woman's husband. Seeletso is offended by the suggestion that she was a prostitute, but vague about what exactly she did there. Once she told me she avoided having more children in Gaborone because she was abstinent. Later she told me about her various boyfriends during that period, one of whom was a rich man who went to jail for stealing millions of pula, the Botswana currency. Sometimes, she said, he would take her to a hotel. Seeletso seemed to have stayed in a surprising number of Gaborone's hotels.

The truth is likely somewhere in between. Seeletso probably did live by sex, but perhaps was not exactly a prostitute. She may have had a few regular boyfriends, such as the rich one who was now in jail, who helped her out financially. And she may have slept with men who hung out at the bars where she spent her evenings. Not all her friends in Gaborone, she admitted, were the most respectable of citizens. They were all "thieves," she told me once with a laugh, and many of them were now in jail.

I suspected that with Seeletso there was also an emotional component to her wild behavior. Her family life was terrible, and she often seemed desperate for attention and love. I also wondered how many men she had infected. As Thabang was born HIV-positive, she must have already been infected by the time she came to live in Gaborone.

The stories Seeletso told about Thabang's father were often also equally inconclusive. Seeletso said his name was Boiki and that he had moved to another village before Thabang's birth. Sometimes she said that he ran away when he found out she was pregnant, and at other times that he left because he had found a job and that he had come to see Thabang after he was born.

Brenda claims Seeletso doesn't know who Thabang's father is and that she was sleeping with many different men at the time, sometimes as many as three in a weekend. "She was just hoping to get money or something from them," Brenda told me one evening over a cup of sweet, milky chamomile tea. The day I met Seeletso, she and Brenda had joked that Thabang's father had been "hit by a train"—a local euphemism, I was told, for the fact that she didn't know where he was.

Seeletso, Brenda told me, was sleeping with men by the age of fifteen, going to local bars and meeting boyfriends. When she got pregnant, she didn't stop. It was only now, after her diagnosis, that she seemed to have calmed down.

On the subject of men, however, Seeletso was quiet. She did admit that she was indeed known as MmaBosch when she lived in Gaborone, but it wasn't because she was having an affair with a white man. Seeletso says they called her that because she had the figure of a white woman, with no behind. When I asked her which type

Botswana men preferred, she laughed and said they liked African women with big curves.

When we finished at the hospital, we went in search of some of Seeletso's old friends. She took me to the house where she had lived with Cynthia, located in a poor neighborhood called Bontleng. By the standards of almost any other African country, the neighborhood would have been considered prosperous. Most people still used latrine toilets, but the houses themselves were sturdy and made of brick, and the area was neat and not strewn with garbage.

We arrived at a house surrounded by a low blue wall, with a sign outside saying: "Traditional Doctor Ngaka." On the next line, was his name: "Doc: Gare Ya Setso," hand-lettered in green paint on a white board.

"Doctor Gare," a pear-shaped man with a short beard and a friendly smile, greeted us warmly and went to fetch his wife, a large woman with an ample chest. We were seated at a plastic table in the yard, in front of a wall of peeling blue paint. Seeletso said she lived with Cynthia in a room in the back, which the two girls rented for about twenty-five dollars a month. When she got sick, they took care of her and the doctor gave her traditional potions.

The couple had never met Thabang, nor did they know that Seeletso and her son were HIV-positive, though they may well have guessed. That day, however, Seeletso told them she had begun taking antiretrovirals. The traditional healer offered to treat Thabang the next time they came to Gaborone and said he thought he could do something to help the child's crippled body. Seeletso seemed amenable to the idea, but told Gare that Thabang was not supposed to take traditional medicines while he was taking antiretrovirals. Later, in the car on the way back, she complimented her friend's powers, telling me that he was a good doctor, by which I think she meant powerful.

Seeletso seemed to have equal faith in Western and traditional medicine. To her, they were equally mysterious, and both required a leap of faith. She believed in antiretroviral drugs because she knew of other people who had improved while taking them and had felt the improvement herself. Yet she had no real understanding of how they worked.

On the way back to Otse, I asked Seeletso if she knew what a virus was and how antiretroviral drugs worked. She said she didn't, but that she just had to trust the government. In stable Botswana, with its generous social welfare system, people tended to have high levels of faith in their government, but I wondered whether people in other, more tumultuous countries in Africa would be as trusting.

19

RIGHTS AND RESPONSIBILITIES

Botswana's antiretroviral program didn't expand as quickly as Dr. Darkoh and other government officials had hoped. They had predicted there would be a small initial surge of patients after the program was launched, as people who were already taking antiretroviral drugs through the private sector migrated to government clinics, where they could get the drugs for free. Later, as news of the program traveled, new patients would join.

Not as many private patients switched to the government program as expected, however, and new patients trickled in only slowly. By January 2003, a year after the program had been launched, there were fewer than five thousand patients enrolled in Masa. The number recruited was far short of the nineteen thousand the government had hoped to treat.[1]

People were also waiting until they were very sick before coming forward, which increased the chance that they would not survive the difficult early days of treatment. In the beginning, the average CD4 count of those enrolling in the program was 50, and many too sick to walk were brought in by relatives or in government ambulances.

It seemed that people were turning to the clinics only as a last possible resort, and many were not coming at all. Across the country, people were still dying every day.

Dr. Darkoh and other government officials were perplexed. They had assumed that once the government began offering the drugs for free, people would come forward to claim them. Indeed, their initial worry had been that more people would seek treatment than the fledgling program could accommodate and they had guidelines determining who would have priority. They speculated that the problem could be that people didn't know the program existed, but this seemed unlikely. Information about Masa had been on the television and radio. Besides, news traveled fast in Botswana, if not always accurately, through the vast interlinked networks of relations and acquaintances. It seemed there was a deeper problem. People in Botswana, it seemed, were still afraid to admit that they were infected, even if help was available.

In early 2003, enrollment in the ARV program did begin to increase steadily, but uptake was still below what had been expected. At centers that offered programs for mothers, many women were still refusing to be tested.[2] The government realized it had to do something to address people's deep fears about AIDS and to force them to confront the scope of the epidemic. Otherwise, Botswana would die. Conventional approaches, however, did not seem to be working.

In March 2003, just a month before Seeletso came home to Otse, an American researcher from the U.S. Centers for Disease Control who worked in Kenya proffered a controversial approach to the problem of stigma in a lecture at the University of Botswana. Dr. Elizabeth Marum and her colleagues argued that, in the context of AIDS in Africa, the balance between public health and individual rights has been skewed and that the emphasis on privacy, which was intended to protect people with AIDS from discrimination, had actually increased stigma by placing them in a special category.

In particular, they believed that the guidelines requiring specific consent and special counseling before a person can be tested for HIV discouraged people from learning their status. In order to slow the spread of the epidemic, Dr. Marum said, it was vital that more people learn their status. Efforts to provide treatment to the millions of Africans already infected could succeed only if people knew they were infected and came forward for treatment. That meant they had to get tested. The WHO had recently launched an ambitious program, dubbed the 3 by 5 Initiative, which aimed to put three million people in poor countries on antiretroviral treatment before the end of 2005.

In a paper published in September 2002 in *The Lancet,* Dr. Marum, well-known AIDS-researcher Kevin de Cock, and other colleagues had argued that the voluntary counseling and testing system that Africa had adopted from the West created a disincentive for people to learn their status. "Unlike other infectious diseases (e.g., syphilis and hepatitis B), for which consent for testing is implicitly assumed by virtue of medical consultation, and diagnosis is encouraged, the diagnosis of HIV infection has often been actively avoided," they wrote.[3]

The Kenya-based researchers proposed that African nations adopt a policy of routine or opt-out testing, where in certain circumstances patients would be given AIDS tests unless they specifically refused. Among those they suggested be targeted were pregnant women, patients at clinics for sexually transmitted infections, and anyone who presented at a hospital or clinic with a suspected AIDS-related infection. No one would be forced to take a test if they refused, but nor would they be asked for special permission. HIV, they argued, should be treated just like any other disease. A doctor didn't ask special permission to test a patient for tuberculosis, cancer, or any other potentially fatal disease.

"It should be normal for everyone to find out their status, and for this to happen we need to change social norms," Dr. Marum told the audience gathered in Botswana, which included Dr. Darkoh and many other prominent people involved in AIDS work in the country. "What we are saying in our article is that the special position we have given to HIV and AIDS contributes in a way to making it a shameful disease, not the opposite."[4] She suggested that Botswana, which had already broken ground by working to make antiretroviral treatment universally available, be the first country to implement a routine testing policy.

Dr. Marum and her colleagues echoed the concerns I had heard repeatedly from people involved in the AIDS fight in Lesotho, and her arguments found a receptive audience in Botswana. Dr. Darkoh and Dr. Khan, who was then director of the National AIDS Coordinating Agency, were soon both convinced. So was President Mogae. Within a few months, Botswana adopted an opt-out testing approach.

In fact, the United Nations had officially adopted a policy of routine testing in November of the previous year, but the idea was still so controversial that no one had yet put it into practice. In November 2002, a month after Dr. de Cock's first paper was published and at a moment when the prices for antiretroviral drugs were falling dramatically and treatment for people with AIDS in poor countries was becoming a possibility, AIDS experts at the United Nations had met to reevaluate international policies and agreed that a routine offer of testing should be made in health-care settings. But it would take almost two years, until June 2004, before UNAIDS made this position public by publishing new guidelines for testing. By that time, following the advice of the group in Kenya, Botswana had already implemented routine testing.

"Many ministries of health were and still are grappling with these issues, not quite knowing what to do, in a way waiting for permission to change and push forward with more routine and diagnostic testing," one member of the Nairobi team told me more than a year later, when support for routine testing was beginning to gain ground. "It either takes a senior leader like the president of Botswana or it takes the international organizations like the WHO and UNAIDS putting out a statement saying this is an okay thing to do."

WHETHER DUE TO the introduction of routine testing, or because more people began to see the positive effects of antiretroviral treatment, in 2003 and 2004, the number of patients seeking treatment for AIDS in Botswana began to increase exponentially. By September 2004, twenty-one thousand people were enrolled in Masa, and an additional seven to eight thousand people were receiving drugs through the private sector. Sparsely populated Botswana was treating more people for AIDS than any other African country.

In Otse, Seeletso and Thabang continued to grow fatter. Six months after she had enrolled in the program, Seeletso looked like a different woman. Her face had filled out, the ugly sore over her eye had nearly disappeared, and she had begun to get a potbelly. Her mother, Matlodi, declared that Seeletso had never been so fat. But as she grew healthier, Seeletso was also beginning to chafe more under the restrictions of her life.

I came looking for Seeletso one afternoon in the middle of September and found Matlodi home with Thabang and her sister Julia, brewing traditional beer from sorghum. Seeletso was visiting friends, but Matlodi promised she would come back soon.

"Seeletso has started to drink and smoke again," Matlodi told me as fat tears began streaming down her cheeks. "And she is seeing boys again. You must tell her to stop these things."

Summer had arrived and the cooking fire had been moved outside from a smoky metal shack. Thabang, who was sitting in his stroller with his feet almost touching the ground because he had grown so much, was fussing because he was hungry. Matlodi ignored him and continued to stir her pungent brew in a large orange vat the size of a trash can. "Seeletso doesn't know how to save money," Matlodi continued. "She just spends it all on drink and cigarettes."

With Matlodi, I could never tell whether she was truly concerned about Seeletso or simply worried that Seeletso would go away, leaving Thabang and taking her food basket with her. Sometimes, she seemed to be shedding a mother's tears for her oldest daughter. Then, suddenly, she would say something that sounded utterly selfish and uncaring.

It occurred to me that had she been born in the era of AIDS, Matlodi, like her daughter, would have been a prime candidate for infection. She was, by all accounts, a wild young thing whose first three children were all by different men. Like Seeletso, she also had a problem with alcohol.

Still, while mother and daughter were alike in many ways, Seeletso seemed to me to be the kinder person, despite her often tough exterior. She bossed me around, to my occasional annoyance, but was also protective of me and watched to make sure my purse was safe and that I was not being harassed too much by her relatives. She didn't trust her brothers. When we were at her house, she would always make me lock my car so that no one stole my CDs or the change in my ashtray. And although she did not always keep Thabang as clean as she should, she was gentle and playful with him. She was sometimes irresponsible, but never cruel.

Matlodi's behavior toward her children, in contrast, often bordered on the abusive. More than once I saw her beat Seeletso's younger siblings, Pono and Dineo, and Thabang was afraid to be left alone with her. If you asked him if he wanted to stay with Matlodi, he would look worried and shake his head no. Matlodi was also lazy. When she was at home, she would rarely get up from where she sat. Instead, she would issue orders to her children, telling them to fetch her things. Often, she spent the day half-dressed, and she never swept the room in which she slept with Seeletso's stepfather and her youngest children. Unlike Seeletso's room, Matlodi's was always filthy and covered in leftover food and dirty clothes. On normal days, she was loud and demanding. She was at her worst when she was drinking.

A few days later, the traditional beer Matlodi was making had finished fermenting. Matlodi opened shop, selling gourds filled with the pungent, yeasty beer to neighbors for 1 pula—about 25 cents—each. Even Seeletso and Seeletso's older brother, Moitlamo, who is known to everyone as "Clicks," had to pay for theirs.

One evening, I arrived looking for Seeletso and found instead a group of neighbors sitting around in her yard, drinking beer. The drinking had obviously been going on for several hours. The grandmother of Mmauwi, the orphan who lived next door, was there begging for beer. A tiny, wrinkled woman with child-sized hands, she had no money, but offered to work in return for a drink. The husband of Seeletso's friend, the woman with whom she watched the soap opera *Passions* every day, was also there. "I need you," he shouted at me, slurring his words. I said I had a husband in South Africa who was very jealous. He told me not to worry, we can use a condom. At this, Matlodi cackled. "Tell him you don't like to break up marriages," she laughed. The man, though, was very drunk. "I am very rich," he said, as if this would convince me. Later, Seeletso said the man was a notorious womanizer, but that, incredibly, his wife didn't know.

Mmauwi came over with her younger sister, Moetsi. The older girl was dressed in a white dress and I told her she looked pretty. She beamed at me, but Matlodi snorted. "This one? This one is not beautiful. It is Moetsi who is the beautiful one." Mmauwi looked crestfallen and ran away.

Matlodi began to pester me about how much money I had. She demanded to know what I paid for my car and how much my rent in Johannesburg was each month. I tried to avoid her questions. When she started demanding that I bring her presents, I decided it was time to leave.

IN EARLY SEPTEMBER, Thabang was admitted to a special school for children with disabilities in Mogoditshane, just outside Gaborone, called the Cheshire Foundation. He was five and old enough to go to school, but none of the ones in Otse were equipped to deal with a student with his special needs. Even the school at Camphill, the center for the disabled based in Otse, said he was too small and weak. He needed to be able to sit up by himself. Otse's social worker applied for a place at the Cheshire school, the only place in the country that could give Thabang the special care he needed.

Cheshire was a residential school, but Seeletso could bring him home on weekends if she wanted. She was excited, both for Thabang and because she would finally be free of the heavy daily burden of caring for him, although she also worried he would be lonely and confused there without his family. Still, she thought it would be the best thing for everyone if he went there.

On September 9, Seeletso packed Thabang's medicines and clothes and went with Brenda and Gill to take him to the Cheshire school. She bade him a tearful good-bye and then went home to Otse in high spirits.

The next day, however, Brenda received a call from the headmaster. Seeletso must come and pick Thabang up, he told her, but gave no other explanation. When Brenda and Seeletso arrived at the school, the headmaster took them into his office and told them that the school did not have the capacity to deal with an HIV-positive student. He gave all sorts of excuses, saying that Thabang might bite another student or one of the teachers and that they didn't have a trained nurse to administer his medication.

Brenda was angry and told the man that it was against the law to discriminate against people with AIDS, but he refused to change his mind. Brenda worried that if they left him there, Thabang would be neglected or abused, so they took him back to Otse. Thabang didn't understand what was happening; he was just angry with Seeletso for leaving him. Seeletso was sad and a little bit embarrassed. "I was hurting so much," she said. She said she had never before experienced any discrimination because she was HIV-positive.

Back in Otse, Brenda called the Botswana Network of Ethics, Law and HIV/AIDS (BONELA), an organization that worked on legal issues related to AIDS. The lawyers there agreed that Thabang had been unfairly discriminated against and offered to represent Thabang and Seeletso. If they had to, they would take the case to court.

Unlike in South Africa, where special laws specifically prohibit discrimination against HIV-positive people, in Botswana there is no explicit legal protection for people with HIV/AIDS. The country's constitution, however, does include a right to nondiscrimination that BONELA had previously argued should include protections for HIV-positive people. The courts, though, had largely hesitated to hand down rulings on the basis of constitutional rights. In labor cases in which the organization was representing employees who had been fired because of their status, the organization had often won on technicalities. Usually when someone was fired because he or she was HIV-positive, the legal process for dismissing the employee had not been properly followed. While such cases benefited the one fired, helping the worker to get compensation or his job back, they did little to advance the larger cause of rights for people with HIV and AIDS.

At the time BONELA took on Thabang's case, it had another big case heading to the country's high court that could potentially establish greater protections for HIV-positive people. The case involved an HIV-positive woman who was selling fat cakes outside a school. She was suing the principal of the school for telling students not to buy her cakes because she was HIV-positive. BONELA argued that the principal had violated her rights by telling students to boycott her stall.

Despite Botswana's supposed commitment to ending HIV-related stigma, BONELA believed the legal framework in the country did not adequately protect people against discrimination. Not only were there no specific laws prohibiting discrimination in employment or access to public services, but there had also been few test cases in the courts to establish legal precedent under the existing laws. This was due in part to Botswana's culture of nonconfrontation.

Unlike in South Africa, where there was a long tradition of protest against injustice rooted in the antiapartheid movement, in Botswana people had never gone into the streets to protest against discrimination or demand better treatment. Most people in Botswana had little sense that they had rights to which they were entitled by law. They had even less of an idea of how to fight for such rights or to complain when they had been violated.

Without Brenda's guidance, Seeletso too would likely have simply just accepted Thabang's expulsion. She was not by nature a fighter, nor would she have known how to contact BONELA. She certainly felt wronged but could not have articulated that feeling in any practical way. Her life, in her mind, was full of wrongs about which nothing for the most part could be done.

THE WEEKEND AFTER Thabang returned home from the Cheshire Foundation, a beauty pageant had been scheduled in the Otse community hall, and Seeletso's cousin Lizzie was competing. There was also a funeral, for a little girl who went to Dula Sentle. The girl's mother had died several years earlier, and she had lived alone with her father, who expected her to do most of the cooking and clean-ing. One night, the girl forgot to open the door when she cooked dinner on a gas-fired stove. The gas burned up all the air in the room, and the girl suffocated.

That was the official story, anyway. But at the funeral, the night before she was buried, there were whispers of foul play. The girl, who was twelve or thirteen, had recently tested HIV-positive. Her mother had died of AIDS some time before, but she seemed too old to have caught the virus from her mother at birth. Nor had she been sick as a child. Some of the guests at the funeral suspected that the girl had been sexually abused by her father and that he had killed her because he was afraid she would tell someone. People said the father just didn't seem right at the funeral.

Seeletso didn't know the girl well, but she dropped by the funeral with me to hear the gossip and see friends. Brenda was there, as were all the girl's school friends, many of whom were still dressed in their uniforms. Some of them I recognized from Dula Sentle.

We didn't stay long, though, because we weren't dressed in the right clothes. At funerals women are expected to wear skirts and to cover their heads, and even Seeletso, who was usually careless about her appearance, felt that it was disrespectful to stay dressed as we were. She was also anxious to get ready for the pageant, which was a major local social event. We had bought some hair extensions in Gaborone a few days earlier, and her cousin had promised to put them in for her before the evening's activities began.

The extensions Seeletso had picked out at an Indian-run store in Gaborone were curly with a bright red tint. A friend braided them as we sat outside the house of Seeletso's aunt. When it was done, Seeletso looked faintly ridiculous, like an African Shirley Temple, her face bordered by bouncy, red curls. But we all said she looked beautiful.

Seeletso was in high spirits. We had left Thabang at home with her sister Dineo, and Seeletso had a rare evening of freedom. Over the previous days she had been moody and withdrawn. I had learned by then that when she was unhappy, she withdrew into herself and said little. She was still upset about Thabang's rejection from the school, but at the time, the bigger problem seemed to be her mother's drinking. All week Matlodi had been selling traditional beer from the house and drinking a fair amount too. Seeletso often bore the brunt of Matlodi's drunken tempers, though Pono and Dineo also suffered. Sometimes, relatives told me, Matlodi would scream at Seeletso and tell her it was her fault for getting AIDS.

Seeletso told me she wanted to get a plot from the *kgosi*, or traditional council, and to build her own house. But houses cost money to build and Seeletso had none. Brenda said she might be able to help, and Seeletso asked me if I would contribute as well. I told her she must get a plot first and then we'd see. She had also been begging me for a cell phone, which seemed the stronger and more immediate desire. Getting a plot wasn't a difficult process. She simply had to find an unclaimed piece of land and then fill out an application for it at the *kgosi*. The months passed, though, and she never went.

That evening, however, Seeletso was preoccupied with other things. She planned to sing a song at the pageant, something by Dolly Parton. She was demonstrating her dance moves when Lizzie showed up in a panic. The pageant was just hours away and she still didn't have a dress.

Another cousin, Serwalo, immediately offered to lend her one, a clingy, silver thing, but Lizzie was skeptical. She tried it on but declared that it made her look fat. Lizzie needed shoes too, so as the sun set, we headed off in my car in search of an outfit. For almost three hours we drove around Otse—which is a tiny place—looking for various friends who might have a dress and shoes. Lizzie's panic increased as the hours ticked by. I was getting tired and becoming annoyed at playing taxi driver. My cell phone, which ran on credit purchased in the form of scratch cards from stores, was almost out of airtime because the girls kept using it to call friends to see if they were home.

Depressed, Lizzie finally settled for Serwalo's silver dress. For shoes, she commandeered mine, which were just black sandals and not very fancy, but better than anything else available. I was left with borrowed flip-flops.

It was almost eleven and the pageant was scheduled to start in an hour, at midnight. But Seeletso and Serwalo assured me that it wouldn't begin for hours. They decided it was time to introduce me to A Thousand Days, the nightclub by the highway. Neither girl had any money, though Serwalo had stolen some Black Label beers from her mother. This, however, seemed to be their usual state. They said they always managed to find someone to buy them beers. As we set off, I was sure that this time they were thinking it would be me.

Seeletso and Serwalo guzzled their beers by my car before we went into the bar. Inside, it was already packed, especially the small courtyard at the back, where the music was thumping. Seeletso immediately began harassing me for money to buy a drink.

Usually I didn't mind paying for things. But in this instance I was uneasy. The doctors had told Seeletso that it was a bad idea to drink while taking antiretroviral therapy. She also seemed unable, or unwilling, to drink in moderation. She had already drunk one large beer and seemed determined to keep drinking until she had reached oblivion. I felt trapped. While it was not my place to tell her how to live her life, I didn't want to contribute to her self-destructive behavior.

In the end, I took the coward's way out and told her a white lie, which I'm sure she saw through, saying I only had a few pula, which we needed for the entrance fee to the beauty pageant later that evening. Seeletso disappeared for a short while; when I next saw her, she was swaying to the music, clutching a beer in one hand and a cigarette in the other. She had no sense of rhythm but didn't seem to care. She was having more fun than I had ever seen her have.

I could easily see what drew Otse's young to this bar. The beat was good and the mood carefree. When I was Seeletso's age, I liked to drink and dance during a night out on the town; it was fun, and in Otse, fun is something that is often in short supply.

I was well aware, however, that there was a seedy underbelly to this seemingly harmless pursuit of a good time. Like Seeletso, most of the young women there, in their skin-tight pants and revealing tank tops, were poor. They relied on men to buy them drinks, which rarely came free. The only currency the young women had was sex, and it was often with sex that they paid. As I looked at the crowd, with the young men dancing together in small groups, their hips jerking to the music, and young women whispering conspiratorially on the edges, I tried to imagine the vast sexual network that must link all these young people together and the fertile breeding ground the virus must have found there. "The girls there, they will sleep with anyone for a few drinks," Brenda's younger brother told me later that night. Seeletso, he said, had the reputation of being just such a girl.

I quickly grew tired of the bar. I was stone-cold sober and probably the only one in the room who was. Shortly after midnight, I dragged an annoyed Seeletso to the community center, where the pageant was supposed to be starting. She insisted that it wouldn't begin for hours and, when we arrived, was proved right. None of the contestants had even arrived yet. We went off in search of Lizzie and found her still working at the Carousel, a small bar across the street from Dula Sentle. We wandered aimlessly through Otse for a while. I was determined not to end up back at A Thousand Days. When we returned to the community center, it was nearly two.

A woman was teaching the contestants how to walk like models and they were prancing around the empty building in a long line, like ballerinas learning a new dance. Seeletso, who was slightly drunk, joined the end of the line and began to mimic their movements in an exaggerated pantomime. The other girls ignored her.

Seeletso's cousin Serwalo arrived with her boyfriend, a man at least fifteen years older who couldn't seem to keep his hands off her. He was chubby, not particularly attractive, and married. Serwalo was strikingly beautiful, with a small, pert nose, smooth skin, and a body with curves in all the right places. She had just finished high school and was applying to go to university in South Africa. I couldn't see what she saw in him. Brenda later told me that the whole family had tried to convince her to stop seeing him, but she had refused. His last girlfriend, Brenda said, was HIV-positive. "All that girl is going to get is AIDS," Brenda concluded with a shake of her head. When Serwalo asked me the next day what I thought of her boyfriend, I told her that I thought she could do much better. She just laughed.

By half past two, a crowd began to gather outside the community center. A woman came around and asked us to pay the admission fee, which was 2 pula a person. I had only a 10-pula note, and she had no change but promised to return when she did. A little while later, I saw Seeletso drinking another beer; she had taken my change and used it to buy herself another drink. This was uncharacteristic of Seeletso. She would sometimes ask for money, to buy spices if we were cooking together or for some chips for Thabang. But she had never before taken any from me. I was tired and annoyed and decided that it was time to leave.

20

BREAKING THE SILENCE

I<small>T TOOK A LITTLE BOY</small> not much older than Thabang to put African AIDS in the international spotlight and give a sympathetic face to the suffering of millions. The stories of Thabang Isaacs and Nkosi Johnson, a young South African also born in KwaZulu-Natal, bear strong parallels. Like Thabang, Nkosi was born HIV-positive to a poor mother and, like Thabang, was denied admission to school because he was HIV-positive. In one significant way, however, their stories diverge: Nkosi died for lack of antiretroviral drugs. Thabang, born more than a decade later, had been given a second chance at life, in part because of the battles that Nkosi fought.

Born February 4, 1989, to a poor mother in rural KwaZulu-Natal, Nkosi was placed into a hospice at a very young age. He was adopted by a white woman with red-hennaed hair, Gail Johnson, who took him to live with her in Johannesburg. In 1997, at the age of eight, Nkosi was refused admission to his local elementary school in the Johannesburg suburb of Melville, where he lived with his adoptive mother, because he was HIV-positive. Gail Johnson took the case to the courts, and Nkosi Johnson eventually won the right to go to school, becoming in the process a powerful symbol of the human toll of the virus.

At the Durban AIDS conference in June 2000, just a few days after Mbeki had questioned whether poverty or AIDS was felling his people, a frail, eleven-year-old Nkosi took the stage and offered, in his tiny child's voice, the most chilling indictment of the South African government's failure to give antiretroviral drugs to pregnant women with AIDS, then the most significant issue on the agenda.

"I hate having AIDS because I get very sick and I get very sad when I think of all the other children and babies that are sick with AIDS," a skeletal Nkosi told an audience of ten thousand AIDS activists and researchers from around the world. "I just wish that the government can start giving AZT to pregnant HIV mothers to help stop the virus being passed on to their babies." [1]

The microphone looked huge next to the little boy's face, and the audience grew silent in order to better hear his words. He wore a diaper and was so small that his belt had an extra six holes punched into it. [2] His words, however, moved people around the world. Less than a year later, on a day that had been designated International Children's Day by the United Nations, Nkosi died quietly at home.

The Durban conference, and Nkosi's speech there, marked a turning point in the battle against AIDS in Africa. While there had been a growing sense of urgency in the public health community about the increasing scope of the epidemic in the last years of the 1990s, that had yet to translate into greater funding or more serious political attention. AIDS was still seen as a tragic, but largely intractable problem.

With the end of the Cold War, the developing world—and Africa in particular—had declined in geopolitical significance, and the flow of aid to the continent dwindled. As Western countries moved away from the politically driven criteria of previous decades, there was also increasing emphasis on funding programs with proven results that could be measured and quantified. With AIDS, the statistics looked bad across the board, and there were few prevention programs that could meet such criteria and little political will to pour more funds into what seemed to be an endless black hole.

The Durban summit, held in a country that had more HIV-positive citizens than any other country in the world, brought into sharp focus the enormity of the crisis and heightened the sense that the world had a moral obligation to do something, anything. Nkosi Johnson and other HIV-positive Africans who went public there also gave the epidemic a new, and perhaps more sympathetic, face. In the West, especially among conservative Christians in America, there had still been a lingering sense that this was an epidemic of choice. But just as Rock Hudson, Ryan White, and Magic Johnson had given the American epidemic an identity that ordinary citizens could identify with, Nkosi Johnson humanized the epidemic in Africa. His tiny voice echoed across even the vast cultural divides that lay between Africa and the West. In the years that followed, right-wing Christians in America would become one of the most powerful lobbies demanding that more attention be paid to the issue.

Durban marked a turning point in the fight against global AIDS. The emphasis prior to that point had been on preventing new infections, something no one was quite sure how to do. At Durban, the focus turned to treatment, which suddenly seemed possible. At the conference itself, the mood was exuberant. A bold new activism, previously unseen in global AIDS, took center stage. "The 60s are back," commented UNAIDS director Peter Piot.[3] The challenge ahead would be enormous, unmatched by any public health effort in the history of the world. Yet for the first time in decades, there seemed to be something tangible that could be done to save lives. The barriers standing in the way of treatment—international drug companies, reticent governments, and stingy international donors— made easier and more comfortable targets than the amorphous confluence of culture, poverty, and ignorance responsible for the spread of the epidemic.

In the months following Durban, a wave of new international initiatives were launched to strengthen efforts to fight the disease. Later that same month, at the G8 summit in Japan, the world's great powers agreed in theory to dramatically increase the amount of funding to combat global health problems such as HIV/AIDS, tuberculosis, and malaria. By April of the following year, at an AIDS summit in Nigeria, rich countries had agreed to create a single fund to coordinate global efforts against disease; although the fund was not created specifically to fund treatment for AIDS, that would eventually become one of its major goals.

The United States government, under its new president, George W. Bush, was among the first to contribute to the new Global Fund to Fight AIDS, Tuberculosis and Malaria, promising $200 million a month after its inception. Within a very short period, however, Bush would expand his ambitions for America's role in fighting the epidemic, but choose a more unilateral method of meeting his goals. The President's Emergency Plan for AIDS Relief (PEPFAR), a $15 billion pledge over five years, bypassed the Global Fund and other international institutions. Launched in 2003, this plan too emphasized treatment, with more than half of the funding set aside for antiretroviral programs. But, to the anger of international AIDS experts and activists, it created an entirely separate bureaucracy.[4]

Within a few years after Durban, the entire mood surrounding AIDS had changed, and there was a new urgency and optimism as billions of dollars poured into AIDS-related programs and doctors fanned out across the continent launching treatment programs. Botswana led the way, becoming the first country to launch a national treatment program, but other countries soon followed. Only South Africa continued to question the need for government-funded antiretroviral treatment. Even after promising in November 2003 that it would launch a nationwide treatment program, the government continued to drag its feet. While the drugs began to become available in government hospitals, the country's health minister, Manto Tshabalala-Msimang, a medical doctor, promoted an alternative AIDS treatment consisting of olive oil, beetroot, and African potatoes.[5]

Although the WHO's target to treat three million people by the end of 2005 went unmet—by the end of the year just under a million people in the developing world were receiving treatment for AIDS, less than one-third of the stated goal—AIDS was no longer an automatic death sentence. In countries like tiny Lesotho, where more than a dozen sites were treating AIDS by the end of 2005, or Botswana, where more than fifty thousand people were enrolled in Masa by the same time, the difference was palpable.⁶ The drugs, however, could only prolong life. They could not cure the disease or solve the conditions of ignorance, poverty, and despair in which it flourished.

IN THE LAST MONTHS of 2004, Seeletso seemed to ricochet wildly between happiness and despair. At times she was thankful simply to be alive and threw herself into caring for Thabang. She talked about her plans to get a plot and how she would get a job when Thabang was finally admitted to the Cheshire Foundation. I was less optimistic about this happening anytime soon: if the case did go to court, it could take years to complete. In her darker moments, Seeletso too seemed to realize that salvation was not just around the corner.

Seeletso was also increasingly falling back into her old bad habits. The snuff she had taken up when she stopped smoking disappeared again, and she had started to bum cigarettes off anyone who would give them to her. Seeletso's drinking binges were also becoming more and more frequent. She would leave Thabang with whoever would agree to watch him and then sneak off for the night with Serwalo or other friends.

Then, on October 29, Seeletso disappeared. She took the bus back to Gaborone and slipped back into her old life in Bontleng. I don't think the trip was planned. She didn't pack a bag or tell anyone where she was going, and as when she had run away the week before her grandmother's funeral, she took nothing with her when she left, not even her medication. Later, she said even she hadn't known how long she would stay away: an afternoon, a few days, maybe a week. In the end, she was away for a month and came home only when her brother Clicks, who lived in Tlokweng, a border town near Gaborone, came to fetch her.

Back in Otse, Matlodi was furious and worried. "I was frightened, so frightened," she told me tearfully when I returned to Otse, a few days after Seeletso came home. "You must talk to her, give her good counseling," Matlodi begged me. "People have told her that if she drinks these pills and smokes and drinks, it will take her to heaven. If she stops taking her pills again, they won't give them to her again and she will just die."

When I asked Seeletso what happened, she was sheepish and told me that she went to "relieve stress," but could give me no further explanation. Perhaps she was unable to explain it to herself. There seemed to be in Seeletso two powerful, contradictory forces at work: hope and despair. One part of her was desperate to live and grateful that she had been given another chance. This rational side of her knew that the destructive lifestyle she had lived before had put her in the situation that she then found herself in, HIV-positive and saddled with a disabled child who would likely need care for the rest of his life. Yet the forces that drove her to that life in the first place had not disappeared. She was still poor, living with an abusive and alcoholic mother in a home where she was sometimes treated as much like a servant as a daughter. Her story, however, would have no Cinderella ending. No prince would come to rescue her from her drudgery.

Sometimes, I think, despair took over and she began to wonder if life was even worth living. Seeletso clearly felt trapped and could sometimes see no other option than to run away. I suspected too that she might have clinical depression, which exacerbated her struggle. She knew what she was doing was self-destructive, yet could not seem to stop herself. The urge to escape sometimes overpowered the will to live.

I recalled something that Dr. Darkoh had told me. "ARV treatment returns you to almost normal," he said. "But it doesn't fix all the underlying problems. The only thing I can promise is that we can keep you alive so you can keep on struggling with whatever it was you were struggling with before."

When Seeletso was in Gaborone, Matlodi had sent someone to the AIDS clinic there to ask them what she should do, since Seeletso was not taking her medicine. They told her to send Seeletso to see a counselor as soon as she reappeared. Her medical card from that visit reports that she looked fine, but that she was "uncommunicative." When questioned by the counselor, I suspect, she had simply gone quiet and retreated into herself. The staff instructed her to return in January and threatened to take her out of the program if she stopped taking her medication again.

For my part, I begged her to at least take her pills with her if she decided she needed another break from her life. I explained that the drugs might not work properly if she kept stopping and starting her treatment, and tried to impress on her why the counselors and doctors were so worried. I doubted that she would listen to my advice any more than that of her doctors or relatives, but I felt obliged to at least try. Seeletso, however, was in a dark mood. When I mentioned something that would be happening the next year, she mumbled darkly, "If I'm even alive then." I had never heard her so pessimistic.

"I don't know what is wrong with this girl," Matlodi concluded, exasperated. "She doesn't want to stay home and drink her pills."

"THESE PEOPLE ON ARVs, they eat too much," the young woman tallying my bill at Baratani Lodge, Otse's only hotel, said. She pointed to the receipt for a meal I had eaten with Seeletso and Thabang earlier in the day, which she had cooked and served us.

I was surprised. No one except her family was supposed to know that Seeletso was on ARVs or even that she was HIV-positive. I asked the woman why she thought Seeletso was taking the drugs. She said she had heard something at school, but that anyway you can tell just by looking at her.

The young woman also told me that she had a friend, who like her was just nineteen, whom she was sure was HIV-positive. At school, someone wrote on the walls that the girl had AIDS, and she said her friend had sores on her mouth that she thought were HIV-related. But the friend continued to deny that she was positive or to seek help. I asked if she would treat her friend any differently if she knew for sure she was HIV-positive. She sighed. "I wish she would just say, my friend, I have AIDS. Then I could help her."

The girl's friend, though, was still in denial. The previous night, the friend had come to Baratani Lodge, where a group of men from Gaborone had gathered for a bachelor party. She spent the night with one of the men, a married man.

The young woman at Baratani confided that she too had recently been tested. She didn't disclose the result to me and looked temporarily sad. She was just nineteen and about to go to university to study accountancy. She had a boyfriend, who was twenty-one, at the nearby police college. I told her it was brave of her to get tested and that even if she was infected, now there was help.

Even with the arrival of antiretroviral drugs, denial was still a powerful force in Otse. I wondered about this young woman's friend. Was she simply afraid to acknowledge that she might be infected, despite signs that were painfully clear to those around her? Or did she know, but feel afraid to confide in anyone? The human dynamics of AIDS are not as simple as is sometimes assumed in the plans for rolling out antiretroviral drugs across the continent. These decisions—to get tested, to seek help, to acknowledge fear—are not always made with the rational part of the mind.

When I was about the same age as the young woman at Baratani and her friend, I once participated in a class project about discrimination against people with HIV/AIDS. We decided that we would all get tested in order to better understand the dynamics of the process. Barring some freak circumstance or strange new mutation of the virus that gave it the power of transmission through new means, there was no possible way I could have been infected: I was still a virgin and had never had a blood transfusion. Yet I was terrified. In those days you had to wait weeks for your results, and I remember it weighing heavily on my mind. In the end, I was too afraid to go back for the results.

Conventional wisdom about AIDS has always held that people should not be forced to learn their status; they must choose to seek out the information. Life, however, doesn't work that way. We don't get to choose when disaster strikes, holding it at bay until we are psychologically ready. It comes and we must do the best with it that we can. There is no other disease, terminal or otherwise, for which a diagnosis is withheld because a patient feels she is not yet ready to hear the news.

I wondered if what that young woman's friend needed was someone to force her to face the fact that she might be HIV-positive, especially because she was endangering not only herself, but others as well. Here was a classic example of Dr. Marum's argument that, in the context of AIDS, we had struck the wrong balance between public health and individual rights. The "right" to privacy was in fact enabling her denial and the denial of an entire continent, and justifying the code of silence.

In Otse, as in many small communities, people often suspected when someone was HIV-positive. As antiretroviral drugs became more widely used, they guessed too when someone was taking them. People knew enough to recognize the signs: when the near dead began walking again and grew fat, it was easy enough to guess the cause. Yet many HIV-positive people still went to great lengths to hide their status.

In Botswana, HIV-positive people spoke about the Masa program in euphemisms even among themselves. When they were going to refill their medicines, they would say they were going for a "top up," borrowing the phrase they used for putting more airtime on their cell phone. Often too they avoided services available in their own communities, like Otse's Home Based Care program and support group.

Though Seeletso continued to travel to Princess Marina for her treatment, she generally seemed largely unconcerned whether people knew she was HIV-positive. She did not advertise the fact, and had not become an activist, but took few pains to hide it either. She kept her drugs on a shelf, where anyone could see them, even though many people were in and out of her room. Unlike many HIV-positive people in Otse, she also openly visited the Home Based Care center. Some of Seeletso's family, however, were more worried than she about what others might think.

One day when we were cooking lunch for Thabang, Clicks came running home in a rage, saying that he had heard that a picture of Seeletso and Thabang had been in *Time* magazine and that the article had said they were HIV-positive. "Everyone will know now that you have AIDS," he yelled. "*Time* magazine is worldwide. Worldwide!"

Seeletso hadn't seen the picture or article, though she remembered posing for a picture with Thabang and her grandmother several years before. She couldn't remember what it was for but wasn't worried. Brenda said that Clicks was just making a fuss; it was Seeletso's choice, not his, and that anyway the picture had been in *U.S. News & World Report,* not *Time.* I reminded Seeletso that the book I was writing could theoretically be published around the world too and asked what Clicks would think. She just shrugged. I had given Seeletso the option of appearing under a pseudonym, but she had always declined. "Maybe someone will read my story and want to help Thabang," she explained. I emphasized that there was no guarantee of that, but still she insisted.

Seeletso's comparative openness, however, remained the exception. The arrival of treatment in Otse had not brought a sudden end to the silence. By September 2005, Otse's Home Based Care program was helping eighty-nine HIV-positive patients, only ten of whom had begun taking ARV drugs. The rest were being monitored but had not yet qualified for the program because their CD4 counts were still too high. The nurses there, however, estimated that this was only a small percentage of the total number of HIV-positive people in the village. Seeletso and other patients who did come to Home Based Care said they often saw people from Otse in the AIDS center at Princess Marina.

"People don't want to come here because they think anyone who comes through the gate is HIV-positive. They are hiding from us," one of the nurses told me. "But the patients see other patients in Gabs and they tell us."

One patient estimated that there were five hundred people from the village on ARV drugs, a number with which Seeletso agreed. This seemed too high to me: it would mean that 7 percent of villagers, including children, were already taking ARV drugs. The government estimated that by this point, about half of the people in the country who needed the drugs were receiving them, but that only a small percentage of infected people had become sick enough to qualify for treatment. I guessed the true number was probably in the dozens, perhaps a hundred at the top end. At least two other relatives of Seeletso's, that I knew of, were taking drugs. But there were certainly many who were going on their own to get treatment and still hiding their infection from other people in the village.

"The Home Based Care, they have a problem, because people are afraid to go there," Seeletso told me one day as we drove away from the center. I asked why she wasn't afraid.

"There is no place to hide," she said with a shrug. "They know. They know."

ALTHOUGH TREATMENT hadn't suddenly swept away the silence and fear, it was saving lives, and the effects could be seen clearly in Otse.

"Sometimes, before, we would have four funerals in a weekend. Now there are weekends with no funerals and the funerals are for old people. Young people aren't dying anymore," Brenda said in early 2005 after a weekend when no one had been buried. Even on my sporadic visits, I noticed it too. On one of my first visits to Otse, in mid-2004, there had been five funerals in one weekend. A year later, there would often be none.

Gill and Brenda also noticed that the number of new orphans coming to Dula Sentle had decreased. When I first arrived, there were around eighty children enrolled in the program; not long before, Gill had predicted that they would have more than three hundred in a few years. New children were still being enrolled, but the flood had faded to a trickle. By mid-2005, they were helping more than a hundred children, but the growth had been steady rather than exponential.

Antiretroviral treatment hadn't stopped all the AIDS-related deaths in Botswana, but there were signs that, across the country, it was beginning to have an effect. Between 2003 and 2004, deaths in hospitals fell by 20 percent. The biggest declines were seen among people between the ages of 25 and 54—the prime ages for HIV infection and AIDS-related death—and in areas with the highest antiretroviral penetration.[7] There were still those who refused to be tested and died unwilling to admit the cause of their illnesses. Some people waited too long before seeking treatment, and there were others whom the drugs simply were unable to help. In those early days, about 9 percent of people who began treatment died.[8]

Men were often more stubborn than women in their refusal to acknowledge that they were sick; nationally, 64 percent of those enrolled in Masa at the end of 2004 were women.[9] Women outnumbered men in terms of the total number of infected, but not by so large a margin. "We have a problem getting the men to come forward," Dr. Darkoh said. "Everyone is insisting that we roll out more programs for women. There's a lobby around it. But it's the men we really need to target."

Still, more people were coming forward for treatment, and many were coming forward earlier. The median CD4 count of people joining the program was, initially, 50. By the end of 2004, it had risen to 86.[10] Most people, however, still waited until they began to be sick before being tested.

Doctors hoped that eventually people would learn their status long before they began exhibiting clinical symptoms. Then they would be periodically monitored and their treatment could be started as soon as their CD4 count fell below 200. Ideally, they might never become seriously ill. That, however, still seemed a long way away. The culture of denial and silence that had developed over more than a decade was slow to change.

Even if Botswana succeeded in virtually halting the number of new deaths from AIDS, many communities like Otse were already reeling from the impact of the ones that had already occurred. Few families were unscathed. Most had already lost members and many were taking care of orphans. In many ways, Otse was lucky. It was a comparatively prosperous village, close to the services offered in Gaborone. It also had Dula Sentle and Home Based Care, both of which had benefited from greater global funding for HIV/AIDS. Yet even there, society was under enormous pressure from the epidemic.

As in Ingwavuma, the large number of orphans was placing stress on many families. In Botswana, the stress was more social than economic since the country was generally more prosperous and the government provided a generous social welfare net. Families in Botswana did not generally go hungry, as the Mathenjwas did in Ingwavuma, but there was an increasing number of cases of abuse and neglect. In Otse too, families often fought over the orphans because of their food baskets.

Seeletso's next-door neighbors, Mmauwi and Moetsi, were members of one such family. They had moved to Otse after their parents died and lived with their grandmother, their older sister, and her young son in a crumbling, one-room concrete building that was among the poorest in the village. The kitchen was a shack of rusted metal leaning against the house. Most of the food in the household came from the food baskets they received from the government.

The girls' grandmother was a drunkard. Once, Brenda gave them some clothes that had been donated to Dula Sentle, but within a few days they were again wearing the same tattered rags. The grandmother later admitted to Brenda that she had sold those clothes for beer. Brenda suspected the grandmother sometimes sold food from their food baskets too. The girls' older half sister, Phena, was no better. Mmauwi, who was eight, complained that her sister beat her. More damaging than the abuse, perhaps, was the neglect. At home, no one took care of the two girls, and they were often left to fend for themselves. Moetsi was unnaturally grave for a child of five. Mmauwi was desperate for attention and clung to volunteers at Dula Sentle. "Can I come live with you?" she would beg in her broken English.

In early 2004, Phena began fighting with their grandmother over custody of the children. She wanted to take the two girls away to her father's home in Ramotswa. The fight went on for months. There were meetings with the social worker, at the village council, and among family members. Brenda wanted the children to stay in Otse, where at least they got two hot meals each day and had the staff at the orphan center to look after them. She had seen similar fights over other children and sometimes wondered if food packages for orphans are such a good idea.

"The only thing that they're fighting for, as far as I can see, is the food basket," she sighed.

In December 2004, the girls went to Ramotswa for Christmas

and didn't return when school began. For months, no one in Otse heard from them. Their grandmother left the village to care for her lands, where she planted corn and sorghum. Finally, in May, Seeletso and I went to track them down. We found them in a sturdy concrete house, painted blue, living with their blind father. They seemed healthy, and Moetsi was going to a day care program run by an organization of women with AIDS.

But Mmauwi complained that she had to do all the cooking and cleaning, and she and her sister slept on the floor with only a single blanket to share. "I want to live with my grandmother in Otse," demanded Mmauwi. "I want to go to Dula Sentle."

21

LIFE, BUT NO SOLUTIONS

Despite her fear of death, Seeletso was too restless to stay in Otse for long. She ran away again in January, though that time, at least, it seemed she had taken her medicine with her.

When I next showed up in Otse, in late February, Seeletso still had not returned. Matlodi told me that before Seeletso ran away, she and her daughter had been at their lands, where they grow their crops. Matlodi sent Seeletso to a meeting at Dineo's school in Otse, but Seeletso never returned. "Even now, I am waiting for her. She is still at that meeting," she said. Then she grew angry. "Who is going to take care of this child?" she complained, pointing at Thabang, who was lying on a gray blanket. Matlodi was paying Mmauwi's grandmother to take care of Thabang in the afternoons. The old woman, though, barely took care of her own grandchildren and was often drunk. More than once I had seen Moetsi, Mmauwi's five-year-old sister, bathing and preparing food for herself. "Maybe I will have to quit this job," Matlodi continued, bitter.

Thabang, who was wearing a T-shirt and nothing else, began peeing in the air, all over the blanket he was lying on. Matlodi simply laughed at him. Thabang laughed too, thinking it was a game.

But no one made any move to clean him up, and he sat there in his own pee.

Matlodi decided she had had enough, that it was time to fetch Seeletso. The next day, I went to Gaborone with Seeletso's cousin Terro in search of her. He had heard that she was back in her old neighborhood and could be found hanging out in the bars near the Pop-In, a small shop. In the bus on the way to Gaborone, Seeletso's cousin was frank in his assessment of the problem. "It's Thabang," he said. "She doesn't like that child." I disagreed. I think she loved and resented him in turns.

Bontleng, where Seeletso had lived, was a poor neighborhood, and the bars there were seedy and run-down. We arrived in the middle of the day, but many of the patrons had already been drinking for hours. Groups of men sat at plastic tables outside or danced, red-eyed, to the music of local bands played from scratchy speakers on portable stereos. "She's doing rubbish," Terro concluded as he glanced around. "That's why she's here. To do rubbish."

There were no women around, except for the bar girls who sold beer from large glass refrigerators. We asked the girl at one place, a bar with no name and a thatched roof, if she knew Seeletso. She shook her head no. Remembering that Seeletso's Gaborone friends had known her by her nickname, I asked if she knew a MmaBosch. "Oh that one," the barmaid said. "She comes here every afternoon. Maybe she will come soon."

We didn't have that long to wait and the girl didn't know where Seeletso was staying, so we moved on, hoping someone else could point us in the right direction. Eventually, a heavily pimpled girl at a phone stall in the parking lot said she knew where Seeletso was staying and gave us an address, house 1912 on a certain street nearby. "She was here yesterday, crying and saying she wanted to kill herself," the girl added as we left.

The house was a poorly built tumble of rooms set behind a blue metal gate. A fat woman was sitting in the yard, having her hair braided. I was about to ask the woman about Seeletso when I spied a flash of turquoise as it vanished over the wall. I realized it was

Seeletso, running away. Terro started to chase her, while I yelled at her not to run away. They both vanished from my sight and I wondered whether to follow. Before I could decide, however, they appeared at the end of the street.

When she reached me, Seeletso threw her arms around me and began sobbing into my shoulder. I let her cry. After about ten minutes, she wiped her eyes and groped in her pocket for a cigarette. She began to smoke silently. I sent one of the little boys who was hanging around to buy us Cokes from the nearby tuck shop and asked Seeletso what was wrong. She just kept smoking, without looking me in the eye. Terro asked her in Setswana if she was taking her medicines. She shook her head no. "I will take you to counseling at Princess Marina," he told her firmly. She just nodded.

Once again, I found it was time to step out of my journalistic role. Seeletso, it was clear, needed a friend. I was worried about her; there was clearly something seriously wrong. We strolled a short way away, to an open plot where there was a half-finished concrete wall. Seeletso sat down and started picking up rocks and throwing them aimlessly. She said she didn't know what to do. She asked me about Thabang and if he was okay. Terro was wrong. Seeletso did love Thabang; she just didn't always know how to express it.

"It's my mother," Seeletso finally said, bursting into tears again. "She doesn't even treat me like her own child." I had seen Matlodi in one of her drunken tempers and heard the stories about her behavior. But I thought there must be something else, something more immediate, that had led Seeletso to claim the previous day that she was going to kill herself. On this subject, however, she would say nothing.

"What do you want to do?" I asked. Seeletso said she wanted to go home, but she didn't want to live with her mother anymore. "I don't want to stay in that place," she said firmly. I suggested we call Brenda to ask her advice. Brenda said Seeletso could stay with Julia, Terro's mother. Seeletso agreed to this, but said she wanted to wash before we went back to Otse. As we walked back to the house where she was staying with friends, Seeletso seemed almost cheerful.

"Are you taking that one away?" the woman in the yard asked with a sneer as Seeletso went to wash. "I don't want her here. She's on treatment. She was sick before." I asked the woman why it would matter if she was on treatment. She ignored my question.

"I don't stay here, so I can't stop her. She stays with those girls, but she doesn't pay," the woman said, pointing at Seeletso's friends. "I want you to take her away." This time I ignored her.

When Seeletso returned, she had changed out of her turquoise top and put on one made of a clingy black material. She said she was ready to go. She took nothing with her but the clothes she was wearing, not even a handbag.

THABANG'S CASE against the Cheshire Foundation had stalled, in part because of Seeletso's repeated disappearances. While she was away the first time, BONELA had contacted the family and asked them to write a statement detailing what had happened at the school and outlining Thabang's history and needs.

Since Seeletso was missing, and no one had any idea when she would return, Matlodi eventually wrote a letter to BONELA on her behalf, but she had not been at the school that day and did not know the details. BONELA wrote a letter to the principal of the foundation detailing their concerns and asking him to explain its policy on HIV-positive students.

The foundation took months to respond, saying that they had to take the issue to their board and that they had been delayed by the Christmas holiday. When they finally did reply, they told BONELA that they had no facilities to deal with students on medications of any sort and that they had asked the Department of Health for a nurse to help administer medications, but until that request was processed they could not accommodate Thabang. In the meantime, they would offer Thabang assistance through their outreach program.

This excuse seemed strange to both BONELA and me, since many disabled students have other health problems that require medication. Seeletso said they were lying because when she dropped Thabang off, they asked her to fill out a form listing the medicines he was taking and when they should be administered. It was only when someone looked closely at this that they had realized that Thabang was HIV-positive.

BONELA was not convinced by the school's excuse either and wanted to pursue the case in court. But Thabang was still a minor and they needed Seeletso, his legal guardian, to agree to be the claimant. When they had tried to contact Seeletso, though, she was missing and no one knew where she had gone.

For months, a communication impasse held up the case. With Brenda's help, Seeletso had tried to call BONELA after she returned to Otse, but had not been able to reach the right person. They had difficulty contacting her in return because she had no cell phone and had been moving among different relatives. By May, still nothing had happened. I had planned to meet with BONELA in any case, so I set up an appointment and drove with Seeletso and Thabang to the organization's offices on the outskirts of Gaborone.

We arrived on a warm afternoon and were ushered into a small conference room with the organization's director and the lawyer who was handling the case. They had not yet met Seeletso or Thabang. They made us tea, gave Thabang some cookies—which he promptly made a mess of—and explained the status of the case.

BONELA, they told us, would be willing to take the case to court, but Seeletso had to be willing to allow her and Thabang's names to be used in the case. Unlike South Africa, Botswana did not allow claimants to file suit anonymously in order to protect their identities. If she proceeded with the case, she had to be prepared for publicity. If the case did go to court, the local media would likely report on the case and use her name, identifying her publicly as HIV-positive.

For BONELA, Thabang was a near perfect test case. The link between his expulsion from the school and his HIV-positive status was clear, as was the harm his exclusion was causing. The Cheshire Foundation offered services that Thabang could not receive anywhere else in Botswana. If the courts ruled in his favor, it could set an important legal precedent that could give people with HIV more protections against discrimination.

BONELA saw the courts as an important route toward establishing those protections. Although Botswana's government was progressive in many ways, including in its stance on treatment, it did not place the protection of individual rights in high regard. Even while Botswana was receiving international accolades for its AIDS treatment programs and its economic success, the country was being criticized for the forced removal of the Bushmen—also known as Basarwa—who lived in the Central Kalahari Game Reserve.[1] In June 2005, the government also expelled a seventy-two-year-old Australian academic, who had lived in the country for fifteen years, for his temerity in criticizing Botswana's electoral system, saying it was undemocratic because it essentially enabled the standing president to choose his successor.[2]

In the area of legal protections for people with HIV, BONELA argued, Botswana lagged behind neighboring countries. "There's not a good legal framework here," Christine Stegling, BONELA's director, said. "Stigma here is still a huge problem." There were also some areas of specific concern: one law, which had been upheld by the courts, gave higher sentences to HIV-positive rapists, even if they did not know they were HIV-positive when they committed the crime.

As she listened to the lawyers describe the process, Seeletso began to cry softly. She was, however, determined to proceed. Through her tears, she said that she wanted the case to go ahead, even if it meant that everyone would know that she was HIV-positive. Her motivations may have been partially self-interested. Only if Thabang went away to school and learned to be more independent could Seeletso ever have anything like a normal life again. Still, it was a brave decision.

In the car on the way back to Otse, Seeletso seemed more cheerful than she had been in months. She talked about trying to get a certificate for some training she had done at a local restaurant, so she could try to find a job. She also had an idea to start a car wash in Otse. "There isn't one in the whole village," she said, excitedly. It was the first time in a long time I had heard her make plans for the future.

I WAS GLAD TO SEE Seeletso happier, but wondered whether it would last. The old demons were still there inside, ready to emerge at the slightest provocation. Just a month before we met with BONELA, Seeletso had run away for a third time. At the time, she was still staying with her Aunt Julia, in the house that had belonged to her grandmother.

The story this time, I was told, was that Seeletso had had a fight with Brenda. Hoping to give her a little income and something to keep her busy during the day, Brenda had given Seeletso some work at Dula Sentle, cleaning and working in the garden. But when Brenda returned at the end of a day away, the staff complained that Seeletso had been taking food from the kitchen and that when they had confronted her, she had replied that she was Brenda's cousin and was allowed to take whatever she wanted. Brenda, however, disagreed and, when she heard the story, yelled at Seeletso, who ran off and cried all day. Seeletso claimed she was only taking tea and the staff were just being mean.

The incident seemed to blow over, but a few days later, after Brenda paid Seeletso for the work she had done, Seeletso again ran off to Gaborone. She said she was going to collect Thabang's medicine but never returned. Two weeks later, Terro and a social worker went to bring her home.

Julia, who was left with Thabang, was furious. "I'm telling you, I was ready to send her and the child away," she fumed to me. "Thabang ran out of medicine and I had to ask Home Based Care to take him to the doctor to refill it." The nurse came to take Thabang to Gaborone, and at the last minute, Julia decided to send Terro to go with them to bring Seeletso home.

"Why is Seeletso doing this?" she asked. "I have tried to understand what causes her unhappiness. Seeletso takes good care of the house. I thought she was happier here. I know my sister can be rude, but any mother who was treated like this would not allow it."

Brenda too was frustrated. She had thought the problem was Matlodi and didn't understand what Seeletso wanted now. "I can't help her if she's going to act like a child," she sighed.

Seeletso was equally silent toward me. She had no explanation for her behavior. I suspected that while things were better at Julia's—Seeletso said Julia was her favorite aunt—she still felt trapped by her life and by Thabang. Although there were more people around at Julia's, there was also more work for her to do. In return for staying there, she was expected to do most of the cooking and cleaning. She must have felt that she was destined for a life of drudgery.

Thabang was getting bigger and stronger everyday, but he was also increasingly difficult to care for. He was getting too big to carry and had outgrown his stroller, though Seeletso still used it. His fits of temper were increasingly bad as well, and he seemed more and more frustrated by his inability to communicate. When he got angry, he had begun to bang his head against the wall, and there was now a small lump on one side of his head.

By this time, he could sit up by himself and walk around with help. He still wasn't toilet-trained and Seeletso seemed unwilling, or unable, to teach him. It seemed easier to simply change his diapers than to carry him to the toilet. Home Based Care, though, was getting tired of endlessly supplying her with diapers and had told her they were cutting her off. Seeletso simply responded by using them only at night. During the day, Thabang would simply go wherever he was.

One thing was better about Julia's house, though. They had a television. While Seeletso had lost her interest in *Passions*—the people in it were bad people, she told me—Thabang could watch for hours, and its presence in the living room relieved her of having to entertain him all the time. All the children in the family would gather after school to watch cartoons, and they would take Thabang with them, which he loved.

OVER THE COURSE of 2005, AIDS treatment centers began sprouting across the continent, even in some of the poorest and most unstable corners: In the Democratic Republic of Congo, by the end of the year more than 6,000 people were accessing antiretroviral drugs. In drought-stricken Malawi, there were more than 30,000.[3] Even South Africa's government, which had resisted providing antiretroviral treatment for many years, had been forced to concede and was treating an estimated 100,000 to 140,000 people.

Yet, the need still far outpaced the supply and would continue to grow as those who had become infected later in the epidemic began to fall sick. Only a few countries, mainly Botswana and South Africa, made any pretense of trying to provide treatment to everyone who needed it. A national treatment program required a functioning national health-care system, something many African countries still lacked.

In most African countries, treatment was being rolled out only at a few small centers, funded with donor money and staffed largely by foreign doctors. While the quality of care at such centers may have been higher, they only reached a small number of people. Whether you lived or died depended on a quirk of fate: the place where you lived. They were also less sustainable. Botswana and South Africa are rich enough to keep funding their AIDS treatment programs even if foreign funding dries up; while countries like Lesotho and Malawi are not. Nor are these boutique AIDS programs contributing to building better health-care systems from which all citizens can benefit.

AIDS is today a trendy cause—perhaps too trendy—and there is more money being poured into it than can be adequately absorbed. A support group in Otse, for example, got a portable building and a brand-new refrigerator from the new Global Fund. According to Seeletso's calculations, the group had three members, who never met. She was one of them. Ingwavuma now has three different home-based care programs, all fighting for the same patients.

This generous flow of aid, however, will not continue forever. Some of the money is being wasted as donors try to push it out too quickly to meet ambitious targets, but I worry too what will happen to many of these programs when AIDS ceases to be the issue of the day. PEPFAR has promised to put two million people on antiretroviral drugs. Who will keep those clinics running when the program's five-year funding runs out? Anyone familiar with the international aid world knows that things go in and out of fashion, new projects open, run their course, and then close. Success is often no predictor of survival. Ann in Ingwavuma told me about a program she once worked on that provided regular deworming at primary schools. The program was highly successful and helped reduce malnutrition rates among students, many of whom were infected by the parasites. After ten months, though, the funding ran out and the program stopped. The same cannot be allowed to happen with antiretroviral treatment.

Still, the mass movement to bring antiretroviral treatment to Africa has done much to change global attitudes about the international community's responsibility to help poorer countries. The international complacency that dominated the 1990s, when the consensus was that there was nothing to be done, has been wiped away. Access to health care is, for the first time, being accepted as a basic human right.

BY THE END of 2005, Seeletso and Thabang were back at Matlodi's place, though they continued to spend a great deal of time at Julia's. Both were growing, Thabang taller and Seeletso fatter. She was, she joked, even considering going on a diet.

The case against the Cheshire Foundation, though, had stalled again, this time because the lawyer in charge had gone on maternity leave. Seeletso showed me a letter that BONELA had finally written to the school in late November, threatening legal action if Thabang was not readmitted. "We would like to point out that antiretroviral medication is easy to administer and does not need any special form of training," it said, and a response in fourteen days was demanded. Far longer than that had passed, but nothing new had happened. Legal deadlines in Botswana appeared to be theoretical at best.

Despite everything, Seeletso seemed more optimistic. She still talked about her plot, and the house she would build there, but on the other hand, she had done nothing to find one or register it, even though I had gone with her to pick up the form. Her idea to start a car wash seemed to have faded too. Now she was more interested in trying to get a job in a restaurant. I wanted Seelesto to be happier and would have helped her with one project or the other, but I could not build her house or start her business for her. I offered to help her fund one of the projects if she came up with a plan, but she never did. She had ideas, but little notion of how to bring them to life. As with her hopes for Thabang, it was not intention but will that Seeletso lacked.

Yet she had not run away for more than six months and seemed, finally, to have found some peace. I hoped it would last, but somehow doubted it would. I suspected that reason and emotion would continue to battle inside Seeletso for many years and that that was simply part of her nature.

Antiretroviral drugs hadn't saved her. They hadn't fixed the things that were wrong with her life or given her the power to control her darker impulses. Perhaps one day she will become resistant to the drugs and will finally succumb to the virus, but for now she fights on. Seeletso's life may often be tortured, but in her own way, she clings to it nevertheless.

"Don't forget us here. Thabang will miss you," she said, waving farewell as I pulled away from her house for the last time. "And send me a cell phone." She was clearly feeling better again.

CONCLUSION

WORLD AIDS DAY, DECEMBER 1, 2006

I LEFT SOUTH AFRICA in early 2006, but tried to keep in contact with Adeline, the Mathenjwas, and Seeletso. It was not always easy, especially since the Mathenjwas and Seeletso did not have cell phones. If I had been out of touch for a while, I would begin to worry that someone had died. Fortunately, that day has not come. The news that has trickled in has given me reasons for both hope and despair.

In early 2006, Adeline brought her son, Bongy, to live with her in Maseru so he could begin school. Adeline continued to work during the day—she found a new, six-month job working for the European Union—and to study at night. She didn't pass all her subjects in her accounting class, however, so had to repeat some of them the next year. But she was determined to pass and get her degree, even if it took longer than she had expected.

In the spring, to my relief, Adeline finally registered Bongy for the children's antiretroviral program at Queen II, which was supported by the Clinton Foundation, and not long afterward he began taking antiretroviral drugs. Adeline was amazed at the change in him. He stopped being sick and began to grow, fast. Adeline too was doing well. By the end of 2006, her CD4 count had risen to over 400. Perhaps the stress had been affecting her health. She was still waiting too for George to pay *lobola*.

In Ingwavuma, Sbuka gave birth to a daughter in May. She must have been pregnant when I said good-bye, though neither I nor Zethu realized it at the time. My parting fear that Sbuka was putting herself at risk, it seems, was justified. The father of Sbuka's daughter was a boy from the neighboring homestead. I was crushed that she had dropped out of school. Khanya too finally admitted that she would never graduate. She got a job as a housekeeper in a suburb outside Durban, which greatly improved the family's finances. Between her salary, her child grant, and Sbuka's child grant they were doing much better. They had given up on trying to get their foster-care grant.

There were other new children too. Ann Barnard got married, had one baby, and adopted another. She said she planned to have a big family.

In Otse, a few months after I left, Dula Sentle—which had been heralded at home and abroad as a model of orphan care—experienced a major crisis. The government of Botswana closed the center, and Gill and Brenda were suspended by the organization's trust, accused of failing to properly register the organization as a child-welfare group and to account properly for donor funding. In addition, the board claimed there had been allegations the Fonteyns had emotionally and psychologically abused children and staff. The center was closed and its buildings abandoned.

From my distant new home in Europe, I was unable to untangle these allegations. The last and most serious I have a difficult time believing. I spent many months in Otse hanging around Dula Sentle. I never saw any indication of abuse, nor did anyone I encountered there ever hint at such a thing. Certainly Gill could be a prickly character. He could be strict with the children and often fell out with people with whom he disagreed. He was also stubborn and a bit of a loner. I could easily see him locking horns with donors and supporters—he often complained about the excessive nature of their accounting requirements—and I would not be at all surprised if he had occasionally quietly bypassed Botswana's often maddening bureaucracy by not doing things exactly according to the letter of the law. I suspect, however—though I do not know for sure since an investigation into Dula Sentle's closure is still under way—that this simply provided an excuse for closing the center and that Gill somehow ran afoul of someone powerful in the government. In Botswana, in my experience, it was necessary to tread carefully. For their part, the Fonteyns denied the allegations and said the center's closure was political.

By the end of 2006, Dula Sentle had still not reopened, although the Fonteyns were continuing to assist orphans from their house. The closure of Dula Sentle, though, had trickle-down effects for Seeletso. Probably in part because Brenda was otherwise occupied and did not have time to follow up, the case against the Cheshire Foundation again stalled. Thabang had grown stronger, though, and could finally sit up on his own, so the school for the disabled in Otse, Camphill, had agreed to take him the following year. Seeletso looked forward to the new freedom that would give her; I was happy for her, but I worried a little that without the regular presence of Thabang, who seemed to be her main anchor to stability, she would again begin to flounder.

Without Brenda's assistance, Seeletso's economic situation became more precarious as well. Although she still received the government food baskets, Seeletso never had any cash and by late 2006 struggled to even find enough money to travel to Gaborone for her and Thabang's doctor's appointments. By then, Home Based Care had also run out of funding and closed, and so could no longer help her. The center's closure also left Seeletso without a source of diapers, though this did not seem to give her additional incentive to toilet-train Thabang.

More than a quarter of a century has passed since AIDS first burst into our consciousness, and it is clear that AIDS will continue to be with us for the foreseeable future. By the most recent estimates, nearly 40 million people around the world are infected, 25 million of them in

Africa. In all but a handful of countries, each year the infection rate continues to grow. A vaccine is still years away, and although we have made much progress in treating AIDS, no cure is yet on the horizon.

Still, over the past five years, new attention to the problems in Africa, and particularly to AIDS, has led to a flood of initiatives and money to the continent. Together, the largest of these programs—the Global Fund to Fight AIDS, Tuberculosis and Malaria, George W. Bush's President's Emergency Plan for AIDS Relief (PEPFAR), and the Bill and Melinda Gates Foundation—have distributed billions of dollars for AIDS relief. The issue has even become a bit of a cause célèbre, with everyone from American Express to Madonna launching AIDS-related projects.

Much good has come from this. Without this money, Seeletso, Thabang, Adeline, and Bongy would all likely soon be dead. By the end of 2006, more than two million people in poor countries who otherwise would have died had been given a new chance at life. We don't know yet whether they will have five years or ten or twenty, but each year, each day extra, is a small victory. The rapid distribution of antiretroviral drugs across Africa and other parts of the developing world demonstrates what can be done if the global community works together to combat a pressing problem and has proved wrong those who say the continent's problems are too vast and hopeless. The battle is far from over. Millions, especially children, still have no treatment or less than adequate access to it—and only a small percentage of infected women have access to antiretroviral drugs, so thousands of HIV-positive babies like Bongy and Thabang continue to be born each year. Still, the picture is less gloomy than it was even five years ago.

There is also a danger to this new focus on AIDS. The amount of money that is flowing into many African countries now is so large that it risks distorting local economies and even the ordinary human relationships that bind communities together. In many places there is so much new money that there is not enough capacity to absorb it. As I saw in all three of the countries where I conducted research for this book, in desperately poor communities even small amounts of money can give rise to enormous jealousy, corruption, and even violence. The stories of Positive Action, rendered ineffectual by its members' greed, of the orphans in Otse, fought over for their food baskets, or of the grandmother in Ingwavuma, brutally murdered after receiving a grant to develop a food garden, should be warning signals about the need for care in distributing such money.

In the haste to address what is undeniably an urgent problem, not enough attention has been paid to building lasting institutions, to protect against corruption and ensure effectiveness. All the energy, effort, and money expended over recent years will be wasted if, in the place of long-term solutions, only quick fixes are offered.

ACKNOWLEDGMENTS

THIS BOOK would not have been possible without the generosity and time of many people. My first, and greatest, debt is to Adeline, the Mathenjwa family, and Seeletso, who opened their homes and their lives to me. I thank them for allowing me to tell their stories. I am, and will remain, in awe of their courage and strength.

Many other people in Maseru, Ingwavuma, and Otse also shared their time and expertise with me. It would be impossible to name them all, but a special thanks goes to Chuck Quehn, Bolelewa Falton, and Koali Job in Lesotho. In Ingwavuma, Zethu Zikalala and Siphephile Mavimbela were invaluable guides and good friends. I'd also like to thank the staff of the Ingwavuma Orphan Care, especially Ann and Paul Dean (formerly Ann Barnard), Vee Dlamini, Thando Mbhamali, and Leigh-Ann Mathys, as well as Hervey and Beni Williams and Maryna Heese. In Otse, Brenda and Gill Fonteyn opened many doors, and first introduced me to Seeletso, Thabang, and the rest of the Isaacs family.

Many friends also lent invaluable moral support, as well as a critical eye, to this project at various stages in its gestation. Heidi Holland offered me a refuge from the chaos of life, which allowed me to complete the book. Adam Roberts—who was working on his own book at the time—was a wonderful ear to bounce off thoughts about the writing process. Anna Koblanck graciously shared some of her own research in Botswana and spent many hours with me discussing the difficulties of writing about AIDS. Thanks also to Ellen Rocco, Gael Lescornec, Challiss McDonough, Alexandra Zavis, Simon Robinson, and Laurie Goering for their support and advice.

I am indebted to my agent John McGregor, who set me on the path in the first place, and to Malaika Adero, my editor, whose careful eye caught many times when the tone of the writing was not quite right.

Finally, I am grateful to my parents, who taught me to care about the wider world. And to Barnaby, who kept me sane during the entire project and gave me confidence when my courage flagged. I know I would not have finished without your support and love.

NOTES

PART I: DENIAL · Maseru, Lesotho

Chapter 1: *Maleshoane*

1. The name *Lesotho* means "place of the people who speak Sotho." Collectively, the people of the country are known as Basotho, while an individual member of the Basotho nation is referred to as a Mosotho. The people of Lesotho speak Sesotho, or Southern Sotho, which is one of three branches of the Sotho language group. There are actually more speakers of Sesotho in South Africa, where it is one of eleven official languages, than in Lesotho, although South African speakers of Southern Sotho would not generally refer to themselves as Basotho. See the introductory notes of Stephen Gill, *A Short History of Lesotho from the Late Stone Age Until the 1993 Elections* (Morija, Lesotho: Morija Museum and Archives, 1993).

2. For an exhaustive history of Maseru, see David Ambrose's *Maseru: An Illustrated History* (Morija, Lesotho: Morija Museum and Archives, 1993). Current estimates of the population of Maseru—and Lesotho—vary widely, since most are based on data from the country's 1996 census and there are debates over how substantial the effect of AIDS and migration have been. The figure of 170,000 is from the United Nations Population Division. See *World Urbanization Prospects: 2005 Revision*, 26 October 2006, www.un.org/esa/population/publications/WUP2005 (25 November 2006).

3. Laurie Garrett, "Mandela Joins Battle on AIDS," *Newsday* (15 July 2000).

4. Tony Barnett and Alan Whiteside, *AIDS in the Twenty-First Century* (New York: Palgrave Macmillan, 2002), 32–33. Barnett and Whiteside, however, point out that there remains a great deal of debate about the average rate of progression from infection to AIDS and from AIDS to death. In the developed world it was believed that an average of ten years usually passed before

a patient progressed to full-blown AIDS. Without treatment, death usually followed within twelve to twenty-four months. In the developing world, where health care is generally poorer and infectious diseases more prevalent, the period between infection and illness was thought to be shorter, between six and eight years. But Barnett and Whitehead report that recent studies cast some doubt on that theory, although there does seem to be some evidence showing that in poor countries with underdeveloped healthcare systems death follows sooner after the advent of full-blown AIDS.

5. This is the official estimate of the country's population from the Lesotho Bureau of Statistics (http://www.bos.gov.ls/) based on extrapolations from the country's 1996 census. Many population experts, however, believe that this number may be too high. They question the method used in collecting the original 1996 data and believe that current estimates may not have fully taken into account the impact of AIDS and migration. Taking into account AIDS, the U.S. Census Bureau (www.census.gov/ipc/www/idbsum.html) puts Lesotho's population closer to two million.

6. CIA, *World Factbook,* 14 November 2006, https://www.cia.gov/cia/publications/factbook/geos/lt.html (25 November 2006).

7. According to the 2006 Human Development Report, Lesotho ranks 149th out of 161 countries around the world in terms of development. See United Nations Development Program, *2006 Human Development Report* (New York: Palgrave Macmillan, 2006). Information about Africa's percentage of the world's poor comes from Elsa Artadi and Xavier Sala-i-Martin, "The Economic Tragedy of the Twentieth Century: Growth in Africa," in *The Africa Competitiveness Report,* Ernesto Hernández-Catá, ed. (Geneva: World Economic Forum, 2004), 2.

8. Ministry of Health, Government of Lesotho, *Health in Lesotho* (Maseru, Lesotho: Ministry of Health, 1993), 19.

9. World Bank, *World Development Indicators 2006.*

10. Ntsau Lekhetho, "Fewer Lesotho Workers Needed in S. African Gold Mines," Reuters (Jun. 21, 2005).

11. United Nations Development Program, *Human Development Report 2005* (New York: Oxford University Press, 2005).

12. The statistic for Lesotho's HIV prevalence rate comes from UNAIDS/WHO, *AIDS Epidemic Update: December 2006* (Geneva: UNAIDS/WHO, 2006), 14. Unless otherwise indicated, throughout this text I have used estimates from the Joint United Nations Program on HIV/AIDS. These estimates are not uncontroversial and are based largely on surveys at prenatal clinics among pregnant women. Often the figures given are estimates of the total number of adults who are believed to be infected, but are mistakenly thought to be percentages of the total population. Since most African countries are disproportionately young, this is a large mistake. In addition, there has been a long debate about how representative infection rates among pregnant women are of the adult population as a whole, especially since there is increasing evidence that women are infected at higher numbers than men. As a result of these criticisms, UNAIDS has repeatedly adjusted the way it

makes its calculations and over recent years has slowly revised downward its estimates of infection rates. Despite these problems, there is no other source of comparative AIDS estimates. The statistics on orphans are from UNICEF, www.unicef.org/infobycountry/lesotho_statistics.html (25 November 2006).

Chapter 2: From the Place Where the Fishes Swim

1. The question of whether AIDS first originated in Africa was a deeply emotional one in the early years of the epidemic, especially for Africans, who felt that AIDS was somehow being blamed on them or that they were being accused of deviant behavior, such as having sex with monkeys. Today, however, there is little scientific doubt that the virus recently jumped to humans from two different populations of African primates. Scientists have learned much about the genetic structure of the virus and now believe that HIV-1 came from a simian immunodeficiency virus that affects chimpanzees, while HIV-2 came from sooty mangabeys. The only remaining debate, and one that we may never know the answer to, is when and how the virus first made the transition from monkeys to humans. Considering that many of the earliest cases seem to have come from Africa, it makes sense that the transition first occurred there. However, there are many perfectly ordinary explanations for such species transmission that do not involve strange sexual behavior. Edward Hooper's *The River* (Boston: Little, Brown, 1999) provides an exhaustive account of the evidence showing an African origin of the disease, although his ultimate conclusion—that HIV was first transmitted to humans through a contaminated batch of a polio vaccine—has been largely disproved.

2. For an account of the outbreak of AIDS in the United States, see Randy Shilts, *And the Band Played On* (New York: St. Martin's Press, 1987).

3. This case was retrospectively diagnosed and first reported by Rask's friend and colleague, I. C. Bygbjerg, in "Letter: AIDS in a Danish Surgeon (Zaire, 1976)," *Lancet* (23 April 1983): 925. For more in-depth accounts of her death, based on interviews with Bygbjerg and others, see Hooper, page 95, and Shilts, pages 3–7.

4. This case was first reported by J. Vandepitte in *The Lancet* on the same day as Rask's case. See J. Vanderpitte, "AIDS and Cryptococcosis (Zaire, 1977)" (letter), *Lancet* (23 April 1983): 925–926.

5. See D. Vittecoq, "Acquired Immunodeficiency Syndrome after Traveling in Africa: An Epidemiological Study in Seventeen Caucasian Patients," *Lancet* (14 March 1987): 612–615. Hooper also discusses these cases further on pages 94–97.

6. Jacques Leibowitch, *A Strange Virus of Unknown Origin,* translated by Richard Howard (New York: Ballantine Books, 1985), 22.

7. For an early report on the Haitian connection, see Lawrence Altman, "Five States Report Disorders in Haitians' Immune Systems," *The New York Times* (9 July 1982): D15. See also two later articles by Altman, "Debate Grows on U.S. Listing of Haitians in AIDS Category," *The New York Times* (31 July

1983): A1; and "The Doctor's World: The Confusing Haitian Connection to AIDS," *The New York Times* (16 August 1983): C2.

8. N. Clumeck, "Acquired Immunodeficiency Syndrome in African Patients," *Lancet* (23 February 1984): 492–497.

9. Vandepitte, 925.

10. B. Lamey et al., "Aspects cliniques et épidémiologiques de la cryptococcose à Kinsahsa: à propos de 15 cas personnels," *Méd Trop* (Marseilles) 42 (1982): 507–514.

11. Leibowitch, 23–24.

12. See CDC, "Epidemiologic Notes and Reports Update on Kaposi's Sarcoma and Opportunistic Infections in Previously Healthy Persons—United States," in *Morbidity and Mortality Weekly Report* (11 June 1982): 300–301.

13. Shilts describes in great detail the struggles of the CDC to fund early research into the disease.

14. See chapter 2, "Health Transition," in Laurie Garrett, *The Coming Plague* (New York: Penguin, 1995): 30–52.

15. To the surprise of many, Lesotho's 1966 election was won by the Catholic Basotholand National Party—which was allied with the country's traditional chiefs—instead of the more progressive Basotholand Congress Party, which had led the country's push for independence and had ties to Pan-Africanists and other national liberation organizations like the African National Congress in neighboring South Africa. But in 1970, just four years after independence, the BNP refused to release the results of a new election that would have toppled them from power. Over the next sixteen years, the BNP prime minister, Chief Leabua Jonathan, gradually consolidated power. For a more detailed explanation of these events, see Gill, *A Short History of Lesotho*.

16. James Smith, "Citizens Welcome Lesotho Coup with Dancing in the Streets," Associated Press (20 January 1986).

17. Alan Cowell, "Lesotho Expels 60 South African Insurgents," *The New York Times* (26 January 1986).

18. Alan Whiteside, *AIDS in Southern Africa* (Midrand, South Africa: Economic Research Unit and Development Bank of Southern Africa, 1990), 9.

19. In response to some of these criticisms, international monetary organizations are trying to make structural adjustment programs more "pro-poor." Although they continue to put conditions on poor countries seeking loans, more attention is being paid to the impact of macroeconomic restructuring on the poor. In particular, the IMF and the World Bank have revised their positions on user fees, agreeing that in some cases essential services like primary education and certain health services should be offered for free. Critics, though, still say not enough is being done and that international lending policies continue to hurt the poor. For an overview of the relationship between user fees, structural adjustment, and health, see Moa Råberg and Harry Jeene, *Selling Out Rights: How Policy Affects Access to Health Services in East and Central Africa* (London: Save the Children, 2002).

20. Ministry of Health, Government of Lesotho, 1993, 22.

Chapter 3: A Man Is a Pumpkin

1. One study among women at a prenatal clinic in Zimbabwe found that 65 percent of women there claimed to have had only one sexual partner in their lives, while another 22 percent said they had had only two sexual partners. More than 80 percent said they were in a monogamous relationship and were living with their partners. Yet their HIV infection rates were the same as the national average, indicating that for many women the main risk factor was being married. See Audrey Pettifor et al., "Early Age of First Sex: A Risk Factor for HIV Infection among Women in Zimbabwe," *AIDS* 18 (2004): 1435–1442. Similarly, a study in Kenya and Zambia found that infection rates were 10 percent higher among married women than among sexually active but unmarried girls, while a study in Uganda found that 88 percent of HIV-positive girls age fifteen to nineteen were married. See UNAIDS/WHO, *AIDS Epidemic Update: 2004* (Geneva: UNAIDS/WHO, 2004): 10. Data on the percentage of women with AIDS comes from UNAIDS/WHO, *AIDS Epidemic Update: December 2006.*

2. World Bank, *Confronting AIDS: Public Priorities in a Global Epidemic* (New York and Oxford: Oxford University Press for the World Bank, European Commission, and UNAIDS, 1997).

3. Elizabeth Reid and Michael Bailey, *Young Women: Silence, Susceptibility and the HIV Epidemic,* UNDP HIV and Development Programme, Issues Paper No.12, http://www.undp.org/hiv/publications/issues/english/issue12e.htm# Anatomy %20as%20destiny? (23 November 2005).

4. UNAIDS/WHO, *AIDS Epidemic Update: December 2006,* 10.

5. Hooper, 158.

6. Laurie Goering, "A Light in the Darkness," *Chicago Tribune* 26, November 2006).

7. For a detailed discussion about how HIV invades the body and destroys cells, see Hung Fan, Ross Conner, and Luis Villarreal, *AIDS: Science and Society, Fourth Edition* (Boston: Jones and Bartlett, 2004).

8. More than 90 percent of Basotho girls first have sexual intercourse with an older man, and in nearly half of those cases the age difference is at least five years. Lesotho Bureau of Statistics, *Reproductive Health Survey 2001* (vol. 1): 29.

9. Young African women are far more likely to be HIV-positive than their similarly aged male counterparts. Women from ages fifteen to twenty-four are three times more likely to be infected than men the same age, and in certain Southern African countries, such as South Africa, Zimbabwe, and Zambia, they are three to six times more likely. See UNAIDS/WHO, *AIDS Epidemic Update: 2004,* 87.

10. Lesotho Bureau of Statistics, *Reproductive Health Survey 2001* (vol. 1): 200–201.

11. T. D. Moodie first made the claim of widespread male-male sex in the mines in 1988 in "Migrancy and Male Sexuality on the South African Gold Mines," *Journal of Southern African Studies,* 14, no. 2: 229–245. There has, however, been very little subsequent study of this topic or its potential relationship to the spread of AIDS in the Southern African region.

12. Hugh Ashton, *The Basotho: A Social Study of Traditional and Modern Lesotho,* second edition (London: Oxford University Press, 1967), 62–63.

13. At the end of 2006, the Vatican was reviewing its stance on condoms and AIDS. See "Vatican's Office for Health Care Has Concluded Study on Use of Condoms in Fighting AIDS," Associated Press (21 November 2006).

14. American President George W. Bush's flagship AIDS program, the President's Emergency Plan for AIDS Relief (PEPFAR) earmarked one-third of prevention money, out of a total $15 billion of international AIDS funding promised over five years, for programs that promote abstinence.

15. Helen Epstein argues that reductions in AIDS infection rates have usually been associated with changes in sexual behavior—in particular a reduction in the number of partners—and that concurrent relationships put people at higher risk for infection. A man, she points out, is more likely to become infected by his long-term mistress than in a single encounter with a prostitute, and more likely to pass it on to his wife than to a casual partner. This theory is boosted by findings that an infected person is most contagious during the first weeks after exposure. Thus if many people were having sex with multiple people around the same time, the virus might spread quickly through these interlinked sexual networks. See Helen Epstein, "The Fidelity Fix," *The New York Times Magazine* (13 June 2004).

Chapter 4: AIDS Strikes Close to Home

1. Without breast-feeding, between 15 and 30 percent of HIV-positive mothers will pass the virus on to their infants. Among women who breast-feed, between 30 and 45 percent will. UNAIDS, "Mother to Child Transmission," http://www.unaids.org/en/Issues/Affected_communities/mothertochild.as (20 November 2006).

2. Kevin de Cock et al., "Prevention of Mother-to-Child HIV Transmission in Resource-Poor Countries," *Journal of the American Medical Association* 289, no. 9: 1175–1182.

3. In late 2004, after Nevirapine had become the standard antiretroviral drug used to prevent mother-to-child transmission of HIV in the developing world, researchers announced that the provision of the drug to pregnant women at birth increased the chance that they would become resistant to the drug later, thus impacting the mother's chance of successful antiretroviral treatment. This finding reignited a long debate in South Africa over whether the government should provide the treatment to pregnant women. See Alexandra Zavis, "Concern about Key AIDS Drug for Pregnant Women Threatens South Africa Program," Associated Press (16 December 2004).

4. Médecins Sans Frontières, "Children and AIDS: Neglected Patients," 15 July 2004, www.msf.org/msfinternational/invoke.cfm?obiectid=C35A2DA2-D4E3-425A879860086416E313&component=toolkit.article&method=full_html (22 October 2006).

Chapter 5: Crumbling Support

1. David Ambrose, *Summary of Events in Lesotho,* 12, no. 1 (2005): 5.
2. A study to test the effectiveness of prophylactic antibiotics for AIDS patients in Africa wasn't conducted until 2004. It showed that daily doses of co-trimoxazole were effective in delaying the onset of the disease in HIV-positive children, despite wide levels of bacterial resistance. See C. Chintu et al., "Co-trimoxazole as Prophylaxis against Opportunistic Infections in HIV-infected Zambian Children (CHAP): A Double-blind Randomized Placebo-controlled Trial," *Lancet* 364 (2004): 1865–1871. In response, WHO, UNAIDS, and UNICEF recommended its use (WHO/UNAIDS/UNICEF, "Joint WHO/UNAIDS/UNICEF Statement on Use of Cotrimoxazole Prophylaxis in HIV-exposed and HIV-infected Children," 22 November 2004, http://data. unaids. org/Media/Press-Statements01/ps_cotrimoxazole_22 nov04_en.pdf? preview=true (22 November 2006)). A 2004 study from Tanzania on the effectiveness of multivitamins in slowing the progression of HIV received attention around the same time and also prompted international health agencies to issue statements in support of their use (Wafaie W. Fawzi et al., "A Randomized Trial of Multivitamin Supplements and HIV Disease Progression and Mortality," *New England Journal of Medicine,* 351 (2004): 23–32). But although many individual doctors across the continent are now treating patients with both multivitamins and prophylactic antibiotics, there has been no wide-scale effort by international agencies to broaden the use of multivitamins. This may be in part because their use was scientifically sanctioned at a time when attention was focused on making antiretroviral drugs more available. Nevertheless, given that scaling up antiretroviral treatment will take years, such cheap and easy interventions should be more widely adopted. Even if we reach a point when antiretroviral treatment is available to all who need it, multivitamins could play a role in helping to slow the progress of the disease and delaying the point at which complex and comparatively expensive antiretroviral treatment is needed.
3. About 45 percent of ART patients experience visible side effects, while 27 percent experience adverse effects, thought to be related to drug treatment, that are detectable only through laboratory tests. But only 9 percent of the former and 16 percent of the latter are considered serious. Sometimes the problem can be solved by switching the patient to a different drug or drug class. See Shaun Conway and John Bartlett, *The 2003/2004 Southern African Abbreviated Guide to Medical Management of HIV Infection* (Baltimore: Johns Hopkins University Division of Infectious Disease, 2003), 50–64.
4. Edwin Cameron, *Witness to AIDS* (Cape Town: Tafelberg, 2005).
5. Nicole Itano, "Concern in Africa over Private Doctors Giving AIDS Drugs," *Christian Science Monitor* (22 February 2005).

Chapter 6: Adeline's Thing

1. Paul Farmer, ed., "Women, Poverty and AIDS," in *Women, Poverty and AIDS: Sex, Drugs and Structural Violence* (Monroe, ME: Common Courage Press, 1996): 4.

2. Lawrence Altman, "New Cases Widen Views about AIDS," *The New York Times* (5 January 1984): A20.

3. Lawrence Altman, "The Doctor's World: AIDS Data Pours in as Studies Proliferate," *The New York Times* (23 April 1985): C3.

4. Leibowitch, 4.

5. Lawrence Altman, "Linking AIDS to Africa Provokes Bitter Debate," *The New York Times* (21 November 1985): AI.

6. Several studies in 1985 and 1987 said they had found astronomically high AIDS infection rates in parts of East and Central Africa. In one, Carl Sazinger and Robert Gallo, from the National Cancer Institute, reported that retrospective testing of blood samples from Ugandan children taken in 1972 and 1973 showed that two-thirds were HIV-positive. The results were later shown to be false. See Hooper, 106.

7. The two articles appeared back to back in the July 14 issue of the *Lancet*. See Phillippe Van de Perre et al., "Acquired Immunodeficiency Syndrome in Rwanda," *Lancet* (14 July 1984): 62–65; and Peter Piot et al., "Acquired Immunodeficiency Syndrome in a Heterosexual Population in Zaire," *Lancet* (14 July 1984): 65–69.

Chapter 7: Awakening

1. Paul Raeburn, "AIDS: The Politics of AIDS in Zaire," Associated Press (31 July 1986).

2. Jon Cohen, "The Rise and Fall of Project SIDA," Science (28 November 1997).

3. Lawrence Altman, "New Support from Africa as WHO Plans Effort on AIDS," *The New York Times* (22 December 1985).

4. For more on Jonathan Mann's tenure at the WHO, see Greg Behrman, *Invisible People: How the U.S. Has Slept Through the Global AIDS Pandemic, the Greatest Humanitarian Catastrophe of Our Time* (New York: Free Press, 2004).

5. Jonathan Mann, ed., *AIDS in the World* (Cambridge, MA: Harvard University Press, 1992): 548.

6. Lawrence Altman, "Key World Health Official Warns of Epidemic of Prejudice on AIDS," *The New York Times* (3 June 1987): Al.

7. UNAIDS, Uganda, www.unaids.org/en/Regions_Countries/Countries/Uganda. asp (30 November 2006).

8. There is currently a fierce debate about what caused the fall in Uganda's prevalence rate. Helen Epstein argues persuasively that reductions in the number of sexual partners played a key role. See "Why Is AIDS Worse in Africa?" *Discover* 25, no. 2 (2004).

9. Ruhakana Rugunda spoke at the Thirty-Ninth World Health Organization Assembly, held May 1–15, 1986. See James Putzel, "The Politics of Action on AIDS: A Case Study of Uganda," *Public Administration and Development* 24 (2004): 23.

10. "Lesotho: Sweeping out the Sweeper," *Time* (13 May 1991).

11. Moe Aung Maw, *AIDS Epidemiology in Lesotho 2000* (Maseru, Lesotho:

Ministry of Health and Social Welfare, STD/HIV/AIDS Prevention and Control Program, 2000).

12. Ministry of Health and Social Welfare and the World Bank, "Strengthening Lesotho's Health Care System, 2001."

13. Family Health International, "HIV/AIDS Behavioral Surveillance Survey: Lesotho 2002, Summary Technical Support—Round 1," 2.

14. Maw.

15. Bethuel Thai, "Mosisili Urges Leaders to End AIDS Stigma," Reuters, in *The Johannesburg Star* (8 March 2004).

Chapter 8: Something Has Turned

1. Nicole Itano, "Britain's Prince Harry Helps AIDS Orphans in Lesotho," Associated Press (3 March 2004).

2. "Lesotho: Not Enough Staff, Poor Infrastructure, but ART Launched," *Plus News* (16 December 2004), www.irinnews.org/pnprint.asp?ReportID=4280 (30 November 2006).

PART II: DESPAIR · Ingwavuma, South Africa

Chapter 9: *Umbulalazwa*

1. For a discussion of the Shepstone system in Natal, see Norman Etherington, "The 'Shepstone System' in the Colony of Natal and Beyond the Borders," in *Natal and Zululand: From Earliest Times to 1910: A New History* (Pietermaritzburg, South Africa: University of Natal Press, 1989), 172. For a description of how this system was extended to Zululand and the Ingwavuma area, see John Laband and Paul Thompson, "The Reduction of Zululand, 1878–1904," in the same volume.

2. Etherington, 174–175.

3. Frank Welsh, *A History of South Africa* (London: Harper Collins, 2000), 450.

4. C. H. Vaughan Williams, "Impact of HIV/AIDS on Deaths Certified at Mosvold Hospital, Ingwavuma, Northern KwaZulu-Natal, from January to August 2003," *South Africa Family Practice* 47, no. 1 (2005): 54.

5. Rob Dorrington et al., *Demographic Impact of HIV/AIDS in South Africa,* Center for Actuarial Research, (2006).

6. Williams, 54.

Chapter 10: Two Waves of AIDS

1. Shilts discusses Dugan's role extensively.

2. Christopher Wren, "AIDS Rising Fast among Black South Africans," *The New York Times* (27 September 1990).

3. Keys Laurinda, "Only 130 out of 33,000 Miners Show Exposure to AIDS," Associated Press (28 August 1986).

4. David Beresford, "S. African Migrant Miners Stricken with AIDS Virus," *The Guardian* (8 April 1988).

5. Whiteside 1990, 15–16.
6. "Botha: Terrorists Bring AIDS to South Africa," Associated Press (20 March 1987).
7. Howard Phillips, "HIV/AIDS in the Context of South Africa's Epidemic History," in *AIDS and South Africa: The Social Expression of a Pandemic* (New York: Palgrave Macmillan, 2004), 34.
8. Virginia Van der Vliet, "South Africa Divided against AIDS: A Crisis of Leadership," in *AIDS and South Africa: The Social Expression of a Pandemic* (New York: Palgrave Macmillan, 2004), 51.
9. Wren 1990.
10. James Brooke, "AIDS Is Now Spreading to Populous West Africa," *The New York Times* (15 April 1987): A5.
11. Virginia Van der Vliet, "AIDS: Losing 'The New Struggle'?" *Daedalus,* 130, no. 1 (2001): 155.
12. Hein Marais, *To the Edge: AIDS Review 2000* (Pretoria, South Africa: Centre for the Study of AIDS, University of Pretoria).
13. Virginia Van der Vliet, "South Africa Divided against AIDS: A Crisis of Leadership," in *AIDS and South Africa: The Social Express of a Pandemic* (New York: Palgrave Macmillan, 2004), 53.
14. Department of Health, South Africa, *National HIV and Syphilis Sero-Prevalence Survey in South Africa (Summary Report),* 2001.
15. Behrman, 48.
16. Andrew Unsworth, "Making Things Happen, Against the Odds," *Johannesburg Sunday Times* (24 February 2002).

Chapter 12: Files and Photos

1. Public Protector, Republic of South Africa. "Investigation of the Play Sarafina II," 20 May 1996, www.polity.org.za/html/govt/pubprot/reportla.html (23 November 2006).
2. Marais.
3. William Mervin Gumede provides a good overview of the Virodene scandal and how it relates to Thabo Mbeki's later stance on AIDS in his 2005 book, *Thabo Mbeki and the Battle for the Soul of the ANC* (Cape Town: Zebra Press, 2005). See also Samantha Powers, "The AIDS Rebel," *The New Yorker* (19 May 2003).
4. Catherine Gorman, "The Disease Detective," *Time* (30 December 1996).
5. Fan, 86–88.
6. See, for example, R. S. Hogg et al., "Triple-combination Antiretroviral Therapy in Sub-Saharan Africa," *Lancet* 350 (1997): 1406. The authors estimate that providing antiretroviral drugs—not including improvements to the health infrastructure—in sub-Saharan Africa would cost 8.3 percent of the region's GNP. Olaf Müller et al. add that the health infrastructure in most of Africa is too underdeveloped to distribute the drugs. See "Antiretroviral Therapy in Sub-Saharan Africa," *Lancet* 351(1998): 68.
7. Carol Paton, "Medicine for Beginners: How ANC Burnt Its Fingers on AIDS Solvent," *The Sunday Times* (South Africa) (29 September 1999).

8. Thabo Mbeki, "ANC Has No Financial Stake in Virodene," ANC website, March 1998, www.anc.org.za/ancdocs/history/mbeki/1998/virodene.html (23 November 2006).

Chapter 13: A New Morality

1. A. T. Bryant's discussion of Zulu sexual behavior in his book *The Zulu People: As They Were Before the White Man Came* (New York: Negro Universities Press, 1970) is written in a style typical of its time and today seems dated, even racist. He describes the Zulu, in regards to sex, as children who have yet to be enlightened by civilized morality. "It never occurred to a Zulu boy or girl that nature's functions and nature's promptings could, in themselves, ever be morally wrong," he writes, and then continues to draw a distinction between the "moral" principles of right and wrong imposed by Christianity and the "social" principles of the Zulu. Despite this clearly Western-centric interpretation, Bryant was likely right in observing that before contact with the West, the Zulus had different sexual prohibitions and customs.

2. Adam Ashforth, "AIDS, Witchcraft, and the Problem of Power in Post-Apartheid South Africa," School of Social Science (Princeton, NJ), occasional paper, May 2001, www.sss.ias.edu/publications/papers/paperten.pdf (22 November 2006).

3. See, for example, Human Rights Watch, "Suffering in Silence: The Links between Human Rights Abuses and HIV Transmission to Girls in Zambia," November 2002, www.hrw.org/reports/2003/zambia/ (23 November 2006).

Chapter 14: The Scourge of Poverty

1. Katherine Floyd et al., "Admission Trends in a Rural South African Hospital During the Early Years of the HIV Epidemic," *Journal of the American Medical Association* 282, no. 11 (1999): 1087.

2. BBC Monitoring, "Mandela Urges End to Silence over AIDS," http://news.bbc.co.uk/2/hi/world/monitoring/225710.stm (22 November 2006).

3. Jonathan Berger, "Litigation Strategies to Gain Access to Treatment for HIV/AIDS: The Case of South Africa's Treatment Action Campaign," *Wisconsin International Law Journal* 20, no. 3 (2002).

4. Mark Heywood, "The Price of Denial," *Treatment Action Campaign*, www.tac.org.za/Documents/PriceOfDenial.doc (22 November 2006).

5. Gumede, 156.

6. Lisa Richwine, "Gore Worked to Soften South Africa Health Law," Reuters (16 April 1999).

7. Department of Health, South Africa, *Minister of Health's Comment on Drug Companies' Withdrawal*, 19 April 2001, www.doh.gov.za/docs/pr/2001/pr0419.html (22 November 2006).

8. Thabo Mbeki, Address to the National Council of Provinces, 28 October 1999, http://www.anc.org.za/ancdocs/history/mbeki/1999/tm1028.html (22 November 2006).

9. "Mbeki Opens Controversial AIDS Panel," Agence France-Presse (6 May 2000).

10. Laurie Garrett and Tina Susman, "Focus on Poverty, not on HIV, AIDS," *Newsday* (10 July 2000).
11. Mbeki Says CIA Had Role in HIV/AIDS Conspiracy," UPI (6 October 2000).
12. Drew Forrest and Barry Streek, "Mbeki in Bizarre AIDS Outburst," *Mail & Guardian* (South Africa) (26 October 2001).
13. Peter Slevin, "S. African Urges Softer Approach to Mugabe," *The Washington Post* (25 September 2003): A18.
14. Many studies have shown a strong correlation between abuse and HIV-infection rates. See UNAIDS/WHO, *AIDS Epidemic Update: December 2004*, 11.
15. Suzanne Leclerc-Madlala, "Virginity Testing: Managing Sexuality in a Maturing HIV/AIDS Epidemic," *Medical Anthropology Quarterly* 15, no. 4 (2001): 533–552.

Chapter 15: Another Death

1. Claire Keeton, "S. Africa Blames Lack of Resources for not Providing Anti-AIDS Drug," Agence France-Press (27 November 2001).
2. Belinda Beresford, "State to Lodge Another Appeal Against Court Ruling," *Mail & Guardian (Johannesburg)* (22 March 2002). "S. African Govt Will Implement Court Ruling on HIV Drugs: Health Minister," Agence France-Press (7 July 2002).
3. Ben Maclennan, "TAC Disrupts Manto's Speech," *The Independent* (Johannesburg) (24 March 2003).
4. Achmat actually made the pledge in 1998, around the time of TAC's foundation, but it did not become public until 2002, when questions were raised about why he had begun to fall sick. See Tina Rosenberg, "In South Africa, a Hero Measured by the Advance of a Deadly Disease," *The New York Times* (13 January 2003).
5. Chris McGreal, "Mandela Hits Again at President's AIDS Policy," *The London Guardian* (29 July 2002).
6. Gumede, 150.

PART III: HOPE · Otse, Botswana

Chapter 16: Homecoming

1. Botswana Tourism, Geographical Information, www.botswanatourism.gov.bw/geographical/geographical.html (22 November 2006).
2. Despite the comparatively free political environment in Botswana, there is little political debate, and local journalists and activists complain that they are under pressure not to criticize the government. Botswana has been particularly touchy about certain issues, such as the recent removal of the Bushman from parts of the Central Kalahari Game Reserve. In 2005, the country also deported an Australian academic, Kenneth Good, who had taught at the University of Botswana for many years after he published a report criticizing Botswana's democracy.

3. Republic of Botswana, *Botswana National Strategic Framework for HIV/AIDS: 2003–2009.*

4. United Nations, Millennium Summit, "Statement by His Excellency Mr. Festus Mogae, President of the Republic of Botswana," 7 September 2000, www.un.org/millennium/webcast/indexe.htm (25 November 2006).

5. *Botswana National Strategic Framework for HIV/AIDS: 2003–2009.*

6. "Botswana Hopes to Provide AIDS Medication This Year, President Says," Associated Press (14 March 2001).

7. Maggie Farley, "At AIDS Disaster's Epicenter, Botswana Is a Model of Action," *Los Angeles Times* (27 June 2001).

8. Agence France-Presse, "Botswana to Provide Free AIDS Drugs; S. Africa Maintains 'No'" (5 June 2001).

Chapter 17: A Second Chance

1. The percentage of patients who become sick with immune restoration syndrome (also called immune reconstitution syndrome or disease) after starting antiretroviral treatment is unclear, but is thought to be related to the patient's CD4 count and the presence of untreated opportunistic infections. One study, though, found that more than 30 percent of patients suffered from immune restoration syndrome. See Samuel Shelburne et al., "Incidence and Risk Factors for Immune Reconstitution Inflammatory Syndrome during Highly Active Antiretroviral Therapy," *AIDS* 19, no. 4 (2005): 399–406.

2. Joep Lange et al., "What Policymakers Should Know About Drug Resistance and Adherence in the Context of Scaling-up Treatment of HIV Infection," *AIDS,* 18, supp. 3 (2004): S69–S74.

3. WHO, *The World Health Report 2006: Working Together for Health* (2006).

4. Ministry of Health and Ministry of Local Government, Botswana, "ARV Therapy in Botswana: Project Description Document" (23 July 2002).

Chapter 18: Forgotten Children

1. Anemia is a common side effect of antiretroviral treatment. See M. Edwards et al., "Characterization of Anemia in HIV-Infected (HIV+) Subjects Treated with Antiretroviral Therapy (ART) with and without Zidovudine in 54 Clinical Trials," 2nd International AIDS Society Conference on HIV Pathogenesis and Treatment, 2005 (24–27 July 2005).

2. Masa, "Program Update for August–September, 2004," Masa Program Monthly Update (Gaborone: Ministry of Health, September 2004).

Chapter 19: Rights and Responsibilities

1. Masa 2004.

2. Botswana has offered prenatal testing and antiretroviral treatment to all pregnant women since 2001, but by 2004 just over half were agreeing to be tested. See Centers for Disease Control and Prevention, "Introduction of Routine HIV Testing in Prenatal Care – Botswana 2004," *Mortality and Morbidity Weekly Report,* v. 53. n. 46 (26 November 2004).

3. Kevin M. de Cock, Dorothy Mbori-Ngacha, and Elizabeth Marum, "Shadow

on the continent: public health and HIV/AIDS in Africa in the 21ˢᵗ century," *Lancet,* 360 (2002): 67–72.

4. Anna Koblanck, *A Few Days More: The Story of a Young Woman Living with HIV in Botswana* (Harare, Zimbabwe: Southern Africa HIV/AIDS Information Dissemination Service, 2005), 96.

Chapter 20: Breaking the Silence

1. Nkosi Johnson's Speech at the International AIDS Conference," Agence France-Press (1 June 2001).

2. Simon Robinson, "Newsmaker: Nkosi Johnson," *Time* (31 December 2001), 52.

3. Laurie Garrett, "AIDS Meeting Impact: S. African Event 'Changed the Face of How Societies Deal with Illness,'" *Newsday* (18 July 2000).

4. PEPFAR, announced in Bush's January 2003 State of the Union address, focuses all its funds on fifteen countries, eleven of which are in Africa. Botswana and South Africa are both PEPFAR countries, but Lesotho is not.

5. Jo-Anne Smetherham, "Manto Gives Her Recipe for Fighting HIV," *The Cape Times* (19 March 2003).

6. WHO, *Progress on Global Access to HIV Antiretroviral Therapy: A Report on '3 by 5' and Beyond,* March 2006.

7. Rand Stoneburner et al., "Declines in Adult HIV Mortality in Botswana, 2003-5: Evidence for an Impact of Antiretroviral Therapy Programs," African Comprehensive HIV/AIDS Partnership (2006) www.achap.org/media/ReDorts/Mortality%20decline%20Botswana%20ART%20Stoneburner%20PPT%20Toronto%20Aug%202006.ppt (16 April 2007).

8. Tendai Gaolathe, "Lessons Learned from Masa: Botswana's National ARV Program," African Comprehensive HIV/AIDS Partnership (2003) www.achap.org/downloads/Presentation5.pdf (16 April 2006).

9. Donald de Korte, Patson Mazonde, and Ernest Darkoh, "Introducing ARV Therapy in the Public Sector in Botswana: Case Study," (Geneva: WHO, 2004), 10.

10. Ibid.

Chapter 21: Life, but No Solutions

1. The government of Botswana first began removing the Basarwa from the Central Kalahari Game Reserve in 1997. The Basarwa, and the international advocacy groups like Survival International who support them, claim they are being evicted to make way for diamond mining. The government says that the Bushmen have abandoned their traditional hunting and gathering life and that their new, more settled lifestyle is no longer compatible with the goal of preserving the delicate natural environment of the park. Stung by criticism over their removal policy, the government of Botswana has often made it difficult for journalists and other groups to cover the issue.

2. Sahm Venter, "Professor Must Leave Botswana," *The Melbourne Age* (1 June 2005).

3. *Progress on Global Access to HIV Antiretroviral Therapy:* 73–75.

INDEX